Companies need to understand how each generation behaves at work, how they want to be managed, and their needs in order to retain them and keep them engaged. Haydn's book will help you unlock the value behind the generations and bring them together for the benefit of your company.

DAN SCHAWBEL, *Forbes* contributor and author of *Me 2.0* and *Promote Yourself: The New Rules for Career Success*

Johnsonville Sausage has always been about the people who ensure we produce the highest-quality products. When Haydn spoke to our leaders, he got us thinking about generational differences in new ways that help us better attract and empower employees of all generations. I'm glad Haydn's put the insights he shared with us into a book that can help thousands of others. You need this powerful book.

RALPH C. STAYER, CEO and owner of Johnsonville Sausage

The secret to future success lies in GQ: generational intelligence. Read this book and get smart about how to connect generations to unleash innovation and productivity.

TIM SANDERS, CEO of Net Minds and author of *Today We Are Rich* and *Love Is the Killer App*

When it comes to troubleshooting workplace issues and facilitating harmonious interactions among employees, FranklinCovey is the undisputed leader, and those who are currently managing four disparate generations need look no further than practice leader Haydn Shaw, whose book *Sticking Points* zeroes in on the areas—like organizational structure and use of social media—where communication is most likely to break down and cause a negative impact on the bottom line.

ALEXANDRA LEVIT, author of *#MillennialTweet: 140 Bite-Sized Ideas for Managing the Millennials*

Sticking Points contains insights and processes that do indeed work. We've had Haydn back many times to teach our managers the tools he has put into this book. I found it so valuable and enjoyable that I invited my wife to come hear his presentation. You'll come back to this book again and again when you run into a new generational challenge. But more important, it will improve your ability to speak the language of other generations at work and in your personal life. A must-read.

JIM THYEN, president and CEO of Kimball International, Inc.

I go all over the world speaking to organizations about leadership, and Haydn has made a slam dunk with *Sticking Points.* He explains why people from different generations think and act the way they do. Why does this matter? When we understand the "why," we can work with people to get outstanding results as teams or individuals. Understanding the "why" enables leaders to celebrate differences and capitalize on the creativity and innovation of each generation. It's a must-read for leaders.

PAT WILLIAMS, senior vice president of the Orlando Magic

Sticking Points provides a practical road map for sidestepping the stumbling blocks that come with a multigenerational workforce. It is a great guide for business leaders feeling the pain of managing four completely different generations. I agree with Haydn Shaw—don't try to change them; lead them. This astute and entertaining book is an important one.

TAMARA ERICKSON, a McKinsey Award–winning author and expert on organizations and the changing workforce

Four generations are challenging associations like the American Business Women's Association to rethink how they attract, retain, and engage their members that are in various stages of their lives and careers. What works for Traditionalists and Boomers doesn't necessarily work for Gen Xers and Millennials. *Sticking Points* is an excellent read that gives organizational leaders, teachers, and families essential tools to help them connect with every generation effectively. Our multigenerational membership loved Haydn Shaw's breakout sessions, and I know you will appreciate his book.

RENE STREET, executive director of American Business Woman's Association National

Understanding the four generations in the workforce is critical today for maximizing customer satisfaction and team productivity. Haydn is a true guide to better understand the differences of this issue and take advantage of the opportunities! I highly recommend this book to anyone who wants a well-researched, easy-to-read, and practical guide to this important subject.

STEPHEN G. OSWALD, CEO of Capital Safety

In his book *Sticking Points*, Haydn Shaw presents timely advice for executives and managers struggling to understand the newest generation of employees. His insights helped us unravel this mystery and provide a path to better communication, greater productivity, and exceptional performance and will do the same for you.

MICHAEL ENGLER, PhD, Chairman/CEO of Cactus Feeders, Inc.

Don't make . . . generational mistakes inside and outside of your business. Let Haydn put a smile on your face as he helps you navigate through the sticking points in every facet of your company and show you how multigenerational leadership wins out.

TIMOTHY P. BAILEY, retired chief credit officer and vice chairman, TCF National Bank

Thinking about my younger teammates—and teenage daughters—as "from another country" makes me smile. And it has improved my ability to listen and understand. This book is a must-read for those who want to work with, live with, and lead other generations effectively.

JENNIFER COLOSIMO, VP of Wisdom at DaVita; coauthor with Stephen Covey of *Great Work, Great Career*

Haydn Shaw's new book *Sticking Points* is definitely the right resource at the right time for twenty-first-century organizational leadership. Having experienced Haydn's practical wisdom at numerous retreats, I have learned that the principles laid out in the book are widely applicable across different types of organizations. I unreservedly recommend *Sticking Points* as a must-read for any organization's leadership team.

ROBERT VAN ALLEN, PhD EE, cofounder of SVS Inc. and executive/program manager for the Boeing Company (retired)

Sticking Points is an excellent book, a valuable glimpse of how generational differences impact organizations. We've brought Haydn to our staff and events we've hosted for other universities because our students and staffs span the generations. Leveraging the generational differences is critical to our success and yours. You need this book.

JUDITH FLINK, executive director of student financial services for the University of Illinois

This generation that has grown up digital continues to bring big changes to the workplace. *Sticking Points* provides a practical way to turn generational tensions into team results so we don't miss the *many* benefits this new generation can bring. Your whole team will want to read and talk about this book.

> **DON TAPSCOTT**, author of 15 widely read books, including *Macrowikinomics: New Solutions for a Connected Planet* and *Grown Up Digital*

Sticking Points by Haydn Shaw helps readers sort out how to get all five generations working together rather than complaining about each other. Insightful and well balanced, this book will make you smile while it explores generational myths and provides a practical process for leading every generation more effectively.

> **KEN BLANCHARD**, coauthor of *The One Minute Manager®* and *Trust Works!*

Haydn's caring, sincerity, and inspirational sense of humor put him in the top one percent of speakers in the nation. Now he's going to the top as an author. *Sticking Points* tackles one of the major problems in organizations all over the world—the friction between generations. And now, in one book, you can gain understanding and learn how to deal with all four generations in a very practical hands-on approach so that your organization can achieve its highest priorities.

> **RUTH WILLIAMS**, author of *How to Be Like Women of Influence* and *Happy Spouse, Happy House*

With over 30,000 employees around the world, it was imperative that we build collaborative and effective teams across multiple functions and geographies. Haydn was able to unlock the obstructionism we saw across generations. His delivery was motivating, and his methods and insights were clear and empowering. With the path illuminated, our teams rose and worked effectively and passionately, from 22 to 62.

> **MATTHEW RUBEL**, former chairman, CEO, and president of Collective Brands (Payless ShoeSource)

In *Sticking Points* Haydn does an amazing service. He not only turns automatic contention between the generations into understanding, but he also reveals the opportunities for creating true synergies. This book is a must-read for leaders of all ages.

> **RON MCMILLAN**, coauthor of four *New York Times* bestsellers, including *Crucial Conversations: Tools for Talking When Stakes Are High*

Sticking Points

STICKING POINTS

HOW TO GET
4 GENERATIONS
WORKING TOGETHER
IN THE 12 PLACES
THEY COME APART

HAYDN SHAW

Tyndale House Publishers, Inc.
CAROL STREAM, ILLINOIS

Visit Tyndale online at www.tyndale.com.

TYNDALE and Tyndale's quill logo are registered trademarks of Tyndale House Publishers, Inc.

Sticking Points: How to Get 4 Generations Working Together in the 12 Places They Come Apart

Copyright © 2013 by Haydn Shaw. All rights reserved.

Interior phone icons copyright © Kathy Konkle, Paul Pantazescu and bubaone/iStockphoto. All rights reserved.

Photograph of computer mouse copyright © Cobalt Moon Design/Shutterstock. All rights reserved.

Photograph of rotary phone copyright © camilla wisbauer/iStockphoto. All rights reserved.

Photograph of smartphone copyright © Miklos Voros/iStockphoto. All rights reserved.

Pie chart illustration copyright © Kamaga/iStockphoto. All rights reserved.

Red phone photograph copyright © Bariscan Celi/iStockphoto. All rights reserved.

Silhouette illustration copyright © 4x6/iStockphoto. All rights reserved.

Author photograph taken by FranklinCovey, copyright © 2010. All rights reserved.

Designed by Ron Kaufmann

Edited by Jonathan Schindler

Published in association with Yates & Yates (www.yates2.com).

Unless a full name is given, names have been changed to protect their owners' privacy.

ISBN 978-1-4143-6471-1

Printed in the United States of America

19	18	17	16	15	14	13
7	6	5	4	3	2	1

To Laurie Anne

CONTENTS

Foreword

I'LL NEVER FORGET THE DAY I was working with an organization where the senior managers and employees were debating the merits of a new approach to how their work might be done. The company's youthful staff had proposed that some of them didn't necessarily need to come in to the office at set times and with set hours. "Let us work when we want," they said. "Just hold us accountable to getting our work done well and on time." But the older senior management team was sincerely questioning whether they would get a full day's work out of these people. The arguments went back and forth and round and round—with no resolution in sight.

I was witnessing a generational sticking point, one of the twelve places the generations are most likely to collide.

We are all seeing generational sticking points pop up in our own organizations or families more and more frequently. As Haydn explains, we've never had so many generations in existence at once, and we're not quite sure what to do about it. That's why we need this book.

I have known Haydn Shaw for more than twenty years, from the time he started at FranklinCovey at the ripe age of twenty-eight. He was one of our two youngest consultants, but honestly, he didn't look a day over twenty! I was still managing a sales team at the time, and my team worried that clients would wonder what they were getting when we first sent Haydn out alone. It didn't take long for us to realize what our clients quickly discovered: Haydn is exceptionally smart, practical, and funny. He quickly became an in-demand presenter and consultant—one of our very best. In short, he succeeded tremendously at what in our business is a very young age, so he knows from personal experience that younger people can make a contribution, and he wants to show us how to let them.

Over the last twenty years I've watched Haydn lead large client projects, develop multiple training programs, and provide thought leadership for FranklinCovey's leadership practice. He has taught my father's *7 Habits of Highly Effective People* program more than almost anyone else in the world. All the while he has been observing and researching generational differences. So in 2008, when FranklinCovey decided to develop workshops on generations, Haydn was already an expert who had spoken to and helped organizations create more productive teams, reduce turnover, and retain top talent by showing them how to sort through their generational differences. More than just spouting theories, Haydn has real-world, hands-on "generations" experience with literally thousands of people, enabling him to connect with people (and readers) in profound ways. As Carl Rogers put it, "That which is most personal is most general."

As you'll see in this book, Haydn has the ability to see the big picture through vast amounts of information in multiple disciplines while simultaneously providing practical insights and tools that can be used immediately. Haydn has the rare gift of taking complex things and making them simple—without being simplistic, which is what he has powerfully done with *Sticking Points*.

When I wrote *The Speed of Trust*, my foremost objective was to help people *build* trust, not just talk about it. That's what I love most about *Sticking Points*. Haydn doesn't simply explain the differences between the generations; he shows us how to use his five-step process to work through and transcend each of the twelve most common generational conflicts— what he calls "sticking points." He beautifully teaches the *why* behind the *what* and helps us gain real understanding of our generational differences, enabling us to leverage today's opportunity of having multiple generations at work at the same time.

Haydn is particularly witty and funny. His approach is to get us laughing at ourselves so we are more open to understanding and trusting other generations. Even though this book addresses a serious topic, you'll catch glimpses of his sense of humor that makes his generational presentations both engaging and penetrating. Haydn's experience and capabilities are what make this book smart and practical; his personality is what makes it interesting and funny.

Most of all Haydn has a vision for organizations empowering people and running with the strengths of each of the generations like no one else

I know. He sees a future for your organization where generations can work together in order to produce extraordinary results. More than anything else Haydn sees generational differences not as problems to be solved but as opportunities to be leveraged.

The problem is that both Haydn and I see too many corporate cultures poisoned by infighting between the generations. We witness simmering fights about checking e-mails and texts in meetings. We hear older colleagues whispering about new hires who don't seem loyal to the organization. We walk into workplaces that can't attract new and younger people to work there or keep the Boomers from longing for retirement.

What excites me about this wonderful book is how it paints a vision of another way—a *better* way. A way to transform a team stuck in generational differences into a team that sticks together.

Sticking Points will be my reference guide for years to come as a go-to resource for both understanding and resolving generational differences. I predict it will become a reference guide for you, too, filled with ideas and insights you can apply from a person you can trust.

Stephen M. R. Covey
MARCH 2013

Preface

WHEN I'M SPEAKING and consulting on generations, people frequently ask me to recommend a book to help them handle generational differences in their workplaces. They say they don't have time to read three or four books. They just want something that's up-to-date and covers all four generations—Traditionalists, Baby Boomers, Generation Xers, and especially Millennials—an easy-to-read book that both managers and associates of all generations will like. They want practical ideas they can put to work, not just research or theories that don't translate into concrete results. When I told them I didn't know of any one book that would do all that, they told me I'd better start writing.

In this book, I wanted to provide a practical resource for those people who approach me—a guide to all four generations, following a methodology that has helped thousands of people deal with the twelve issues most likely to pull teams apart.

This book is specifically written for the workplace context, but it has much broader applications. Generational differences don't just show up in the conference room. They surface in the home, on the school or nonprofit board, and at religious organizations. Anywhere people get together, what I call the "ghost stories" of the different generations impact the way they think. When we understand why another generation thinks the way they do, we are much more likely to appreciate their differences and speak their language. We are much more likely to stick together.

A quick note about my research. This book is . . .

- based on conversations and interviews with thousands of people from the four generations as well as the latest published research.
- about all four generations (with extra attention to Millennials since they are new) so the whole team can read it together and then put it to work.
- fast to read, with a touch of humor. (If we can't laugh at our generational differences, they'll always irritate us.)
- practical. If you can't apply what a book recommends, what's the point?

To make it practical, I've included . . .

- comparisons of how generations think, which a major client described as "the answer key to the generations."
- a five-step plan for leading rather than managing generational differences.
- ways to apply this five-step plan to each of the twelve generational sticking points you face at work (or home).
- answers to the most common questions I get asked about generational differences.

Generational tensions are inevitable, but they don't have to leave you stuck. This book will help you to get the four generations working together in the twelve places they tend to come apart.

CHAPTER 1

Sticking Together or Coming Apart

CINDY SNEAKED OUT before the conference wrapped up. Seeing me by the registration table, she looked at her watch and asked, "Can you answer a question about your presentation? I've got a big problem on my team."

"Sure," I said. "We have a few minutes before people start coming out."

She glanced at her watch again and started in. "For six months I've been working with Human Resources, trying to figure out what to do with Cara. I'm leaving the conference early to finalize the paperwork to fire her. But after listening to you, I'm wondering if maybe there's something generational about this. I lead an information technology department, and Cara surfs the Internet three hours a day."

"Sounds like a lot," I said. "If she's surfing that much, her work must not be getting done. Who on your team is picking up the slack?"

"No work falls to other people," Cindy said. "She actually carries the heaviest workload in my department. She supports more software programs and more users than anyone else."

"Oh," I said with surprise. "Seems strange to fire your highest producer. Do her customers complain about her work?"

She hesitated. "No . . . she has the best customer satisfaction scores of anyone in our department. The vice presidents often tell me to do whatever

1

it takes to keep her because she is the best in my department. That's why Human Resources and I have been trying so hard to figure out how to make it work with her. But we are stuck."

"If she does more work and has better results than anyone on your team, why are you firing her?" I asked.

"Because she sets a bad example for the rest of the department. I have other techs asking me why they can't surf the web if Cara can. Plus, we pay her for a full day, and she's not working three hours of it. What if everyone did that? At first I offered to promote her since she is so good; I knew that would fill her plate. But she says she likes the job she has. I've coached her for a year now that she needs to stay busy. I've offered her extra projects, but she says it wouldn't be fair."

I finished her thought. "She says that being able to surf the Internet is her reward for getting her work done faster. She shouldn't be punished by having to do 30 percent more work than everyone else without 30 percent more pay."

Cindy almost shouted, "That's exactly what she said!"

Cindy was in the middle of a sticking point.

• • •

"My wife and I have two kids in their twenties, but they are certainly not like we were," Stan, a fifty-six-year-old accountant, stated once we had found a seat. We'd met in the food line at an open house for a recent high school graduate. At first when people find out I do leadership training and consulting, they nod politely. But when I mention I've been researching the different generations for twenty years, they can't stop talking.

As I started eating, Stan continued. "By the time I was twenty-five, I already had a house, a kid, and another on the way. But my kids don't look like they're ever going to settle down."

The brisket was good, so I kept eating and listened to Stan. He went on, "Our oldest son, Brandon, is a good kid, but he's taking his time figuring out what he wants to do. He's twenty-six, and he moved back home five months ago because he says things are just too expensive on his own. Living with his parents doesn't seem to faze him or his friends. I would have died of embarrassment. And I know his mother would never have dated me if I'd lived at home, but it doesn't seem to bother his girlfriend, either. She's a really nice girl with a good job, but after dating for four years, they never talk about marriage. Most of my friends were married by twenty-six; most of Brandon's are still dating."

"That seems about right," I said. "The average age for marriage has jumped. My oldest son had thought about getting married at twenty-two, and everyone said he was crazy. *I* thought he was crazy, and I got married at twenty-two. Actually, his *grandmother* thought he was crazy, and she got married the day before she turned seventeen. It's a different world."

Stan hadn't touched his food. "I'm not saying he should get married. He has moments of maturity, but I don't think he's ready for commitment yet. He hasn't finished his college degree or found a job that he wants to stick with, and he still plays a lot of video games. It's not getting married later that I don't understand; it's that he and his girlfriend don't want to get serious. I'm a little worried about what's going to happen to him and his friends."

Stan was stuck (and his brisket was getting cold).

•　•　•

Hector had asked if we could talk at a seminar lunch break, and he got straight to the point: "Haydn, my team is stuck. We had an important presentation recently that started out fine but ended in disaster."

Hector Perez was a forty-three-year-old vice president of a new division formed to help his midsize manufacturing company move into green technology. Even discouraged and noticeably tired, Hector's hands never stopped moving. He waved his fork like an orchestra conductor as he talked: "Larry Broz, our CEO, is great. He asked me to fly in my team, who are mainly Generation Xers like me, to make our pitch to the management team for increasing the research and development spending on green technologies. Larry's why I left a great company to come here. He may be almost seventy, but he thinks as young as I do. And my team did great. They looked professional, they knew their stuff, and even when the executive team began to throw out strong challenges, they listened and responded like they were old pros.

"But then the meeting crashed, and our proposal went with it. One of my team members, Rachel, was texting under the table. She finished quickly, but later, when the head of operations launched into one of her pet topics, which we've all heard many times before, Rachel began texting again, in full view of the others in the meeting. The head of operations then lectured Rachel, Rachel defended herself, and I tried to make a joke about my team texting in my meetings to ease the tension, but that got the head of ops even more fired up.

"The whole meeting just imploded," Hector said. "Once the CEO got the head of operations calmed down, we met for another hour, but it was awkward, and the energy was gone. People were still thinking about Rachel using her cell phone rather than the strategy. Larry finally put the meeting out of its misery and asked the executive team to submit additional comments in writing."

Hector continued, "Rachel was just doing what our whole team does in our own meetings. She texts while I'm talking, too, but it doesn't bother me because I know she's dialed in to what we're doing. On the flight home, two of my people agreed that Rachel should have left her phone alone but complained that senior management is out of touch with how people communicate now. I'm stuck in the middle. The senior execs want me to keep my team in line, but my young team members wonder if they're just spinning their wheels here, if this is the place for them long term. If senior management can't adjust to smartphones, will they ever be able to embrace these new green technologies they want us to implement? I came here to make a difference, not keep the peace."

Hector was stuck between dueling generations.

• • •

Cindy's and Hector's companies didn't know it, but they had run into seven of the twelve most common generational sticking points I've identified from interviewing and working with thousands of people. And Stan's family was tangled in four different sticking points as well. Each generation in these situations thought the others were the problem. The groups tried in vain to ignore or avoid their generational differences. Typically, as at Hector's company, the generation in charge tells a younger generation to get it together, hoping that will solve the problem. But it never does.

These groups' approaches predictably didn't work, and they weren't sure why or what to do about it the next time. Generational friction is inevitable today, and "the next time" will come more and more often and create more and more tension. If only the companies and family I described had known the following:

- For the first time in history, we have four different generations in the workplace (and five in families). These generations might as well be from different countries, so different are their cultural styles and preferences.

- Of the four approaches organizations can take to blending the generations, only one of them works today.
- Focusing on the "what" escalates tensions, while focusing on the "why" pulls teams together.
- Knowing the twelve sticking points can allow teams to label tension points and work through them—even anticipate and preempt them.
- Implementing the five steps to cross-generational leadership can lead to empowering, not losing, key people.

But they didn't know these things. And neither do most organizations or families. Sticking points are inevitable, and they often get teams and families stuck. But they don't have to. *The same generational conflicts that get teams stuck can cause teams to stick together.*

Stuck in the past or sticking together going forward: it's a matter of turning a potential liability into an asset. And it's not that hard to do, as you will soon discover. (In later chapters, I'll pick up the stories of Cindy, Stan, and Hector and share the advice I gave them about working through their generational sticking points.)

"THEY DON'T GET IT"

The most common complaint I hear from frustrated people in all four generations is "They don't get it."

"They," of course, means a boss, coworker, or family member from a different generation who the speaker believes is the cause of a problem. And in my experience, "it" usually refers to one of the following twelve sticking points—places where teams get stuck:

1. communication
2. decision making
3. dress code
4. feedback
5. fun at work
6. knowledge transfer
7. loyalty
8. meetings
9. policies

10. respect
11. training
12. work ethic

Anyone in today's workforce can identify with most, if not all, of the twelve sticking points.

"They don't get it" is usually a sign that a sticking point is pulling the team apart. Team members of the same generation begin tossing around stereotypes, making jokes to each other about the "offending" generation. Each generation attempts to maneuver the others into seeing the sticking point their own way.

And that's the first mistake—viewing a sticking point as a problem to be solved rather than as an opportunity to be leveraged. The goal becomes to "fix" the offending generation rather than to look for ways to work with them. The irony is that when we say another generation doesn't get it, we don't get it either.

Once we get it, we realize that these sticking points are more than intergenerational differences. They are catalysts for deeper understanding and appreciation that can make teams stronger and better balanced. Sticking points can be negative if you see them as problems or positive if you see them as opportunities for greater understanding and flexibility. Sticking points can make things worse or better depending on whether the four generations can work together in the twelve places they naturally tend to come apart.

We'll spend the next two chapters looking at why generational sticking points usually get teams stuck, and we'll see how we can change them into the emotional glue that sticks teams together to achieve exciting results.

FOUR GENERATIONS: THE NEW REALITY

Generational friction is inevitable today because we've never before had four generations in the workplace.

Different researchers label the generations—or more technically, "age cohort groups"—using different terms. For simplicity's sake, I've summarized the most common names along with each generation's birth years so you can see where you and others fit.

I'm using the term *Generation X* (or *Gen X* for short), even though the members of that generation don't like the label. Who can blame them? It came from the title of a book about a lost and rootless generation—and *X* is

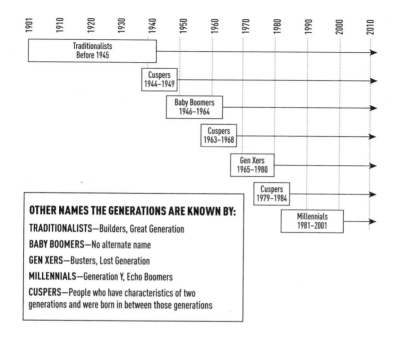

often a symbol for something that's missing or an unknown factor. But unfortunately, that's the name that has stuck.

Not everyone would agree with the dates I assign the generations. Some of us disagree by a couple of years, especially about the length of Generation X.[1] Age cohort groups are determined by the way a generation buys, votes, and answers surveys, so of course there is no easily identified date when the Boomers ended and the Gen Xers began.

To deal with the transitional years when it is impossible to separate generations because people have characteristics of both, marketers developed the term *Cuspers*. For example, I am a Cusper, born in 1963—just when the Baby Boomer generation was ending and Generation X was beginning. Cuspers are a blend of both. I identify in some ways with Boomers and in other ways with Xers. (My wife jokes, "You overwork like a Boomer, and you are cynical like an Xer. I've married the worst of both worlds.")

While Cuspers can create problems for marketers who can't tell which generational pitch to aim at them, Cuspers are often able to bridge generations. They have one foot in both camps and can sometimes serve as translators and negotiators between generations.

I mentioned earlier that there are five generations in the home. The fifth generation (children of the second half of Gen Xers and the first half of Millennials) doesn't yet have an established name or even a start date. We assume that the Millennial generation will be about the same length as the Boomers and Xers, but that may not be the case. Assuming the fifth generation starts somewhere from 2002 to 2004, those children are already consumers and influencers of massive amounts of government and parental (and grandparental) spending. They may not be in the workplace, but they certainly are consumers.

For the first time in history, there are four generations in the workplace and five in the marketplace. This new phenomenon complicates our work and our relationships because while people of all generations have the same basic needs, they meet those needs in different ways. The rest of this book will detail the commonalities and differences among the four generations we find in the workplace.

SEVEN WAYS THE GENERATIONS WILL INCREASINGLY IMPACT YOUR ORGANIZATION

If you've never paid much attention to generational differences, here are seven organizational realities you need to be aware of. I'll divide them into internal and external impacts.

Internal Impacts:
1. *Conflicts around generational sticking points.* How do you get four generations of employees to play nice together in the sandbox? Increasingly, organizations are recognizing that younger employees don't see things the same way their elders do and that it's impossible to create policies that don't annoy someone. How do you get through the differences and get back to work? Generational friction is inevitable; generational problems are avoidable—that is, if you and your team have a working knowledge of why the generations are different and of how to lead them rather than simply manage them.
2. *Managing and motivating different generations.* Whether it's older supervisors trying to motivate younger employees or younger supervisors trying to direct people their parents' age, generational differences complicate things. While people are motivated by similar needs, how they seek to fulfill those needs differs. And that causes challenges in engaging and motivating different generations.

3. *Replacing the Baby Boomers in the war for talent.* Who will you hire following the coming exodus of Baby Boomers? Even in economic downturns, organizations compete for the best employees, what's commonly called the "war for talent." Traditionalists have already largely left the workplace. Over the next decade, many of the Baby Boomers will follow—and the ones who return will do so on their own terms. Who will replace them in your organization, and how will you adjust to the younger generation's different approach to work? How will you transfer the Boomers' experience, job knowledge, and customer relationships? Further complicating the shift, lower birthrates in the industrialized world and longer life spans could create a labor shortage over the next two decades.[2]

4. *Succession planning.* Do you trust Generation X to run the place? The president of one of the United States' thirty largest banks confided to me, "Anywhere we have a Boomer in the succession plan for the top spots, we're pretty confident. But if it's a Gen Xer, we don't know. We just aren't sure they get the business." It's a common sentiment. Organizations made their peace with Gen Xers ten years ago, after a decade of fretting and calling them "slackers." But handing over the keys to the company causes differences in work ethic and loyalty to resurface. In the late 1990s, succession planning was a hot topic as organizations began to do the math on Boomer retirements. But it faded with the global downturn of 2002. If your organization is typical, well over half your leaders will retire in the next decade. You can't put it off any longer. Ready or not, you must have a succession plan.[3]

5. *Leadership development.* Where will you get your leaders? Generation X is a much smaller generation, and Xers do not tend to stay in one company throughout their careers. As we'll see, the leadership development processes that served the Boomers are not working for the next generation.

External Impacts:

6. *Shifting markets.* What do the different generations want? You thought your website was great, so why isn't it working? We all know generations buy differently. That's the basis of generational market research. If your organization must market to multiple generations, you need to understand what appeals to each generation and learn to speak their language.

7. *Connecting with five generations of customers.* Most people relate well to two of the generations but not four or five. Will your salespeople miss half your customers? How will you prepare your employees to satisfy five generations of customers?

THE PEOPLE ISSUE OF THE NEXT DECADE

This generational math adds up to the people issue of the decade for your business—or hospital or government agency or political campaign or military unit or church or school or nonprofit or foundation or symphony or association or family.

In many ways, the impact on nonprofit organizations will be more intense sooner. Successful businesses can buy a little time with higher pay. Most nonprofits don't have that luxury, especially after the Great Recession that began in 2008 restructured the economy. They need to know about sticking points now. Here are some organization-specific generational challenges that will need to be dealt with in the immediate future:

- *Hospitals and medicine.* Gen Xers and Millennials did not have Sputnik and the space race to drive national passion in science. The average age of nurses in many places is increasing as medicine struggles to attract and retain Gen X and Millennial nurses. Some hospitals are already forced to hire temporary surgeons due to the shortage.[4] (Think of the implications as the Baby Boomers hit their high-medical-need years.) Whereas businesses like Hard Rock Cafe can pick a demographic target, hospitals must serve all five generations. Without generational understanding, a highly skilled Millennial nurse can bring down customer satisfaction scores with a Traditionalist patient just by being more informal in language and approach. What to a Millennial is friendly can seem disrespectful to a Traditionalist.
- *Government.* Millennials went into government studies in much higher numbers than Gen Xers but have not been staying in government jobs. I tell my governmental clients that they have an "empty middle." With well over half their staff and most of their managers eligible to retire in the next seven years, and relatively few Gen X managers to take over, they have a generational gap that will be a challenge to fill.
- *Political campaigns.* Capturing the vote of the two younger generations was key to Barack Obama's coming from obscurity to

the presidency and then to his reelection.[5] In the 2008 election, the first BlackBerry-carrying president lured away one of the three founders of Facebook, who at twenty-four led the customization of social-networking technology and changed the rules of politics. One example: Obama's Vote for Change site registered over one million voters with only a few part-time staff. In the past that would have required two thousand full-time staff.[6] Campaigns at every level learned from his victory and raced to adopt technology-driven, grassroots-based campaigns. In Obama's reelection, his campaign put even more focus on social media but added precision data mining that will set the playbook for the future.[7] Campaigns that don't take seriously all generations and their communication technologies will struggle.

- *Military.* A United States Army commander told me in 2004 that the boot camp staff's most hated recruiting slogan was "An Army of One." Recruits came in expecting the army to accommodate their goals and preferences.[8] He and his peers begged the recruiting office to go back to "Be All You Can Be" (used 1981–2001), but that slogan has ceased to resonate with the younger generations. The Army switched slogans to "Army Strong" in the fall of 2006 because they missed recruiting goals due to the Iraq Conflict. When recruits knew they would most likely be shipped off early in their career, the self-fulfillment promises of "Be All You Can Be" couldn't be met.

- *Religious organizations.* People often turn to religion for comfort and guidance in a changing and sometimes confusing world but find that with five generations, it is impossible to keep everyone on the same page. Younger generations are not willing to wait for styles and approaches to change—they simply go somewhere else or stay home. Because religious organizations survive only if they are able to attract the next generation, this may be the most important issue they face.

- *Schools.* Similar to hospitals, K–12 schools struggle to attract and retain Gen X and Millennial teachers. In many areas, the dropout rate for new teachers is 50 percent. Internally, faculty struggle just as businesses do to understand the different generations. One med school professor told me she asked her dean if she could record herself teaching so she could work on research rather than offering ongoing classes. The school no longer required class attendance, so half her students didn't show up. (He said no.)

- *Nonprofits/foundations.* Without business-level salaries, nonprofits and foundations have to motivate and inspire each generation if they hope to win in the war for talent. Moreover, the generations have different ideas of what volunteer involvement looks like and how organizations should be run. Add to that the changing expectations of donors, and the same changes that have impacted political campaigns will continue to change fund-raising.
- *Associations.* When I ask my association clients to name their key challenges, these themes emerge: How do we get younger members to join? How do we get them to attend and, better yet, volunteer? And how do we deal with the tensions between generations when younger members try to jump in but don't want to do things the way they've always been done?
- *Families.* Raising children is definitely different today. Teens spend hours online with fifty friends and have to be forced to go outside. You know it's a different world when your child asks for the "Totally Stylin' Tattoos Barbie" for her (or his) birthday.

All organizations have to understand sticking points to ensure that their teams stick together instead of being stuck in generational conflicts. Sticking points are unavoidable; staying stuck in them is a waste. With the right tools and understanding, they can instead be huge opportunities to make our organizations more effective.

CHAPTER 2

Blue Screen of Death: The Difficulty of Leading Four Generations

IT'S THE END of the world as we've known it. Flip-flops prove that. They are the footwear of choice for Millennials, our newest generation in the workforce. Millennials wear them regardless of the weather. They say flip-flops are comfortable, and they will not be deterred by frostbite. Just as different countries have different clothes, so do the different generations. Nothing symbolizes this like flip-flops.

Personally, I don't get flip-flops. I've tried them, but I hate that strap between my toes. I'm more Boomer when it comes to men in sandals. I think men have ugly feet—big, knobby, hairy toes—that ought to be covered up in shoes. But I know that's just the generation I'm from; we wore tennis shoes, not sandals. (I'm not being sexist, by the way. Many women have ugly feet, and I think they ought to cover them up as well. You know who you are.)

To my generation, flip-flops were shower shoes you wore at the campground to avoid touching the same floor that the family two campsites over walked on with whatever weird stuff was growing on their feet. You threw away the flip-flops when you were done. But I just attended another wedding where the bridesmaids were all in formal gowns and matching flip-flops. The mother of the bride couldn't bear to have her daughter wearing cheap flip-flops and admitted to spending three hours hand decorating them with lace and beads. (There are now websites that will do the decorating, so parents, you can relax.) Flip-flops symbolize the new world we're in because shoes mean different things to different generations.

Flip-flops also symbolize this new world because they illustrate how words don't mean the same thing to the four generations. My father's generation doesn't call them flip-flops; they call them "thongs." My kids used to kick off their flip-flops at my parents' house, and my father would ask them to move their thongs before someone tripped. They'd laugh their heads off. "Dad, Grandpa calls them thongs!"

It's an awkward family moment explaining to your father what a thong means today.[1]

It's the end of the world as we've known it.

THREE REASONS IT'S MORE COMPLICATED TODAY

People ask me if experts are making too much of the generational divides. When I was teaching a management course to a team of internal trainers, their manager got quite upset with me because I kept answering his team's generational questions. He told his team that good management works with every generation and that generational differences were inflated by consultants looking to make a buck. He insisted that his trainers were not to address generational issues when their classes brought them up. And his attitude is fairly common. Many people wonder, *Why the big deal? What's so different now?*

Four generations is new. For most of history there have been three generations with much clearer ways to transition power and money. Until the industrial age, most assets were land or livestock, so people waited until their parents (or at least their father) died or officially transferred assets and authority. Unless they left the farm to seek their fortune, children waited patiently.

My grandparents were typical. They married and moved into the farmhouse with my grandfather's parents, and my grandfather took a job in town as a mechanic. My grandmother spent the first ten years of her marriage working alongside her mother-in-law, and fifty years later had not a negative word to say about her. They knew it wasn't their house or their farm or their business. When there were only three generations, "wait your turn" worked.

But now we have four generations. The time-proven process of "wait your turn" is history.

Let me offer three underlying reasons. The first is that people live longer.

In 1900, the life expectancy was forty-seven years.[2] Today, most people are just getting warmed up at forty-seven. One million cancer deaths have been prevented in the United States since 1990.[3] Previous generations used to hear, "Be patient; he won't live forever." Today, he might as well. Younger generations would have to wait into their seventies to take control. Since the Boomers, no generation has been patient. People are no longer willing to wait that long.

Second, there has been a huge acceleration in the speed of information, resulting in generations developing much more quickly and younger generations contributing significantly at earlier ages in knowledge-worker jobs. Not only is information far more accessible, there's far more of it, and it changes at lightning pace.

In an economy built around farming, change was incremental. The generations had very similar experiences and fewer generation gaps and tensions. In an industrial economy, the pace of change went faster. The automobile arrived. Then the radio. Then missiles. That meant that generational experiences changed rapidly. After the spread of television and the start of the Information Age, generations got even shorter.

In a knowledge economy, change is rapid. The personal computer. The Internet. The cell phone. Digital music. Remember the Walkman? It did its share to form a generation, and now ask kids what a Walkman is. They have no idea. Generational spans are reduced. The world used to be more orderly, where the people who had power had access to information and the rest of us had to ask. Now anyone with a smartphone can find information that only those at the top could access before. That allows every generation to contribute good ideas based on relevant data. Pervasive information levels the playing field. Everybody can be challenged by anybody, and those of us who have raised children know that they enjoy challenging us.

Finally, the "wait your turn" approach no longer works because we raised the last three generations as consumers. They were taught to question authority, shop for the best deal, and expect to be entertained. In the famous 1924 sociological studies in Muncie, Indiana, parents' top priorities for their children were for them to be good church members, religious, and obedient. In 1999, when sociologists did detailed studies for comparison, the top two desired qualities were tolerance and independent thinking.[4]

So get ready: flip-flops are coming to the workplace. Already there are organizations that allow flip-flops on Fridays if the employee gives money to charity. Here's my prediction: in ten years, flip-flops will be formal business wear. Women will wear flip-flops to formal cocktail parties. (They do already, depending on where you live.) Of course, these will be $250 flip-flops with a whole lot of bling, but flip-flops nonetheless.

How do I know flip-flops will be acceptable business wear? Simple: the world is not making any more Baby Boomers. Baby Boomers went out of production a long time ago.

I made my "flip-flops as formal business wear" prediction at a large insurance company. An executive shook her head at that, so I said to her, "You're thinking, *Over my dead body,* aren't you? Well, statistically speaking, you're probably right." Just as the Traditionalists finally gave way on suits and ties in most jobs, Boomers will give way on many things that right now they can't accept. It just takes time for enough Millennials to join the workforce to shift the balance. Those of us who don't understand why Millennials love flip-flops will get used to them (even if we never like them ourselves).

The bottom line is clear: the new generation will bring change, and smart organizations don't fight what they can't stop. They figure out how much of another generation's approaches they can embrace without hurting the business, and then they get back to the real work. Usually they just need an interpreter to help them understand some basic information about the generations so they can keep their teams together when generational differences start pulling them apart. Then they begin to figure out what to do.

One person who needed an interpreter was the chief information officer of a huge IT division who had hired me as a consultant. He was frustrated about the lack of engagement in a change-management process he had started up. "Haydn," he said, "we've decided to form four teams to follow up on the employee engagement survey we did, but people are not signing up for the teams. What's the problem?"

"Boomers," I said.

"But *we're* Boomers!"

"You don't mean to be the problem, but you are. Your expectation is that everyone who has been pushing the organization to improve and wants to do something about it has one option—sign up for one of your four teams. That's how Boomers got their voice heard: they joined committees. Except most of your folks are Xers or Millennials. They're not going to sign up for that."

"But we need to get them engaged. We're offering them a chance to have real influence."

"What if they don't want influence that way? You're only giving them a Boomer option, and they're not going to take it."

"But what are we going to do?" he said. "We need to have some kind of systematic process for input. We can't listen to 160 people."

"It's possible," I said. "It really is. Let me lay out for you what they would sign up for and how they want to do it."

Once I did that, and the leaders got it, they came up with ideas for doing things differently. Most of us can figure out better approaches once we understand the other generations.[5]

When I tell this story in my presentations, there are always some Boomers saying, "I wish *I* had known there were other options besides joining a committee. I've sat through a lifetime of those meetings." You probably know how those committee meetings go. "For a start, let's create our team charter." Three months later, the committee is still arguing over the wording. "Should we use *too* or *and*?" Of course, some people are really into it. "Wow. I just feel we're building a really cohesive group." But the more action-oriented members are looking for sharp objects to poke into their eyes because nothing is getting done.

The younger generation says, "Why do I have to sign up for this whole dreary process? Can't I just find other people with ideas, figure out the issues we need to work around, and get it cranked out—without any more than three face-to-face meetings?"

DIFFERENT COUNTRIES

That IT department makes a good illustration of my basic premise. Neither generation had any understanding or flexibility with the other. The Boomer leadership team could only interpret their department's lack of committee work as "they don't care," whereas the Xer and Millennial teams couldn't imagine why the leadership would ask them to suffer through what they considered an excruciating process. They could only assume "they don't care." They were two different decision-making cultures from two different worlds missing each other.

The truth is, we were raised in different countries, but we don't realize it. We think, *We all speak English, and most of us didn't grow up in different nations, so this shouldn't be hard.* But even if the people on your team came from the same town and attended the same schools, they did not grow up in the same place. The 1924 town that Traditionalists grew up in was very different from the one their grandkids experienced in 1984. They were taught differently in school, they've seen different events on TV or their laptops, they have different customs, they grew up in different houses, and they had different ways of interacting. If we miss that, we get frustrated and wonder what is wrong with others for not responding like we do. Frustrations lead to stereotyping.

Once we begin talking in stereotypes, conflicts get worse fast. Generations start talking down to each other, but they do it loudly and slowly, like the stereotypical "ugly American" abroad. There really are such people. They are ugly because they don't try to understand the cultures of the countries they visit; they try to get what they want the same way they do at home. "Doesn't anybody here speak English?" they ask. And then they talk slowly and loudly, as though the other person is an idiot.

You see that between the generations, too. A younger employee is asked if she can come in and help the boss troubleshoot a computer problem so the boss can get a proposal in the mail today.

The boss says, "All I know is I get the blue screen of death."

"Now here's what you need to do," the employee answers, very slowly. "You'll—need—to—reboot. Do—you—understand?" She thinks to herself, *You don't understand a word I'm saying, do you?*

Or a manager shows his frustration when the Millennial employee who he's been assigned to mentor asks why he can't work from home on Fridays. Speaking slowly and a little too politely, he says, "Because it's not our policy," as if that answers it.

"But why is that our policy when studies show that people who work flexible schedules get more done?" the Millennial says, also a little too politely.

On the way home, both of them may realize they were talking down to each other. They got the blue screen of death—the computer error screen that halts all activity—trying to communicate. Unfortunately, they probably won't feel bad about it because each believes the other is to blame. They don't know enough to reboot and try it again, but with respect this time.

We talk about generational diversity in ways we would never speak of other differences, and we do it without giving it a second thought. "You know how entitled these new employees are." "The older executives are so rigid." We use stereotypes and labels and put people into boxes. We wouldn't talk that way about gender. We wouldn't talk that way about ethnicity. But when it comes to generations, we forget to show respect or at least to keep our mouths shut. Four generations is so new that we don't know what to do about it, so we resort to stereotypes to vent our frustrations. That's understandable, but stereotypes only make matters worse.

If we are going to get through this next decade, we have to understand that we are natives to only one generation and immigrants to the other three. We might as well not be jerks about it.

18

It's okay to think about a different generation in the same way we might think about a different country—*Nice place to visit, but I wouldn't want to live there.* Of course we will feel more comfortable with our own generation's customs, music, approaches, and values. Our own generation will always feel like home. But that doesn't mean we can't visit other cultures and learn to appreciate them and to speak their language.

One corporate president told me this was the most helpful thing I said in my presentation. He realized how much a product of his own generation he was despite his Gen X and Millennial children, and he began to feel bad that he was not understanding his people and his family. "But when you said we're only native to one generation, I realized I can't be blamed for being from the country of Boomer. I can only be blamed for not learning about your country or for making you do it my way. That's bad leadership."

He got it. When you realize you are in a different country with a different language and different values, you find someone who can translate and teach what you need to know to find your way.

FOUR APPROACHES

There are four approaches to the four generations. The approach we take determines the results we get. Which approach are you using? Which approach is your boss using? Your organization? Which approach do you need to use to get the results you need?

1. Ignore Them

When a generation first hits the workplace, it's easiest to ignore them. Their numbers are small, so they are easy to miss. Even more, since they are a minority, they tend to adapt to the dress, communication styles, and approaches of the other generations. They drive to work in flip-flops and change to shoes in the car. We don't see the flip-flops, so we don't think anything has changed.

One group of executives assured me that their Millennials were not like what I described. "They never grumble that we require suit and tie." But if these executives ran into them in the store or saw them around their homes, they would be shocked. Or some notice the difference but believe what I hear from many business owners: "It's my sandbox. They had better learn my way if they want to play in it."

If you want to ignore generational issues, it's easy: don't hire people you don't understand. Hire people like you . . . until they're all dead.

I had taught about half my session in Phoenix when a guy said, "Based on what I've learned about the generations, I've got five more years to flip my business and get out. I don't want to deal with these generational differences, so I'm just going to hire Boomers or Xers who think like Boomers."

"At least you have a plan," I said. "Just make sure you sell to a very careless buyer. If you get a buyer who does due diligence, she might figure out that you don't have a sustainable business model. All your employees with the knowledge to run the company will be about to retire. If she notices, it will cut the street value of the business by 25 percent. Let's hope you find a buyer who is kind of stupid."

He paused. "I had a really good plan until I talked to you."

This is far from an extreme example. In the past year, I've heard fifty managers or executives tell me they are done hiring Millennials. But with close to 50 percent of postcollege Millennials already in the workplace, it's hard to ignore them. Once we can no longer ignore a generation, we have three remaining choices.

2. Fix Them

When there are too many members of another generation to ignore, it's tempting to try to fix them. Some organizations brag to me of their training programs for Millennials. If the programs help them understand customers and employees of different generations, I'm all for them. Every organization needs tour guides. But if only the Millennials are learning about other generations, I dig deeper into what the programs are covering. Most of the time, they are trying to "fix" the Millennials. The employers behind the programs believe Millennials are broken and need to be less like themselves and more like the older generations.

Fixing goes both directions. Over half of all younger-generation employees disparage the abilities of older employees, just as almost 75 percent of older workers disparage the abilities of younger employees.[6]

Most of us have had some experience with trying to fix people in family life, and we know how effective it is. Have you ever tried this? "Honey, I just want to take a moment out of my busy day to help you improve." Even dogs are not excited when they overhear you talking about getting them fixed.

We spend too much unproductive time in our organizations and families trying to fix the other generations when they don't think there is anything wrong. Here's a very important point, especially for business leaders: no matter how hard you had it, your younger employees didn't experience it, and so it's not real to them. So go easy on the "back in the day" stories. If your kids would roll their eyes, your younger employees probably want to.

3. Cut a Deal with Them

Once half a new generation hits the workplace, power begins to tip. The new generation begins eating lunch together, and it doesn't take long for them to realize that everyone else at the table is changing from flip-flops into shoes in the parking lot. Then they begin to ask each other why. "If we work in an office or a customer service call center and don't see customers, why can't we wear flip-flops?"

Once half of the new generation is out of school and in the workplace, managers are forced to do something about the dress code (or work-from-home policy, or sales approach, etc.). The older generations begin cutting a deal with the new generation. We saw the same pattern when the Gen Xers entered the workforce. Ignore, stereotype, and try to fix (we called them "slackers" for a decade), and then finally cut a deal—and casual Friday spread to most organizations.

On a practical level, some generational differences can be solved by cutting a deal. But it is no longer the solution it was with Baby Boomers. Boomers faced an employer's market and had to defer to the older generations who made the hiring decisions.

When the massive surge of Boomers hit the work world, it was intensely competitive. One company president told me that his senior year in college, he went on thirty job interviews and got two offers. "A third of my graduating class didn't have a job when they finished school. We were the first Baby Boomers in the workplace, so of course we did what they said. They had the jobs, so we wore the ties."

But there was a limit to that. The Traditionalists believed neckties were essential for men outside the home. You know what a necktie is? It won't be long before you only see them in museums. Boomers were not as enthusiastic about ties. Boomers began, very gradually, to experiment with dropping the tie. And the Traditionalists were genuinely shocked. Religious organizations spent ten years fighting over whether you had to wear a tie to church, and millions of Boomers just quit going. (Unlike previous generations, Boomers didn't wait their turn; they dropped out of church or joined congregations that didn't require ties.)

Over time, as the balance of power began to tip, organizations cut a deal about neckties. When Gen Xers entered the workplace, the deal making accelerated because there weren't as many of them and the labor market needed them. Many just wouldn't work at a place where they had to wear a tie.

"What if you only wear the tie when you're with older clients?"

"Okay, for how long?"

"The whole meeting, but only if they are wearing one."

"Why do you Traditionalist guys wear ties at all?"

No answer made sense to the Gen Xers because it was just part of the uniform. Slowly, society cut a deal and said, "You don't have to wear a tie, except in certain jobs and on certain ceremonial occasions." (The *Wall Street Journal* ran an article a few years ago on the conflicts over suits and ties in high-end law firms, long the land of the formal dress code. Newly employed Millennials questioned why they had to dress up if they weren't meeting clients. The law firms were surprised. One New York law office buys new employees a suit, ties, and shoes.[7] "We're lawyers: we wear ties.")

The same deal-cutting happened in American society at large with women and girdles. Girdle sales dropped suddenly in the late 1960s. After hundreds of years of women wearing corsets, Boomer women decided not to wear them, and sales fell off a cliff. One Boomer woman said she looked her mother in the eye and said, "I'm not strapping myself into latex for any man." Yankelovich, one of the pioneer generational market research companies, claims the girdle launched their generational approach to marketing. The president of Playtex called in a panic and wondered what to do since his wife had announced at dinner that she was throwing out her girdles. Sales had plummeted in six months.[8] Mass marketing gave way to generational market research and targeted campaigns.

Every new generation negotiates a deal with their elders. Gen Xers came along and said, "We're not going to relocate." Their Traditionalist and Boomer bosses were shocked. They had relocated seven times in twelve years to move ahead. An early Boomer friend of mine thought he had won the lottery when he got hired by IBM right out of college. People were pounding his back and congratulating him. IBM shipped him off for four five-week training sessions in Atlanta. *Twenty weeks* of his first year he was gone. "Because IBM was such a family-friendly company," he told me, "they gave us a half hour every Saturday on the company's phone to call home and talk to our families. Neither my wife nor I ever questioned it."

The Xers cut a new deal on relocating. There's an episode of *Friends*, the ultimate Xer TV show, where Chandler Bing, one of the few characters with a corporate job, falls asleep in a meeting. Somebody asks him to move to the Tulsa office. He wakes up and says yes without knowing what they asked. Later on he realizes what he did. When he tells his girlfriend, Monica, that he's moving to Tulsa, she says go ahead, but she's not moving with him. The whole premise of the episode is that only if he were asleep would an Xer say yes to Tulsa without asking his spouse or partner. Contrast this attitude with the Boomers, who would have been jumping for Tulsa like dogs for a piece of bacon:

"Tulsa? Is it a promotion?"

"No, it's a lateral move."

"Do I get a raise?"

"No."

"Do you pay my moving expenses?"

"Half."

"Okay, I'll go, because it will look good on my résumé. If I don't go, there are fifteen other people who would jump at the offer."

Boomers remember someone pulling them aside and whispering, "Don't be too picky; they'll only offer you a promotion two or three times. The next one could be worse."

But the Xers said, "Thanks for the offer, glad you have confidence in me, but this city works better for my home life."

"You're telling us no?"

"Yes, but thanks. Think of me when you have something at this office."

"But we need someone to go to Tulsa. Who's going to go to Tulsa?"

So the Boomer ended up hiring someone in Tulsa and then flying a week a month to help him get ramped up. Because there were so few Gen Xers, organizations had to quit insisting people relocate. Today, audiences are shocked that anyone would agree to off-site training twenty weeks their first year. Over time we cut a deal with the Xers, and most of us don't remember the way it was before. Boomers haven't called them "slackers" for ten years, though in delicious irony I've heard Gen X managers call Millennials "slackers" and not even remember where they got the word.

We need to remember that thousands of Traditionalists fought casual, and now most workplaces no longer require the tie and jacket. Boomers worked long hours and relocated, and today we take for granted that candidates have to talk job offers over at home before they can give an answer on relocation. Thousands of Boomers and Gen Xers will fight adjusting to the more networked and casual style of the Millennials, and in ten years they won't remember their organization did it any other way. Smart organizations know things will shift, and they will do it gradually and with understanding rather than holding on to old habits until generational tensions erupt and they have no choice. They move from cutting a deal to the only approach that takes full advantage of the sticking points.

4. Lead Them

The problem with cutting deals is that you can't do it with all four generations at once. Even though managers are spending more time than ever in meetings to recraft policies, no matter what they come up with, someone will be upset. You can't cut one deal that engages everyone. Some organizations are experimenting with cutting many deals, but that becomes craziness to manage. And that's the problem—managing it.

Throughout history, managing has worked. Each of the first three approaches is management. Managers ignore, managers determine what should be fixed, and managers cut the deals and then announce them. Even if they get feedback and do focus groups, they are ultimately the ones who decide how to change the policies. They keep control over the rules, but they have to spend more and more time doing so in this multigenerational, information-driven workplace. Managing down isn't getting the same results anymore. Information is too pervasive, the environment changes too quickly, and employees who are used to thirty coffee choices in the average supermarket don't get it when they come to work and are told what they have to do and how they have to do it.

So what's left? What's left is to lead.

Years ago I heard Colin Powell describe what it takes to lead an army. You could summarize his remarks this way: "Love your soldiers. Wake up in the morning and love your soldiers. Go to bed at night thinking about your soldiers." The husband of one of my colleagues worked closely with Powell during the Gulf War in 1990 and 1991. He and the other soldiers under Powell would have done anything he asked night or day. No question. That's leadership.

Leaders love their people. If we love people, we won't try to change them. We can only lead people if we quit trying to change them, and we can't quit trying to change them until we appreciate them, and we can't appreciate them until we understand them. Leadership starts with understanding. Once we understand others, we realize that if we had been born where they were born and raised in the situation they were raised in, we would think a lot more like they do. Maybe, just maybe, they're not so weird; maybe their differences have to do with their experiences. Maybe they came from a different world. And then it clicks: that's where we must start, no matter what generational differences we face. Understanding is the antidote to the relational poison of fixing.

The Boomers were the last generation that responded to management; Gen Xers and Millennials respond to leadership.

The problems with management have been explored for thirty years. For at least that long we've known why leadership is necessary in the Information Age to drive employee engagement, innovation, and new markets. Yet many organizations still use Industrial Age thinking and approaches to squeeze out results.

The Millennials will change that. Gen X required a more humane management approach and less control, but because there were too few of them and they were not in upper management, organizations could continue to manage rather than setting the vision, the goals, and the values and then leading accordingly. The younger generations may put up with management in a recession when jobs are scarce, but they respond to leadership.

Frankly, Boomers also respond better to leadership (as Stephen Covey, Jim Collins, Warren Bennis, and a host of others have demonstrated), but they were the last generation to start work in the Industrial Age. They carried typewriters into college dorm rooms. And they entered hierarchical organizations. In 1950 almost 20 percent of men were veterans of World War II, and those who weren't had been heavily engaged in the war effort. Plus, many had been raised in hierarchical families in rural communities where they were taught children should be seen and not heard. Of course managers would direct large organizations the same way they had been managed at home or in both world wars. And it worked. Management built large, successful organizations.

So even though Boomers respond better to leadership, they learned early on to "buck up" and function with management. But the new generations are from a different world. They will continue to push organizations toward what the leadership books have been telling us the past three decades.

WHO'S GOING TO KNOW WHERE THE PIPES ARE BURIED?

What approach are you and your organization taking—ignoring, fixing, cutting a deal, or leading? How much longer do you think you have until you are forced to lead? Why wait? The landing is easier if you don't have to force the plane down at the last minute in the midst of full-strength, four-generation turbulence.

I was teaching in an oil refinery, and a whole group of Boomer supervisors complained to me that the younger employees just didn't get it. "When we joined thirty years ago," one of them said, "we had to do all the dirty work and pay the price before we got any chance to make decisions. The younger generation just doesn't want to do that. In fact, most of them are talking like they don't expect to be here long. There's no loyalty. What do we do to keep them here for thirty years?"

"Why is that important?" I asked.

"Somebody in this refinery has to know where all the pipes are buried. In an emergency, we need somebody with that kind of knowledge, or this town could blow up."

"I see your point. What have you tried?"

"In each department we've tried mentoring a couple of guys who we thought would stay around. But they don't want to hear our stories and wait their turn like we did. When the old guys used to put their arms around our shoulders and tell us we were management material, we would listen to their stories—hundreds of times. You figured out how things really worked that way. What's wrong with these young guys?"

"When you were about to graduate high school, did your fathers tell you to try to get a job here at a huge, stable company?" I asked.

"Yeah. And when we got the job, they knew we were set for life."

"Most of you have children," I said. "Are you encouraging them to work here?"

They all looked around. "I told my kids to stay in college," one of them said. "I don't necessarily want my children working around hydrocarbons."

Somebody else said, "You know, for the past fifteen years people have speculated this place will get sold. It's not the same kind of refinery it was when I started."

"Let me see if I understand," I said. "What you're asking is 'Where do we find the stupid Millennials?' You want me to help you find the stupid ones who don't know this place has been up for sale. If you can get the stupid ones, you only need to mentor two just like the old guys did when you came, when this was a good job that people would happily stick to for thirty years. But if you don't want stupid ones, you'll have to train seven or eight people because you won't know how long they will stay."

Somebody said, "But that's a lot more work, training seven or eight people instead of just one or two like they did for us! It's not fair that we have to work a lot harder than the guys before us had to. We want you to tell us how to find the ones who will stay."

"Guys," I said, "let's have a moment of silence, because everybody needs to pout when they face a reality they don't like. You're going to have to work harder at this than the generation before you did. You're going to have to train seven or eight people, knowing that they will probably turn over. But if you care about this town and you want somebody to know where those pipes are in an emergency, you'd better get working."

Later one of them pulled me aside and said, "Thanks for this. I've always prided myself as a mentor, but I was thinking of retiring. I thought I had lost my touch. I get it now that I have to change my approach. These Millennials are a lot like my kids. I figured out how to talk with them at home. I can do it at work."

That's leadership: understanding other generations and how the world looks from their point of view, learning how to solve problems with them without first trying to "fix" them. Sometimes you can negotiate a deal. Mostly, you have to get the different generations talking to each other and working through their frictions. It's not that hard to move from management to leadership, but it does mean stopping and understanding why the generations approach life differently. It means understanding five steps for leading through those differences. And it means moving past leadership stereotypes so that anyone—supervisor or not—can lead through the twelve sticking points at work.

CHAPTER 3

Getting Unstuck: Five Steps for Leading through the Twelve Generational Sticking Points

THE YOUNGER MEMBERS of the team in charge of the conference where I was speaking were sitting against the back wall of the auditorium, working on their laptops. When their regional director, Mary, an older Baby Boomer, asked what she could do to keep her younger employees engaged in their weekly staff meeting, they suddenly looked up, their interest piqued.

I had just finished giving a presentation on generational differences to four hundred leaders in Phoenix, and Mary was interviewing me, asking me questions the audience had submitted—what to do to get a younger employee to show up on time, whether organizations should allow Facebook during office hours, and so on. But as we were reaching the end of the interview, Mary threw in one of her own questions.

Her team stared in surprise as she admitted that for the past three years, she worried she had lost her touch. Throughout her career, people had told her she was great at leading meetings, but now her Millennial and younger Gen X employees worked on their laptops during meetings, rarely looking up. Despite feedback from some older colleagues who complained that this behavior was rude, she knew her younger employees didn't mean any disrespect. But she did wonder at times if they were listening, and she missed the energy, excitement, and engagement that brainstorming and eye contact had created on her teams in the past.

I took about five minutes to answer her question. I gave a quick summary of how the four generations see the sticking points of meetings and respect and assured her that coming unstuck would be easy. We wrapped up with one last question from the audience, the conference took a quick break, and then the next speaker began his session.

I sat in the back row to listen. Mary's young team members were still there, whispering about her question. They were surprised that she felt they weren't engaged. They wondered what their team could do to make meetings better for everyone.

Later, as we were all packing up, Mary's team asked me to go into a little more depth on how the generations see meetings. I watched her team work through their sticking point before they left the auditorium.

It took them twenty minutes. All they needed was a process.

Let's take an in-depth look at the process I outlined when I answered Mary's question—the process I outline whenever I help teams through their generational sticking points, which will help you and your teams as well.

ANYONE CAN LEAD

Having four generations at work causes scores of conflicts every day, but in my work with organizations, twelve sticking points come up most often:

1. **Communication:** What is the best way to interact with my coworkers?
2. **Decision making:** How do we decide what to do?
3. **Dress code:** How casually can I dress?
4. **Feedback:** How often and in what ways do I want input?
5. **Fun:** How much fun at work is allowed?
6. **Knowledge transfer:** How do we pass on critical knowledge to new employees?
7. **Loyalty:** When is it okay to move on?
8. **Meetings:** What should happen in our meetings?
9. **Policies:** Are policies rules or guidelines?
10. **Respect:** How do I get others to respect me?
11. **Training:** How do I learn best?
12. **Work ethic:** How many hours are required, and when must I work them?

While there are many more sticking points we could address, learning how to deal with the twelve most common will teach us how to handle any others we encounter. Furthermore, if we know these twelve sticking points, we can watch for them and avoid needless tensions. Even better, sticking points can be turned into the glue that holds the four generations together in the twelve places they come apart.

But here is an important distinction: knowing what the twelve sticking points are isn't the same thing as knowing what to do about them. That's why having a process makes all the difference. It's easy for us to allow sticking points to become conflicts that leave us stuck; but with the right tools, it is equally easy for them to become places of renewed unity for our teams and families.

If you are going to be effective with four generations, you'll need to quit trying to fix or cut a deal with the generations and start leading. If you don't think you can lead because you're not a born leader or you don't have a management position in your organization, you miss a great opportunity to make a significant impact. Whoever you are, whatever your role, you can help your colleagues work through generational differences by using the five steps. In this chapter, I'll explain the five steps, and in chapters 8–19, I'll apply them to the twelve generational sticking points.

THE FIVE STEPS FOR LEADING THROUGH GENERATIONAL DIFFERENCES

Here are the five steps for leading through the twelve sticking points the four generations encounter:

1. **Acknowledge:** Talk about generational differences.
2. **Appreciate:** Focus on the "why," not the "what," and the common needs.
3. **Flex:** Agree on how to accommodate different approaches.
4. **Leverage:** Maximize the strengths of each generation.
5. **Resolve:** Determine which option will yield the best results (when flexing isn't enough).

Let's go into each of the steps in more detail, illustrating how to use them with colleagues or family.

1. Acknowledge: *Talk about generational differences.*

Competitive advantage goes to the team that can bring differences and frustrations into the open, where they can be resolved.

Consider this example. Someone on your team comes to you because she can't communicate with the person in the next cubicle. Her cubicle neighbor always has his earbuds in while he works. "We've always just talked to each other over the cubicle wall," she says. "But Josh never responds because he doesn't hear me with his earbuds in. I have to get up and go to his desk, and then he has to pull one of those things out of his ear before we can talk. Sometimes he looks annoyed, like I'm bothering him or something. What's wrong with these young employees?"

Instead of trying to manage the situation by immediately making a new policy—"No earbuds during work"—bring it to the team: "A couple of people have mentioned the difficulty of communicating through our cubicles due to people wearing earbuds or headphones while they're working. Obviously, headphones aren't going to go away anytime soon, so let's talk about this. I've learned it's part of a common generational difference. We definitely need to keep information flowing all day, so let's talk about how we do that now that more people use headphones."

Once you've put the hard feelings on the table and emphasized the common need, don't be surprised if there is dead silence for a moment. Don't fear silence, even if it's awkward at first. You've brought the problem into the open, and it's now time for the generations to talk (if you can keep them from fighting, that is).

2. Appreciate: *Focus on the "why," not the "what," and the common needs.*

Appreciating other generations keeps generations talking instead of fighting. If we put a generational sticking point on the table and then let people talk, usually their first reaction is to complain about what is wrong with another generation. A generational fight can break out in two minutes. That's why we have to quickly introduce the common need and switch from "what" to "why."

In the example above, "We definitely need to keep information flowing all day" reminds the team of their common need to communicate. We all have the same basic needs, but the generations try to meet those needs differently. When people are caught up in a generational sticking point, emotions escalate, and people forget that they have far more similarities than differences. When that happens, the tensions appear bigger than they really are. Emphasizing the common need early on redirects the goal from "fixing" another generation (so they do it my way) to resolving the sticking point. Appreciating common needs settles down the emotions so we can start talking about the whys.

When I teach how to deal with generational differences, I may have to redirect a group from talking what to why twenty times before they get the hang of this new way of thinking. When they do, they make quick progress. The secret is simple: whats divide; whys unite. Try it with your team and watch the unhelpful stereotyping and judging ease and communication and understanding grow.

Continuing with the previous example, now that you've got the problem on the table, ask why: "Why do you prefer to talk over the cubicle wall?" "Why do you prefer to work with headphones? Why don't you think it's more convenient to talk across the cubes?" (By the way, the answer I've heard from hundreds of Millennials and Xers is that Boomers chatter all day, and the younger generations can't concentrate. They use music to drown out the conversations. Plus, they think it's faster as well as less distracting to use e-mail to communicate. Recently an Xer told me that when an older colleague asks three times a day if everyone saw the e-mail that just appeared, she wants to scream.)

Until the people on your team understand why other generations work differently, they will remain irritated, and the team will pull apart rather than stick together. Getting stuck complaining about what is different is the biggest cause of generational tensions. Sadly, focusing on the differences is so common that I have seen generational training programs built around the whats. They give long lists of characteristics of each generation and techniques to manage them. Instead of beginning with understanding, they begin with differences.

The Baby Boomer head of diversity for a large food company told me that my speech on generations the year before changed things for her. She discovered she didn't want to fix the Millennials now that their behavior made sense. She said, "I no longer see them as feeling entitled. They have just been marketed to so much. When you said Millennials expect a toy in the bag with every meal, it clicked for me."

So when colleagues or direct reports come to you with a what that's bugging them about another generation, let them vent for a moment and then refocus them on the why. Coach them to talk to the "offender" themselves about why the what is happening. Remind them that they are going to the other person not to change him or her but to understand. You will be surprised how often this simple step will take care of the situation. Simply understanding where the other person is coming from resolves many conflicts. At the very least, it drains the emotion out of the discussion so the team can sort out better solutions.

3. Flex: *Agree on how to accommodate different approaches.*

Once people acknowledge and appreciate their differences, they can decide how to flex for each generation. Consider training, for example: the four generations prefer to learn differently. Once those preferences are recognized, the team can offer multiple training options. Organizations have been arguing over classroom versus online training for fifteen years. Don't argue—flex. Offer them both, let people choose, and then verify they have gained proficiency. The common need is not *how* people learn but *that* they learn.

Should all policies be flexible? Of course not. So how do you decide what to flex? *By determining which policies are based on a business (or organizational) necessity.* Everything else can flex. Many policies are nothing more than how the generation in charge prefers to do things. And sometimes the policies remain in place long after the generation that wrote them has retired.

When it comes to generational sticking points, the hardest thing for many people is separating their preferences from the needs of the organization. The first two chapters are full of examples of people who weren't able to tell the difference between them and escalated the inevitable generational frictions into conflicts that could have been avoided.

Clear definitions can protect your team from generational preferences masquerading as business policies.

BUSINESS NECESSITY:
Anything that will make you lose your foot, customer, money, or funding.

GENERATIONAL PREFERENCE:
Anything that is not a business necessity.

If the policy doesn't prevent you from losing a foot, a customer, money, or funding (if you are a nonprofit), then it's a preference and should be flexed to accommodate different generational approaches.

Take wearing flip-flops in the workplace as an example. Should you flex the dress code to allow flip-flops? In a factory, your workers could lose a toe wearing flip-flops (steel-toed flip-flops defeat the purpose), so no flip-flops is a business necessity. Neither should hospital personnel be allowed to wear them. It seems silly to imagine doctors scrubbing both hands *and* feet before surgery. Food service organizations should also prohibit flip-flops. Watching my burrito get made by a guy with grease under his toenails would take away my appetite. Salespeople shouldn't wear them if their customers don't like it. I'm sure you could think of a few other situations where flip-flops would cost you your foot, your customer, your money, or your funding. Of course, if the company's goals or your customers' expectations—and therefore its business necessities—change over time, then the policy must change as well.

One woman on a webinar said she thought banning flip-flops is a business necessity because she found the noise they make distracting, which diminished her productivity. When I asked if any other types of sandals in her workplace made flapping noises, she said yes—but they weren't as distracting. The others on the webinar wouldn't let her get by with it. They questioned her acoustical distinctions until she finally admitted that she didn't think flip-flops looked professional and that they shouldn't be worn at work. Though her desire for a professional workplace was admirable, she illustrated how easy it is to camouflage a generational preference as a business necessity.

Confusing a generational preference for a business necessity makes organizations inflexible; it can also cost them money. I was presenting to a large group, and when I started talking about flip-flops, one group whispered and laughed and didn't stop for five minutes. When I finished, I headed to their table, curious as to what made them call a meeting in the middle of my talk. They said they were the managers of one of the top spas in town and had a no-flip-flop policy. Their younger staff members were baffled by the policy since they gave their clients flip-flops to wear. They also argued that since they had been voted the city's best pedicure, wouldn't it make the spa more money if their clients could see their toes? So when I spoke about how inflexible organizations can get about dress codes, they realized they had turned their generational preference into a policy. They couldn't quit laughing at the irony that of all businesses, flip-flops made perfect sense for spa employees because clients expected an informal environment and flip-flops provided free advertising for their pedicures. In the middle of my presentation, they decided that their no-flip-flop policy would change the next day.

Smart organizations listen when the different generations help them see where they are losing money because they have mixed up business necessities with generational preferences.

In contrast, some people would rather lose money than flex. A couple of years ago I spoke to two hundred small business owners on how to keep their younger employees motivated and loyal because they had seen drops in productivity that hurt their businesses. About halfway through the presentation, some of them disagreed so strongly they stopped me. "If it's my business and I pay them," they asked, "why should I have to flex for these younger generations? They should flex for me. I started my own business to be able to run things the way I want."

My response was, "No problem. If you can find employees who want to play by your rules, and your rules make your business a success, then there's no need to change."

Their next question made it clear they were missing the point: "So how can we get our younger employees to do it the way we want?"

I almost laughed out loud. These business owners were insisting on running things according to their preferences and were surprised to discover that their younger employees ignored them or quit. It's human nature, but they chose their own emotional comfort over business success. Organizations have a few necessities, but most things are preferences.

4. Leverage: *Maximize the strengths of each generation.*

At best, cutting a deal produces a compromise, but maximizing differences produces leverage. Just as a physical lever can allow a single human to move a boulder, leveraging generational differences so that one person's strength makes up for another's weakness provides a large impact from a small team.

The father of modern management, the late Peter Drucker, said one of the goals of management is "to make human strengths [increase] performance while human weakness is neutralized and largely rendered harmless."[1] Each generation brings different strengths to the team, and smart leaders arrange the various strengths on their teams in such a way as to neutralize weaknesses, leveraging those strengths so the whole is greater than the sum of its parts. Effective leaders combine people from multiple generations to accomplish more than if they recruited from only one. And recent research in France discovered that mixed groups of younger and older employees had the highest levels of cooperation.[2]

It's easy, however, to miss the strengths and leverage the irritations. At the processing center for a very large bank, a Gen X manager said, "We did a team-building exercise a couple of months ago that my boss found on the Internet. We broke up by generations. Each of the groups wrote down what they liked and what annoyed them when working with the other generations. Each generation filled up a flip chart and a half of things that irritated them about the others, but no generation recorded a single thing they liked about working with the other generations."

And no wonder—they started in the wrong place. They started with the "what" and not the "why," and then they stayed stuck on annoyances rather than contributions. Sticking points can pull us apart, as this department learned, but they can also help us stick together by appreciating and leveraging our generational differences. Leadership means bringing out the positive in what others think are negatives.[3]

After speaking to one of the largest golf course–management companies in the world, I opened the floor for questions and answers. A manager asked, "How can I get my younger employees to show up on time to open the course at 5:00 a.m.?" I responded that I would be surprised if you could get many Millennials to show up at 5:00 a.m. since they had probably been out until midnight the night before. My suggestion was to give that assignment to a Traditionalist who goes to bed by 10:00 p.m., produces less of the sleep hormone melatonin, and therefore can't sleep past 5:00 a.m. even if he wants to. Let him open up, turn things over to the Millennials at nine (or ten), and then head out to golf or drive the course as a ranger.

Sometimes we make things harder than they need to be. If you keep your eyes open over the next couple of weeks, you'll notice twenty examples in your organization where generational strengths could be better leveraged. Leveraging the strengths of each generation builds a better team, so start turning sticking points into the glue that sticks your team together.

5. Resolve: *Determine which option will yield the best results (when flexing isn't enough).*

It's not possible to flex away every irritation or sticking point. Flexing allows you to "meet in the middle" when each generation accommodates the approaches of the others, but with over half of the twelve sticking points (decision making, dress code, fun, knowledge transfer, loyalty, meetings, policies, work ethic), flexing doesn't solve most of the problem. If there are four generations in the workplace, you can't rotate a policy every four weeks in order to please each generation. Therefore, when flexing isn't enough, we have to resolve the issue. For example, you'll need to select the decision-making process that fits the situation, develop a plan to transfer knowledge, and figure out how to make the meetings work for everyone. Understanding and flexing will make it far easier to come to a resolution, but you will ultimately have to decide how you will move forward in those situations where everyone's preferences can't be accommodated.

THE FIVE STEPS IN ACTION

Let's see how the five-step process played out with Mary's team from the beginning of this chapter. They were stuck because they had different expectations about meetings. The Millennial team members who had heard Mary's question approached her after the session to apologize—they'd had no idea that working on their laptops during meetings bothered her. Once the sticking point between generational meeting styles was acknowledged (step 1), they immediately brainstormed creative ways to flex (step 3) the format of the meetings to meet everyone's needs. (And here's the kicker: they didn't stop packing up. They talked while they worked. Once people get it, the process goes quickly.)

But flexing couldn't solve all the issues; some of them had to be resolved. Increased understanding (step 2) made it painfully clear that no amount of flexing would please everyone. The Boomers on the team wanted meetings with agendas and full eye contact from all members. The Gen Xers wanted shorter meetings and to use e-mail to report progress instead of everyone taking a turn to verbally report. And the Millennials were happy to sit in the meetings as long as they could accomplish other work on their laptops when their participation wasn't needed. Better understanding allowed them to leverage their generational differences by agreeing to drop the verbal reports but keep the first ten minutes of fun and small talk (step 4). But that still left the problem of what to do about the computers. Knowing that everyone wasn't going to be satisfied with any decision, they agreed that computers in meetings were allowed as long as everyone stayed engaged and participated and team members didn't later request information that was covered in the meeting, which would be a sign they had not been listening (Step 5).

The computer question that couldn't be "flexed" away got resolved so the team could move forward—for now. A year from now the team will have new people, new technologies, different ratios between the four generations, and other unforeseeable changes. That means the obvious: today's resolution will become tomorrow's sticking point and will require new flexibility and new resolutions.

• • •

As you can see from Mary's story, the most important thing is to focus on why each generation prefers a different approach rather than on what they don't like about the other generations' behavior. And I've noticed that when teams understand other generations better, they will often resolve issues on their own, saving the organization from grinding out more policies. So if you are in a management role, stop trying to control the generations. Quit thinking you are the one who has to cut a deal. Your team can figure out the twelve sticking points while you work on other important decisions. That's the beauty of leadership.

This book will prepare you to apply the five-step process to the twelve sticking points. The first two chapters made the case for step 1, Acknowledge, by showing the mess created when we ignore generational differences. The next four chapters will go deeper into step 2, Appreciate, and get you thinking "why" rather than "what." They will give you crucial information and understanding about the generations that will make it possible for you to use the five steps to lead through your generational sticking points effectively at work and at home. That's the focus of part 2, where we'll roll up our sleeves and look at how to apply the five steps to each of the twelve main generational sticking points so you can help your relationships go from stuck to sticking together.

PART 1

Ghost Stories

Understanding the Four Generations

INTRODUCTION

Telling Ghost Stories

THE CHICAGO WATER TOWER is home to a famous ghost story. The Great Chicago Fire of 1871 left a third of the city homeless but did not burn down the limestone water tower. Legend has it that one of the water tower workers stayed, pumping water even after the others had fled the encroaching flames. Not realizing the building would be spared, he ran upstairs and hanged himself rather than be burned alive. Through the years, many have claimed to see his ghost hanging from a noose in the tower's upper window.[1]

Although this famous ghost story adds excitement to bus tours, the real ghost is the Chicago fire itself because its memory and impact still cast shadows throughout the city. The Great Chicago Fire explains why the city is larger (the rubble from the fire was dumped into the lake, expanding the shoreline) and why building codes became stricter. Historical events are like ghosts because their impact lingers long after the events are over.

Each generation has its own historical ghost stories, especially the "I remember what I was doing when . . ." moments. Traditionalists world-wide remember what they were doing when they first heard their country joined World War II. All of us remember what we were doing on September 11, 2001, when we heard that the World Trade Center's twin towers were

43

hit. These stories help us make sense of momentous events and explain who we are today and why. They live on like ghosts.

We don't fully appreciate another person until we understand his or her ghost stories. Couples tell each other their ghost stories for hours and then find themselves falling in love. They *stay* in love by explaining their current lives with ghost stories. "I don't know why you can't remember to put things away after you get them out!" the wife grumbles. The husband replies, "You know I'm not naturally organized like you are. I never have been. Don't you remember when I told you about the time I was ten . . . ?" When we understand a person's ghost stories, we appreciate that person more (or at least have less desire to strangle him or her).

In the same way, we won't appreciate another generation until we understand their ghost stories. The historical events during a generation's childhood years shape their values, worldview, and definitions of success. Their shared experiences are what distinguish them as a generation in the first place. That's why they use their ghost stories to explain themselves to other generations.

Thousands of people have found the material in the next four chapters transformational. I'll tell stories about the four biggest ghosts of the Traditionalists, Baby Boomers, and Gen Xers, but I'll relate six ghosts for the Millennials because they are the newest generation and consequently the least understood.[2] Certainly the older generations will benefit from the next four chapters of ghost stories. Even if we experienced the events described, we sometimes miss their significance for our relationships today. But the Millennials didn't live through most of these events—a major disadvantage for them. That's why these next four chapters are critical to their ability to relate to the older generations.

Telling ghost stories helps get four generations working together in the twelve places they come apart. But it's easy to take ghost stories too far. We'll look at two ways people do that before we get into the ghost stories themselves.

GHOST STORIES, NOT URBAN LEGENDS

In 1935 an alligator was caught and killed in an East Harlem sewer. From this one incident, an infamous urban legend emerged: tired of their pet alligators, New Yorkers flushed them down their toilets, and the alligators ended up in the sewer. After decades with no sunlight, the blind and albino gators became even more ferocious, feeding on anything they bumped into. The Department of Environmental Protection continues to educate people that alligators can't last through the winter in a cold climate, but the urban legend won't die.[3]

As this story illustrates, urban legends start with a kernel of truth (an alligator *was* caught in the sewer), add natural human fear (scary creatures in dark places!), and then stir in ignorance (of the habitat of alligators). Generational "urban legends"—stereotypes—get started in a similar way.

For example, consider the generational stereotype I often hear in my consulting work: that Traditionalists and Boomers resist new technology and are holding the rest of the team back. What's the kernel of truth there? Well, since there are always employees who put off learning the new technology in any software rollout, it's inevitable that some of them are older. The fear that often drives this stereotype—at least the "holding the rest of the team back" part—is that competitors will adapt to and adopt new technologies faster. What most people who hold this stereotype don't realize, however, is that half of all Boomers and 20 percent of Traditionalists sleep with their cell phones close at hand.[4]

Or consider the more recent stereotype that Millennials will hurt the team because they don't want to work in an office. The kernel of truth here is that *some* Millennials certainly do want to work from home more often. The fear is that their supervisors won't have the ability to hold them accountable if they can't see what the employees are doing. What surveys actually show, however, is that more than half of Millennials *want* to come in to work.[5]

Urban legends are inevitable, but fearing to go to the loo in New York City is avoidable. Similarly, generational friction is inevitable; generational problems are avoidable. Facts overcome urban legends. But how do we move people beyond the urban legends of stereotypes to understanding the facts about other generations? The best way is through interaction with people from other generations—telling each other our ghost stories. Unfortunately, we've all seen how similar people sit together at informal company settings. Since this interaction probably won't happen informally, we'll need the five-step process I outlined in chapter 3 to lead our teams toward results.

A company vice president once asked me for my most practical suggestion for increasing effectiveness with the other generations. I told him the highest-impact thing he could do was to reduce stereotyping in his division. Like urban legends, generational stereotypes take on lives of their own that lead us to withdraw or disengage from other generations. These stereotypes make us paranoid, and so we create the negative interaction we fear.

Or we spend a lot of time and money trying to fix something that is not broken. For example, PricewaterhouseCoopers (PwC) learned in their twelfth annual CEO survey that 61 percent of CEOs thought their company had challenges recruiting Millennial employees. CEOs see flexible schedules as critical to their ability to attract and retain talent. But as PwC's survey of new college graduates and many other surveys show, the younger generations value other things more than flexible schedules. Surprisingly, Boomers and Traditionalists value them even more than Millennials. (See more on this in chapter 19.)

These CEOs are trying to build their recruitment strategies around urban legends instead of around what Millennials really want. Wasting time and money on recruiting strategies is avoidable if we replace urban legends with facts.

GENERALIZATIONS, NOT STEREOTYPES

I asked my contact at a government agency why one of their Human Resources people didn't come back to my presentation after the first break. He told me she didn't like anything that put people into categories. And actually, I agree with her. Putting people into categories is stereotyping, but using generalizations is helpful.

Sherlock Holmes described the difference between the two to Dr. Watson this way:

> While the individual man is an insoluble puzzle, in the aggregate he becomes a mathematical certainty. You can, for example, never foretell what any one man will do, but you can say with precision what an average number will be up to. Individuals vary, but percentages remain constant.[6]

The generational comparisons I make throughout the book describe large numbers of people but fail to predict or explain any one individual. Generational research necessarily generalizes, oversimplifies. It's a valid generalization that Millennials are more likely to have a tattoo than members of other generations. But you'll only embarrass yourself if you ask every Millennial you meet to see his or her tattoo, because only 38 percent have them.[7] The percentages generalize, but thinking you've pegged a teammate because you know the percentages for that generation is stereotyping. Averages do not determine how any individual person will behave.

I've always been a fan of Ralph Stayer, the CEO and owner of

Johnsonville, because of the way he grew a small family butcher shop into an almost-billion-dollar company based on trust and empowerment long before those were popular management buzzwords.[8] So I was thrilled when I learned Mr. Stayer was able to attend a session I was leading for Johnsonville's leaders and new interns. I gave the group a list of generational preferences and asked them to select the ones that most matched their own. Ralph showed me his totals. With a grin on his face, he asked if he had done something wrong. Even though he was a Traditionalist by age, all his preferences but one matched the thinking of Millennials.

"Mr. Stayer," I said, "not only do I not think it's wrong, I think it's the explanation of how you've been so far ahead of your time. You were leading like a Millennial before anyone had even given them a name." Generalizations give us a place to start, but as we can see in Ralph Stayer's case, they don't do justice to any individual. That's why we must show respect and listen so we understand the person, not the label.

The point is, we don't get into trouble generalizing; we get into trouble making inaccurate generalizations. We all have generalizations about generations, some of them the equivalent of urban legends. But if we can understand the legitimate ghost stories that influence the generations, we will be a long way toward understanding why the generations behave the way they do. Nothing will help you reduce stereotypes and build bridges with other generations better than learning the important stories that have haunted them throughout their lives, and then telling some of your own.

CHAPTER 4

Traditionalists: Keep Calm and Carry On

BORN BEFORE 1945

Traditionalists (Born before 1945)

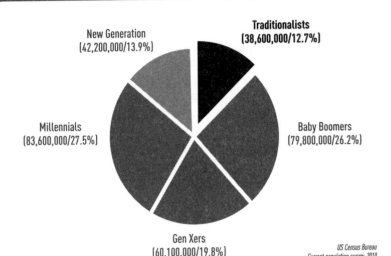

New Generation
(42,200,000/13.9%)

Traditionalists
(38,600,000/12.7%)

Millennials
(83,600,000/27.5%)

Baby Boomers
(79,800,000/26.2%)

Gen Xers
(60,100,000/19.8%)

US Census Bureau
Current population survey, 2010

Names
- Builders
- Matures
- GI Generation
- Silents
- Radio Generation
- Greatest Generation

Teen Years
- 1920s, 1930s, 1940s, 1950s

Key Events
- Standard Oil broken up (1911)
- World War I (1914–18)
- Prohibition (1920–33)
- First popular talking movie (1927)
- Sliced bread introduced (1928)
- The Great Depression (1929–39)
- The New Deal (1933–39)
- Move from the farm to the suburbs (1901–70)
- World War II (1939–45)
- Atom bomb dropped on Hiroshima (1945)

Top Television Shows
- None: networks didn't broadcast to the entire United States until 1951.

Top Music
- "Yes! We Have No Bananas" (Billy Jones, 1923)
- "The Prisoner's Song" (Vernon Dalhart, 1924)
- "Charleston" (Paul Whiteman and His Orchestra, 1925)
- "Tip-Toe thru the Tulips with Me" (Nick Lucas, 1929)
- "Smoke Gets in Your Eyes" (Paul Whiteman and His Orchestra, 1933)
- "Pennies from Heaven" (Bing Crosby, 1936)
- "A-Tisket, A-Tasket" (Ella Fitzgerald, 1938)
- "Boogie Woogie Bugle Boy" (The Andrews Sisters, 1941)
- "White Christmas" (Bing Crosby, 1942)
- "The Gypsy" (Dinah Shore; The Ink Spots, 1946)

What Makes Your Generation Unique?
Top five responses Traditionalists give about themselves:
- World War II, the Great Depression (14%)
- Smarter (13%)
- Honest (12%)
- Work ethic (10%)
- Values/morals (10%)[1]

Nervously tapping her clipboard, a frazzled Generation X meeting planner recently asked me, "Can you skip the section on Traditionalists[2] since there aren't many left in our organization? We're running behind, and we need you to cut fifteen minutes off your speech so we can end the day on time."

"I can," I replied, "but you won't see the same impact. It would be better to trim a little from each section because your younger employees won't understand the Baby Boomers without understanding the generation that trained them." Her puzzled expression told me she needed what I was going to say about Traditionalists as much as anyone.

We can't ignore Traditionalists because they still exert enormous influence on organizations. First, the youngest of the Traditionalists are still in the workplace, especially in leadership roles, and will be for another ten years.

Second, Traditionalists are still somebody's customers, voters, parishioners, or patients. (They can be your customers, too, if you understand who they are and therefore how to reach them.)

Peter Drucker, the father of modern management, grasped the older generation's importance in his final book, *Managing in the Next Society*:

> In the developed countries, the dominant factor in the Next Society will be something to which most people are now only just beginning to pay attention: the rapid growth in the older population and the rapid shrinking of the younger generation.[3]

Most important, you cannot understand the other generations without understanding Traditionalists because they built the organizations we have today and trained the Baby Boomers.

A manager in a large insurance firm summarized it well after hearing the historical influences that shaped the four generations: "Our company is like a car. It has a Traditionalist body, a Boomer transmission, and Generation X wheels, but it runs on Millennial fuel."

Therefore, you can't understand the organization you work in, the Boomers who lead it, or how to push for changes to it unless you understand the Traditionalists' ghost stories.

THE TRADITIONALISTS' FOUR BIGGEST GHOST STORIES
Ghost Story #1: The Great Depression

When I was twelve, my grandmother Emily moved in with us. Many times she would tell us as we ate dinner, "You kids should appreciate how much you have. When I was your age, we only had oleo on Sundays. The rest of the week we had lard on our bread." But it never had the impact on me she hoped. First, I didn't know what oleo was. (Oleo, I eventually learned, is margarine.) Second, I couldn't imagine a world where *margarine* was a luxury.

You can't understand the Traditionalists unless you understand how the shift from the Roaring Twenties to the Great Depression (beginning in 1929) left an entire generation cautious, thrifty, and focused on saving. With little welfare and no Social Security, millions of people barely fed their families despite sacrifice and hard work. Anyone who has Depression-era parents or grandparents has heard slogans like "Waste not, want not" and "Make do and mend." Many of the oldest Traditionalists continue to reuse their tea bags even after years of economic stability. When my other grandmother finally went to a nursing home at age eighty-nine, my aunt and uncle moved in to the family farmhouse and threw out approximately 2.3 billion plastic Cool Whip containers from the cellar. My grandmother figured if there came a time when she didn't have enough food, she would certainly have containers for what little she did have. One workshop participant told me his grandfather saved gallons of used tractor oil in case they would ever need to heat their home with it. They had done without, and they never wanted it to happen again.

The Great Depression made Traditionalists more economically conservative, and that conservatism spread to other areas of life. During the Roaring Twenties women's hemlines rose, but the Great Depression brought them back down. The Depression brought a greater focus on family. Puzzles, badminton, and (ironically) the board game Monopoly became national fads. The Great Depression made Traditionalists more conservative and cautious in every area of life.[4]

Ghost Story #2: World War II

The Great Depression taught Traditionalists to sacrifice and show patience. That lesson served them well during World War II. The most popular war in US history, World War II united the country like no other war before or since. Families gathered around the radio for war news, saved their cooking grease, and prayed for their men to come home. Those fighting in the war believed in the sacrifices they were making. Soldiers jumped out of Higgins boats on the beaches of Normandy on D-Day knowing that most of them would die but convinced death in victory was better than life lived under a totalitarian regime. So the Traditionalists learned to sacrifice their individuality for the cause—to sit down, shut up, and do what they were told.

Traditionalists didn't complain and often think younger people get upset about trivial things. Since we live in a different world, complaining about the food in the cafeteria or "food wagon" is a staple of office small talk: "Google has five chefs and different cuisines. I wish *we* worked at Google. We have the roach coach where the hamburgers and the fajitas all taste the same." Traditionalists who ate cold C-ration meals in foxholes would have little patience for those who complain that the corporate cafeteria has too few low-calorie selections. (Can you imagine someone in a foxhole in World War II whining that "last month's Spam had a nuttier, more piquant flavor to it"?)

Before World War II ended, almost 15 million people had served in the United States military. It took the largest government program in history and millions of people who sacrificed their own individual goals and dreams to win the big war. As a result, Traditionalists had far more confidence in their leaders and large organizations than we do today.

The ghost of World War II still roams the hallways of our organizations. World War II proved that large, hierarchical organizations could get things done. The Traditionalists came home from the war leading the way they were led. They ran hierarchical organizations using a command-and-control approach that expected employees to fall in line, prove their loyalty, and do their duty. They saw no need to chase off the ghosts of command and control until the information and service economy rewarded change, speed, and in-the-moment decision making.[5]

World War II introduced large numbers of women to mission-critical jobs outside the home. Before and after World War II, women working outside the home were relegated to jobs that were considered nonessential. But during the war, there was no choice but to replace men with Rosie the Riveter. "I've found the job where I fit best," a woman brags on a wartime government recruitment poster. After the war, she would be taken out of the job where she fit best and put back into "women's work" so a soldier could have a job. The wartime need for female workers brought thousands of women from the farm to the city. As we'll see in the Traditionalists' next ghost story, when the war was over, many did not go back.

In summary, because of World War II, Traditionalists witnessed the power of large government programs, larger-than-life leaders, and the accomplishments of a unified nation where everyone did his or her duty. They didn't question authority at home because the threat overseas was far more terrifying. Though greater acceptance of working women would take another generation, the seeds of change sprouted in World War II. Most of all, Traditionalists learned the power of sacrifice and patience. Ironically, the most famous British poster from World War II was produced in case Germany invaded Britain, but it was never used. It later became so popular because it captures the wartime perspective of the Traditionalists: "Keep Calm and Carry On."

Ghost Story #3: The Move from Farm to City

The third large ghost that shaped the Traditionalists was the rapid migration from farm to city. While this shift gained momentum through the first half of the twentieth century, the transition from an agricultural to an industrial workforce accelerated after World War II. Johnny came marching home from the war and married Rosie the Riveter. She told him she was not going back to the farm and the outhouse now that she had lived in town and used indoor plumbing. So she took him out to the suburbs to see the prefab houses with all the modern conveniences. These post–World War II subdivisions sprang up on the periphery of every major American and Canadian city.

At the beginning of the twentieth century, two-thirds of the United States and Canada lived on farms or in rural towns. By 1970, almost three-quarters lived in the city and suburbs. In my seventeen years of education, no one discussed this massive migration from the farm to the cities that has made incredible but often unnoticed impacts on our lives. I'll focus on the four impacts that most relate to generational sticking points.

1. LIFE ON THE FARM MAKES IT EASIER TO INSTILL WORK ETHIC.
I recently asked a group of Minnesota hog farmers to tell me the difference between growing up on the farm versus growing up in the city. One said

the city provides immediate gratification, and I see his point. In the city, you get paid a week or two after you work. On the farm, you plant in the spring and get paid months later in the summer or fall. In the city, you can have Chinese food delivered at 1:00 a.m. On the farm, Chinese comes out of a can if you get hungry in the middle of the night.

But I suggest it's just the opposite: the farm, not the city, taught the Traditionalists immediate gratification. On the farm, when the alarm goes off at 4:30 a.m. and it's time to milk the cows, there's no calling in sick. The popular '70s drama *The Waltons* gave many people a window into what the Depression was like. So let's imagine that the teenage John-Boy Walton doesn't get out of bed at 4:30 a.m. to milk the cow when Grandma Walton calls up the stairs that it's time to get up. (John-Boy is having girl trouble, so he is depressed and doesn't want to get up.) After calling two more times, Grandma Walton hurries upstairs and drags John-Boy out of bed. She knows the immediate consequences of not milking the cow—they don't get biscuits for breakfast. *That's* immediate gratification: if you get up and work, you will get to eat. In contrast, when I ask people what time their kids would need to wake up if they want a glass of milk, they tell me 3:00 in the afternoon. The suburbs don't create the same connection between work and reward. Farm life gave the Traditionalists the strongest work ethic of any of the four generations.

Today there's a huge delay instead of immediate gratification. I saw that in my own home when my thirteen-year-old son, Max, asked why he had to quit playing his Xbox and do his algebra homework. I responded with the typical dad reasoning: "So you can get good grades so you can get in to advanced classes in high school so you can get in to a good college so you can get in to a good grad school so you can get a good job and be assigned good projects and become a manager by age thirty-two." He looked at me and said, "But that's twenty years away. I can be a master of Xbox now." He was right, but I unplugged the Xbox and made him start on his homework anyway. Is it any wonder that Traditionalists developed the most admired work ethic? They saw the immediate connection between what they did and what they got. They believed "You take care of the farm, and the farm will take care of you."

2. LIFE ON THE FARM PROVIDES MEANINGFUL ADULT ROLES AT A MUCH EARLIER AGE.

Unlike the twenty years that my son may have to wait between seventh-grade algebra and his first significant promotion at work, there was no waiting period to begin making meaningful contributions on the farm. If you could do a man's or a woman's work in the field or the home, providing for the family, you were considered a man or a woman. Today, most teenagers go to school instead of to work—often to college and graduate school. That means a lot of young people don't enter the full-time workforce until their mid- to late twenties and aren't given key responsibilities for another five years after that.

Whereas Traditionalists were considered adults at eighteen, surveys show that today's adults don't think young people become adults until around age twenty-six. And twentysomethings push the date back even further: they also don't see themselves as adults until around age twenty-eight.[6] Because it takes so much longer to be taken seriously as an adult, psychologists refer to this new period of freedom and self-exploration as "delayed adolescence."

That's how they label a thirty-two-year-old man with a responsible job, two preschoolers, and a mortgage who plays computer games four hours a day on the weekends. That comment always causes some mother-in-law in my seminars to find me after the presentation and ask, "When is my son-in-law going to grow up? He's a wonderful father and a great guy, but he plays computer games like a college kid, and it really worries me." I tell her to give it five more years, and he'll probably be down to an hour a day. Most likely he doesn't yet have the same pressures at work that guys his age did thirty years ago.

That's why the term *delayed adolescence* isn't accurate or helpful. It implies the twentysomethings are refusing to let go of adolescence because of some character defect. Instead, sociologists have identified a new stage from ages eighteen to twenty-eight, which they call emerging adulthood because it comes after adolescence and before early adulthood. Because it takes longer to get an education and society doesn't consider young people adults until their late twenties, it's harder to find meaningful adult roles until later in life compared to past generations.[7]

Not understanding that these changing dynamics have created this new life stage can cause people to be judgmental at work and worried at home. Stan (from chapter 1) and his wife worried that something was wrong with their son Brandon because, in his midtwenties, he wasn't serious about finishing college, choosing a career, or committing to a wedding date. We will continue to see the impact of this new life stage on families and organizations throughout the book. The farm provided the first half of Traditionalists meaningful adult roles at a much earlier age. When that ended with the move to the cities, emerging adulthood began with the next generation, the Baby Boomers.

3. LIFE ON THE FARM MADE IT HARDER TO COMMIT CRIMES, ABUSE DRUGS, AND BECOME AN UNWED MOTHER.

The migration from the farm to the city enabled many of the social ills that often get blamed on declining morals. Let's be clear: rural settings have always had their share of problems. But it's harder to rob someone if he or she knows who you are. And opium and cocaine were temptations of the city. Most farm people didn't have access to them even if they wanted them. They may have gotten a little tipsy on dandelion wine or moonshine, but drugs didn't impact rural areas until decades later.

Similarly, unwed mothers were much less common on the farm earlier in the century. Currently, nearly 40 percent of mothers are not married, the highest ever recorded in the United States due to the increase in women in their twenties and thirties having children without being married.[8] It is easy to forget that as many as half of all women were not virgins when they married in the 1920s, but quick weddings were often arranged before the pregnancy began to show.[9] (Maybe morals have declined less than we imagine.) On the farm parents had a pretty good idea who a child's father was, and the young couple could make a living, whereas in the city neither may have been true.[10]

4. LIFE ON THE FARM IS DRIVEN BY THE SUN, NOT THE ELECTRON.

When my grandfather on the farm thought there had been too much talking and not enough working, he would say, "Let's go—we're burning daylight." He knew the daylight was precious, and farming was a race against the sun to get everything done.

Today, we live in a 24/7 world, powered by the electron instead of the sun. A college junior can play foosball at three in the afternoon and crank out his homework at three in the morning. Traditionalists grew up on the farm or had farm-born relatives who instilled the "early to bed and early to rise" ethic. Today, only 2 percent of Americans work on the farm. Millennials are two generations away from the farm and wonder why it matters when they get the work done as long as they get it done.

My research has revealed that work ethic is one of the three biggest sticking points in today's workplace (see chapter 19). Without knowing it, many times people are complaining about the ghosts of the farm rather than the output of the Millennials. For some Boomers it doesn't matter how much a late riser produces. If she is not at her desk by 8:00 a.m., she doesn't have the work ethic the Boomer manager wants. We get stuck over work ethic when the real issue is "sleep ethic." *When* versus *whether* work gets done is a genuine sticking point.

Ghost Story #4: Mass Marketing and Confidence in Experts

The pre-Traditionalist generation was regionally based because they had little immediate contact with the "outside world."[11] But radio changed things for the Traditionalists. Some call Traditionalists the Radio Generation because it became their link to the broader world. And it did something else: it created the voice of "the expert." With the radio came not only news and entertainment but also mass marketing.

The golden age of radio (1920s–1940s) was also the golden age of mass marketing. Each radio show was sponsored by a single company. Week after week, the stars of that show plugged the sponsor's products before and after each episode. With whole families gathered around the radio in the evening, this mass marketing created powerhouse brands.

Traditionalists have always valued the guidance of experts. Previous generations either made their own essentials or purchased them at a dry goods store. City grocery stores carried multiple brands to choose from, so Traditionalists turned to trusted experts for guidance. "If Lux soap was good enough for 'four out of five' households, why shouldn't it be good enough for ours?" "If big-band leader Benny Goodman, on *Camel Caravan*, said that doctors examined over two thousand smokers and found not a single case of throat irritation from smoking Camels, why would I doubt the experts?"

The Traditionalist generation began regionally isolated in 1901 and ended with an unprecedented national unity that had won World War II. And who got them through those years? Experts—Roosevelt during the Depression with his radio "fireside chats" and the scientists and engineers who created the weapons that ended the war. Traditionalists grew up trusting the voice of experts—they didn't question their doctors or their lawyers. (Many Baby Boomers have told me that they accompany their parents on doctor visits because to this day their parents won't ask questions.)

Traditionalists ended their childhoods trusting in experts, confident in their leaders, and tuned in to mass advertising. No wonder Traditionalists were shocked when their Baby Boomer children began questioning the experts they trusted. Archie and Edith Bunker, sitting at the piano and singing "Those Were the Days" on their weekly television sitcom, were a perfect picture of how the Traditionalists felt when their children disagreed with them on almost everything.

THE GREATEST IS NOW SMALLEST—BUT STILL IMPORTANT

The generation that newsman Tom Brokaw called "the greatest" because they saved Western civilization from the scourge of Axis aggression is now the smallest in the workforce.

Younger leaders, managers, and workers need to know about the Traditionalists' ghosts: the Great Depression, World War II, the move from farm to city, and the echo of mass marketing and the voices of experts. Those apparitions still surface in the halls of businesses, in family gatherings, in nonprofit board meetings, and at the polling booths. The Traditionalists' commitment to sacrifice, hard work, orderliness, structure, and authority brought us through times when it seemed the world might fall apart. Their alternative title, "Builders," is apt: they built the world we live in today.

CHAPTER 5

Baby Boomers:
Do Your Own Thing

BORN 1946-64

Baby Boomers (Born 1946–64)

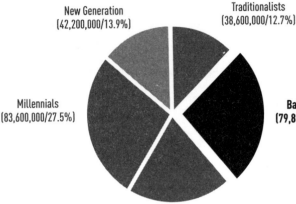

New Generation
(42,200,000/13.9%)

Traditionalists
(38,600,000/12.7%)

Millennials
(83,600,000/27.5%)

Baby Boomers
(79,800,000/26.2%)

Gen Xers
(60,100,000/19.8%)

*US Census Bureau
Current population survey, 2010*

Names
- Baby Boomers

Teen Years
- 1960s and 1970s

Key Events
- Surge of births after World War II
- Robust economic expansion
- Television
- Civil rights movement (1955–68)
- *The Feminine Mystique* (1963)
- Vietnam Conflict (1954–75)
- Woodstock (1969)
- The Watergate scandal (1972–74)
- US and USSR limit nuclear warhead testing (1976)
- Love Canal evacuation (1978)

Top Television Shows
- *Gunsmoke* (1957–61)
- *Bonanza* (1964–66)
- *The Andy Griffith Show* (1967–68)
- *Rowan & Martin's Laugh-In* (1968–70)
- *Marcus Welby, M.D.* (1970–71)
- *All in the Family* (1971–76)

Top Music
- "Mack the Knife" (Bobby Darin, 1959)
- "I Can't Stop Loving You" (Ray Charles, 1962)
- "I'm a Believer" (The Monkees, 1966)
- "Aquarius/Let the Sunshine In" (The 5th Dimension, 1969)
- "Joy to the World" (Three Dog Night, 1971)
- "Killing Me Softly with His Song" (Roberta Flack, 1973)
- "Love Will Keep Us Together" (Captain and Tennille, 1975)

What Makes Your Generation Unique?
Top five responses Baby Boomers give about themselves:
- Work ethic (17 percent)
- Respectful (14 percent)
- Values/morals (8 percent)
- "Baby Boomers" (6 percent)
- Smarter (5 percent) [1]

How Boomers See Themselves at Work
Top-ranked terms used to describe coworkers in the same generation:
- Strong work ethic
- Competent
- Ethical
- Ability to handle a crisis
- Willing to take on responsibility
- Good communication skills[2]

"Baby Boomers are so arrogant."

Tim's voice was so intense that I put down what I was reading and looked up at him. The stocky Gen Xer and I were on a flight to Boston, and he had introduced himself about ten minutes ago. I'd told him I was on my way to consult with a client about helping generations leverage their differences into organizational strengths. We talked for a few minutes, and I returned to my newspaper while he answered e-mail. Obviously he'd opened an e-mail that struck a nerve and wanted to talk about it.

So I asked, "What do you mean, 'Boomers are so arrogant'?"

"I'm not talking about you," he said. "You don't look old enough to be a Baby Boomer."

"Actually, I'm half Boomer and half Xer. I was born right in the middle. But why do you think the Boomer half of me is arrogant?" I was grinning, so he felt safe enough to answer.

"Take this e-mail," he said, jabbing at his laptop. "I and three others were asked to research better ways of teaching science. We worked for six months researching how to teach physics to high school juniors rather than seniors so they're better prepared for their college placement exams. But the Boomer teachers think the way they have always done it is better. I just got this e-mail saying my school isn't going to try our new approach."

I replied quietly, "Bummer. It's disappointing to put in a lot of work, only to have your idea shot down without a trial run. Sounds more like they disagree with your approach than that they're arrogant."

"No," Tim insisted, "the Boomers are arrogant. They think that every other generation needs to listen to them because they are bigger, smarter, and harder working than everyone else. They act like they're special. What's so special about the Baby Boomers other than they're a huge generation that can throw their weight around?"

I took a shot at answering him: "Well, Boomers were told they were special from the time they were babies. That, as well as the sheer size of their generation, definitely makes them confident—and that can come off as arrogance. But you'll never understand how to work with them or influence them unless you understand why they were told they were special. The decades the Baby Boomers grew up in, especially the older ones, were more than special. They were *magical*."

That caught Tim's attention. I wasn't exaggerating. They *were* magical. During the Boomers' childhood years Tinker Bell would open *The Wonderful World of Disney* television program by splashing fairy dust across the screen with her wand. "When You Wish upon a Star," the program's theme song, transported viewers to a world of endless possibility and hope. Young Baby Boomers grew up as the most optimistic generation in American history, and they had good reason:

- Kids grew up with their grandparents and sometimes great-grandparents due to increasing life spans.
- Penicillin and vaccines eradicated and controlled long-standing health threats.
- The world was at peace.[*]
- Television constantly marketed to, captivated, and entertained them.
- The postwar economy boomed, and the middle class prospered.
- Families drove across the country on two-week-long vacations in the summer because they could afford cars.
- Boomers grew up believing that the world was theirs for the taking if they worked hard—and if the Russians didn't blow them up.

---

[*]Boomers lived through the Cold War and were regularly reminded of the threat of nuclear attack, watching films on bomb shelters and doing air raid drills at school. In addition, television brought the Vietnam Conflict into people's living rooms, daily magnifying its impact. But after the devastation of two world wars, which involved much of the world and were "total wars" (where everyone in a nation is enlisted in the war effort and is personally impacted), the Korean and Vietnam Conflicts involved a few nations and a comparably small percentage of adults. Because it was contained halfway across the world, the conflict did not threaten the daily lives of most Boomers as the Civil War and both world wars had done, or as terrorist threats do today to a lesser degree. Vietnam's impact was not its size, but how it became a flash point for the generation gap. The Boomers grew up in a time of relative peace that has continued for what is now the longest stretch in US history.

THE BABY BOOMERS' FOUR BIGGEST GHOST STORIES
Ghost Story #1: The Boom of Babies

The first Boomer ghost is the biggest—literally. Never before in history were so many babies born so quickly. A British visitor to America in 1958 said, "It seems to me that every other young housewife I see is pregnant."[3] Traditionalists married at a significantly earlier age (20.1 years for women and 22.5 for men) than people did before the war. Johnny came marching home from the war, missing his girl and wanting to settle down and start a family. Having been sobered by the carnage he saw overseas, he was serious about building a society strong enough to prevent future dictators. And society wasn't ready for what happened next:

- Hospitals weren't ready. Newlyweds could afford to have babies right away due to the GI Bill, which helped veterans get education and housing—and the birthrates boomed. Extra beds were pushed into the nurses' lounge because so many babies were being born and hospitals didn't have enough beds. One writer declared, "Having a baby in one of the nation's war-madhouse areas [by a military base or industrialized area] is a desperate adventure second only to war itself."[4]
- Schools weren't ready. Because the Census Bureau didn't expect the boom to last, schools weren't prepared for the number of students enrolled. The first wave of Baby Boomer grammar school kids sometimes sat two or three to a desk and shared textbooks. The first wave of Baby Boomers learned to compete to get a seat at lunch, a spot on the Little League team, and later a dorm room at college and a job after graduation.
- Colleges weren't ready. Colleges and universities didn't have enough faculty or living space to accommodate ballooning enrollments. Fortunately, the growing presence of fraternity and sorority houses provided more places for students to stay. Unfortunately, the wild parties at those houses, as portrayed in the movie *Animal House* (1978), became every dean of students' nightmare.

When Boomers act like workaholics (and expect you to as well), you have to remember how overcrowded hospitals, grade schools, sports teams, campuses, and job markets taught them that you have to compete to get what you want. Everyone made the park district Little League team in third grade, but only the best got to play, and only the very best got a trophy. The Boomers learned that if you didn't put in the hours, somebody else would.

When Boomers come across as domineering, you have to remember that they are used to getting heard. The sheer size of their generation made them the center of attention. Marketers referred to them as the "pig in the python" because just as a pig reshapes the python as it moves its way through the snake, Boomers would reshape markets and business or political priorities at every stage of their lives. They reshaped childhood—smaller families meant they were the focus of their parents' attention and dreams. Marketers doted on them while rock-and-roll radio stations multiplied to give them the music they craved.

Boomers have reshaped each stage of their adult lives as well. They pushed off buying their first houses and saving for retirement, redefined parenting styles and roles in marriage, reworked everything from the coffee shop to religious organizations, and have stayed active (and Botoxed), hoping to hold on a little longer. And this huge generation is now reshaping retirement—they plan for retirement, but they don't plan to retire. According to a Yankelovich survey, Boomers think old age begins at 79.5—two years past the current life expectancy![5] Boomers seem to have voted among themselves to redefine old age out of existence. (Where on earth would people get the idea that Boomers are arrogant?) They don't think of themselves as getting old, nor do they want other people treating them like they are. Boomers have always felt special and powerful, and institutions and advertisers have reinforced that idea by adjusting to please their biggest market.

Ghost Story #2: Affluence

"For the first time, a civilization has reached a point where most people are no longer preoccupied with providing food and shelter," *Life Magazine* announced in their 1959 year-end issue.[6] Affluence is the second ghost story you must understand if the Boomers are going to make sense. They grew up in one of the most economically optimistic times in history.

World War II caused the US economy to focus almost exclusively on wartime necessities. The postwar economy boomed because people (especially soldiers returning from the war and starting families) needed things that hadn't been available during the war: furniture, cars, washing machines, houses, clothes.

Because the war wasn't fought on American shores, our factories and transportation systems were in place, whereas much of Europe's and Asia's infrastructure had been destroyed. The economy boomed because the United States simply stopped producing bullets and started producing over a third of all the world's manufactured goods. In addition, the boom of babies grew the market. All those babies needed cribs, houses, and diapers. Baby food sales jumped from 2.7 million cases in 1941 to 15 million in 1947.[7] Almost overnight the political slogan "a chicken in every pot and a car in every garage" was coming true. By the 1950s many even had a dishwasher and a television. The country thought this new generation would not need to strive for the American dream as their parents had—they were born into it.

The ghost story of affluence explains many of the Boomers' distinctive values. No longer worried about survival, Baby Boomers changed their value system from sacrifice to self. Affluence also strengthened the Boomer focus on self because parents no longer needed to have lots of children to support the farm. They could channel their expectations and their attentions into their 3.5 children. As a result, Boomers were the first generation to be raised in an era that emphasized that people are special. In 1940, only 20 percent of men and 11 percent of women agreed with the statement "I am an important person." In 1990, 62 percent of men and 66 percent of women agreed.[8] Instead of hearing, "Who do you think you are?" as the Traditionalists had, the Boomers were told they were special. It's no surprise that Boomers are idealistic and confident.

Affluence funded the focus on self and the optimism that made the Boomers' growing-up years magical. It created "Great Expectations," to use the title of Landon Jones's award-winning history of the Boomers.[9] For example, the Boomers didn't save money the way their Depression-era parents had. The economy was booming, and they were confident the money would be there when they needed it. (That may be why a March 2011 Associated Press–LifeGoesStrong.com poll found that the median retirement savings for Boomers is only $40,000—24 percent have saved nothing.[10]) They felt that they were witnessing the dawning of the "Age of Aquarius" (to borrow the title of the worldwide hit song of 1969).

Ghost Story #3: Television

Historians suggest that John F. Kennedy's assassination in 1963 was the first time the nation cried together, because of the real-time connection provided by television. When Franklin D. Roosevelt died in office, people were sad once they heard the news. But when they learned Kennedy died, strangers stopped on sidewalks, watched televisions playing in store windows, and wept together. Television gave people a personal connection with Kennedy that they didn't get with Roosevelt on the radio. Radio made Roosevelt trusted; television made Kennedy loved. How the nation mourned is only one way television powerfully reshaped the world Boomers grew up in.

For the first time, television allowed the entire country to see the same thing at the same time. And when the "thing" was Kennedy's funeral or the first moon landing—powerfully emotional events—the nation shared common experiences as never before. Unlike radio, where individual people form different pictures in their heads as they hear a story, television assures a much stronger common experience, since everyone sees the same image. That's why MTV launched their channel in 1981 with photos of the Apollo 11 moon landing, because everyone had seen it live or replayed dozens of times. They didn't need a caption to identify what they saw—everyone knew the footprint in the moondust was Neil Armstrong's. Since there were only three major network television channels (yes, Boomers grew up with only three networks!), the entire nation saw the same stories the same way at the same time.

Boomers grew up in houses where the average television set was on six hours every day.[11] Political scientist Paul Light estimates that by age sixteen, the average Baby Boomer had viewed between twelve thousand and fifteen thousand hours of television.[12]

Gen Xers grew up with scores of channels on cable and Millennials with hundreds, not to mention the content we are making on our own. More video is uploaded to YouTube in a month than the big three television networks have broadcast in sixty years.[13]

Today a thousand people could be watching a thousand different things on TV or the Internet.[14] When the Boomers grew up with only three networks, everybody watched the same thing, especially if it was a major event. It's hard for Xers and Millennials, who grew up with so many sources of information and entertainment, to grasp how having only three television channels powerfully connected the Boomers and scripted their common language. *Gilligan's Island* may have been corny, but Boomers can still sing the theme song because it was one of the few shows on.

Ghost Story #4: The Generation Gap
Parents in the '60s never knew what hit them. They thought they were giving their children a better life than they'd had by making the world "safe for democracy" and by providing new suburban homes and educational opportunities. But the teenage Baby Boomers questioned their par-

ents' beliefs (and those of their teachers and leaders), listened to rock and roll, grew their hair long, and tried to spend all their time with friends in what seemed like their own world, embarrassed to be seen with their parents. After generations had struggled to keep their kids safe, fed, educated, healthy, and free, the Traditionalists were finally able to give their kids all these wrapped up in a bow called the American dream—and the kids rejected it. The Traditionalists couldn't believe that educational achievement dropped while drug use, teen pregnancies, and crime rose.[15] By 1974, over 40 percent of Boomers said they would be better off without their parents.[16] Traditionalists had no idea that the suburban lifestyle, affluence, and education they gave their children would cause a shift in thinking to a mind-set so different from the past generations. Previous generations had their squabbles, but this generation gap felt like a canyon that even Evel Knievel couldn't jump.

Social forces were pulling the generations apart. The move from farms to suburbs that World War II sped up created a new subculture—the teenager. Before World War II, the word *teenager* was rarely used, because teens were seen simply as younger versions of adults rather than as their own subgroup. After World War II, marketers focused on this new population segment that was no longer dressing, dancing, or buying like their parents.

It's easy to see why. Farm life provided teenagers opportunities to take their places in adult society once they could do the work of adults. Additionally, the farm put their parents at the center of their lives. But once families moved to the suburbs, the Boomer kids had many more sources of influence. On the farm, teens worked much of the day around their parents, but in the suburbs, parents headed to jobs while teens went to school and spent more of the day with their peers than their parents. Suddenly the home was only one of many influences competing with teachers and the media.

The Traditionalists never imagined education would undercut their values and create a gap with their children. In college history classes, Boomers learned that George Washington did not cut down a cherry tree and that Thomas Jefferson did more with his evenings than write political treatises. At the same time, television put President Nixon's Watergate scandal into their living rooms and made Boomers even more skeptical of government. They had information that led them to question things their parents had never doubted or considered. The same families who had gathered around the television to see Tinker Bell with her magic pixie dust were now battling around the television right along with *All in the Family*'s Archie Bunker and his long-haired son-in-law, "Meathead."

The generation gap signaled a massive shift in values far more important than the music, tie-dye, or protests that usually get the focus. The leading researcher of the Baby Boomers, Daniel Yankelovich, titled the 1974 summary of his research *The New Morality: A Profile of American Youth in the '70s*. He found three significant changes in values. The first two—moral norms ("sex, authority, religion, and obligations to others") and social values ("money, work, family, and marriage")—are well known, but the third, self-fulfillment, was an underlying shift from emphasizing duty, obligations to others, and pursuit of financial security to greater focus on self. Yankelovich said self-fulfillment "is the individual's way of saying there must be something more to life than making a living, struggling to make ends meet, and caring for others."[17] Parents and their adolescents have always irritated each other, but the adults think, *It's just a phase; they'll grow out of it.* But the Boomers didn't grow out of it, because society was effecting a profound shift in their focus—from sacrifice to self-fulfillment.

It takes cash to become the "Me" generation, and Boomers were the first generation to have the money, time, and freedom to explore self and search for meaning. If the Boomers had a slogan, it was "do your own thing." I still remember buying, at age nine, an LP called *Isaac Hayes Live at the Sahara Tahoe* that I found in the discount bin at the grocery store of my small town. For all nineteen minutes, he sang, "Do your thing" over and over, encouraging the Boomers not to let anything stand in their way. This central commandment of the new morality was printed on psychedelic posters, spray-painted on overpasses, and written into television dialogue. The generation gap marked the shift from "do your duty" to "do your own thing."

The media (and thus much of the population) focused on the smaller ghosts of the Boomers' youth—sex, drugs, rock and roll, and the Vietnam protests. But those realities did not cause the generation gap. No more than 2 percent of Boomers joined civil rights or antiwar protests or the counterculture.[18] Television's focus on the counterculture magnified its size in the minds of Traditionalists. Woodstock (1969) and the Monterey Pop Festival (1967) were symptoms, not causes, of the generation gap. Affluence allowed a much more profound shift to self over sacrifice, optimism over caution, and the new morality over traditional religion.[19]

The Boomers are still shaped by the value of self-expression. They value youth because keeping fit and staying young provides the vitality necessary to continue pursuing meaning and self-fulfillment long after they retire. They still value hard work after competing with so many others, and that makes them worry the younger generations aren't willing to pay the price to succeed.

Their optimism and high expectations made them idealists more than pragmatists. That's why they still value fairness because everyone deserves a chance to fulfill their potential regardless of their gender, ethnicity, or background. Boomers weren't rebels against the core values of democracy and free enterprise as much as they were opponents of anything that created limits and got in the way of self-expression.[20] For example, they championed the civil rights movement as a way to fix the system so the United States "would live out the true meaning of [its] creed: . . . that all men are created equal," as the Reverend Martin Luther King Jr. said in his famous speech at the Lincoln Memorial. They thought all people deserved the right to pursue their dreams—so the system had to be fair.

Finally, Boomers value communication and understanding with their own children. They promised themselves that they would not let themselves get out of date like their parents and would listen to their children. So they parented the second half of Xers and the first half of Millennials differently, with more dialogue and less "because I said so."

Boomers value being cool much more than their parents did, so they listen when their children tell them that their clothes don't work. When I ask my Boomer audiences who has gone back upstairs and changed an article of clothing because their teenagers told them it was out of date, almost everyone (including myself) puts up a hand. Boomers learned from their children as well as taught them.

THE SECOND WAVE: CHOPPIER THAN THE FIRST

The four ghosts of size, affluence, television, and the generation gap explain why Boomers think the way they do. But before we move on to the Generation Xers, we need to acknowledge that the two ends of the Boomer generation—the oldest and the youngest—had different experiences and opportunities. Just as the beginning of the Boomer generation has more in common with Traditionalists, the end of the Boomer generation has more in common with Generation X. Society changed dramatically in the twenty years that produced the Baby Boom.

The second wave of Boomers missed out on the benefits of the first wave. Financially they aren't as well off as the older Boomers, who got the best jobs, ran up the price of housing and investments, and may get more Social Security than they paid in.

Even more, the first wave came of age with the optimism and idealism of the Kennedy years (known as "Camelot"), the success of the space program, and *Leave It to Beaver* and *The Mickey Mouse Club*. The second wave grew

71

up with Watergate, the Arab oil embargo, "stagflation," *Rowan and Martin's Laugh-In*, and *Maude*.

As a result, many second-wave Boomers feel left out of the typical portrayals of the generation in news articles and movies. Molly Grimsley of Fairfax, Virginia, had her letter to the editor published the week after *Newsweek's* cover story "Ready or Not, Boomers Turn 60" appeared:

> Speaking as one who was born in 1959, I am very tired of continually being lumped in with the Baby Boomer generation. I have nothing in common with those born from 1946 through the mid-1950s. I have no memory of JFK or Lyndon Johnson. The first president I have a strong memory of is Nixon. I never watched *Howdy Doody* or Jackie Gleason. My television choices ran to *Green Acres, Gilligan's Island, Get Smart,* and *The Brady Bunch.* I have hardly any knowledge of 1960s folk music (can't stand it) or rock and roll: I grew up with bad '70s music and disco—thank goodness the Clash and Sex Pistols came to the rescue![21]

The second wave of Boomers grew up with the same belief in their potential[22] and the same belief in the American dream as the first wave. What they lacked was the same sense of optimism that all problems would be solved if they were only better, smarter, and tried harder. The *New York Post* captured their shock and frustration:

> Independence Day, 1979, the American paradox is bleakly apparent. As a nation, we appear to have become steadily more dependent on forces seemingly beyond our control, losing confidence in our ability to master events, uncertain of our direction.[23]

Pat Caddell, the pollster for the Carter administration, found that for the first time Americans believed the future would be worse than the present.[24] A political cartoon from 1979 shows a couple beaming with joy, finally reaching the gas pump after waiting in line for two days, only to have a chunk of Skylab fall from the sky and crush their car. Little orphan Annie might have been singing "Tomorrow" enthusiastically in the record-setting 1977 musical, but the United States was more skeptical about the future's possibilities.

Americans responded to the threats on their optimism about their financial future not by putting aside their emphasis on the self and returning to the self-denial and sacrifice of the Traditionalists but by ushering in a decade of conspicuous consumption headlined by the Yuppies (Young, Urban, Upwardly Mobile Professionals). The bestselling *Yuppie Handbook* announced the new rules: "The name of the game is the best—buying it, owning it, using it, eating it, wearing it, growing it, cooking it, driving it, doing whatever with it."[25] Rather than give up their "great expectations," Boomers turned from self-exploration and building a better world to outcompeting everyone else so they could get a bigger piece of what seemed like a much smaller pie.

The second wave of Boomers was choppier than the first wave; it flowed over far more rocks on its way to the ever more distant American dream. Those rocks created the big ghosts for Generation X. It seemed that Tinker Bell was out of pixie dust.

DON'T STOP BELIEVING

Tim, my airplane seatmate, is not alone in thinking that Boomers are arrogant. There are far more Boomers than Xers, and Boomers are often the bosses today. Certainly Boomers do not lack confidence and are not ready to yield their place, and when they do, they will not go quietly.

The Boomers' ghost stories make it clear that *special* is the right word, not *arrogant*. The Boomers grew up thinking they were special—that the world was theirs for the taking if they worked hard and stayed true to their inner selves.

Not only is *special* a better word, it's far more helpful to the other generations trying to influence this massively influential generation. Instead of resenting the Boomers' sheer numbers and therefore dominant place in society, Gen Xers and Millennials will get much farther with them if they understand how to speak their language. Tim and his committee spent all their time researching better ways to communicate science to students and neglected to research better ways to communicate with their older colleagues. The other generations have to do for the Boomers what they ask the Boomers to do for them—understand why they think the way they do. Every generation has to figure out what they're going to do with the world the previous generation handed them. Like every other generation, Boomers are simply reacting to expectations placed on them by the previous generation. Boomers began with magic and pixie dust and ended with cracks in the national confidence. But through it all, they have never lost their optimism and commitment to meaning, self-exploration, and self-expression. It was never about rebellion or long hair. They started their lives wishing upon a star, and they've never stopped. This massive generation challenged and reshaped the world we live in and will continue to do so for decades to come.

CHAPTER 6

Generation X:
Get Real

BORN 1965–80

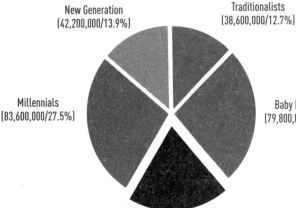

New Generation
(42,200,000/13.9%)

Traditionalists
(38,600,000/12.7%)

Millennials
(83,600,000/27.5%)

Baby Boomers
(79,800,000/26.2%)

Gen Xers
(60,100,000/19.8%)

US Census Bureau
Current population survey, 2010

Names
- Generation X
- Gen X
- Baby Bust
- Busters
- Slackers

Teen Years
- 1980s and 1990s

Key Events
- Double-digit inflation (1979–81)
- Iranian hostage crisis (1979)
- The Sony Walkman (1980)
- AIDS (1981)
- MTV (1981)
- Household borrowing grows twice as fast as income (mid-1980s)
- Space shuttle *Challenger* explodes (1986)
- Berlin Wall torn down (1989)
- Persian Gulf War (1991)

Top Television Shows
- *Dallas* (1980–84)
- *The Cosby Show* (1985–89)
- *Rosanne* (1989–90)
- *The Simpsons* (debuts 1989)
- *Friends* (debuts 1994)
- *Seinfeld* (1994–95)

Top Music
- "My Sharona" (The Knack, 1979)
- "Ebony and Ivory" (Paul McCartney with Stevie Wonder, 1982)
- "That's What Friends Are For" (Dionne and Friends, 1985)
- "Another Day in Paradise" (Phil Collins, 1989)
- "Dreamlover" (Mariah Carey, 1993)

What Makes Your Generation Unique?
Top five responses Generation Xers give about themselves:
- Technology use (12 percent)
- Work ethic (11 percent)
- Conservative/traditional (7 percent)
- Smarter (6 percent)
- Respectful (5 percent) [1]

How Gen Xers See Themselves at Work
Top-ranked terms used to describe coworkers in the same generation:
- Confident
- Competent
- Willing to take responsibility
- Willing to put in extra time to wrap a job
- Ethical [2]

At *Donkey Kong's* peak, sixty thousand arcade machines were in use worldwide.[3] The game came out in 1981, as Generation X entered their teenage years, and surprised the gaming world with a hero who was neither handsome nor endowed with superpowers. Rather, he was a middle-aged construction worker who needed to rescue his girlfriend, Pauline, from the gorilla Donkey Kong by climbing scaffolding and jumping over barrels. In *Donkey Kong Country*, the 1994 update, the famous gorilla had to swing over chasms on vines to save his hoard of bananas.

No matter what version, gamers had to master successively harder challenges if they were to get the girl or the bananas. Even more, the technology behind the games themselves changed so quickly that new versions of *Donkey Kong* required buying new gaming consoles or computers just to play them. This meant Generation X teens had to learn both new equipment and the game's new levels. Players might die hundreds of times before they gained the skills necessary to conquer each level, but with patience, concentration, and caffeine, they would make it to the end.

Donkey Kong is a great metaphor for Generation X. If Tinker Bell's pixie dust symbolizes the almost magical optimism of the Baby Boomers, *Donkey Kong* symbolizes the unrelenting challenges that Generation X had to overcome, as well as the technological tools that seemed to give them a way to do it. Generation Xers grew up in a world that was running out of pixie dust. Divorce, latchkey kids, multiple recessions, global competition, missing children on milk cartons—Gen Xers learned to roll with the bad news and land on their feet. Their lives matched their video games because Donkey Kong had to swing from vines and then land on his feet or fall to his death.

Because every *Donkey Kong* player would, from time to time, miss the landing and fall off the side of the cliff, smart gamers hedged their bets. They collected enough coins along the way to get another life so they could come back to the same level rather than having to start over at the beginning of the game. Life for Xers was similar when it threw surprises at them that were often beyond their control.[4] So Gen Xers became realists hedging their bets. They found new families, constantly learned and rewired their lives, and cautiously enjoyed things today rather than betting on an idealized future that might never happen:

- Instead of relocating seven times in ten years as the Boomers had, they stayed put so they could be close to their friends, who had become their families.
- Instead of coming in early and staying late to prove themselves at work, they pushed their organizations to install technology that would help them get work done faster so they could get on with their lives.
- Instead of jumping into home ownership, they traveled.
- Instead of conspicuous consumption, they chose the simpler "grunge" look or wore khakis to work.

But what Gen X saw as realistically coping with life's never-ending challenges, the older generations saw as cynical—and whiny. Even the name *Gen X* is partially a slam. When it first became obvious that this new generation didn't think like Traditionalists or Baby Boomers, no one knew what to call them because they were still an unknown. Douglas Coupland first called them "X," the unknown in algebra, and to their (and his) horror, the name stuck. His 1992 novel *Generation X: Tales for an Accelerated Culture* described disengaged, pessimistic but well-educated twentysomethings who could neither find a job in their field nor find their way to the good life the Boomers had.

If the name *Gen X* was harsh, at work they got called worse. Told they would be the first generation in US history to make less than their parents,

Xers focused on life outside work. As we saw in the last chapter, Baby Boomers coped with the same discouraging events by competing harder for the shrinking pie, while the Traditionalists who led the organizations believed that if we all pulled together and worked harder, we could still win. Neither generation understood that Gen X didn't want to dedicate themselves to a game they thought they had no chance to win. Because Gen Xers wouldn't play the way the Boomers did, the older generations called them "slackers" for their first ten years in the workplace.

As a result, no generation feels as misunderstood as Generation X. Before my workshops begin, I will frequently have a Gen Xer pull me aside and ask, "Is this going to be another session where you tell us that we are the problem and need to fit better into our organization?" Often at the beginning of my speeches on generations, Gen Xers are looking down, waiting to be slammed for not working hard enough, showing loyalty, or liking meetings. But when I explain the Gen X ghost stories, they start looking up and nodding unconsciously. Finally, they look at other Gen Xers around them as if to say, "He gets us. He doesn't think we're the problem."

They feel misunderstood because they never saw themselves as whiny slackers but as open-eyed realists. And they've always wondered if the Traditionalists and Boomers know the difference. They grew up in *Donkey Kong*, not *The Wonderful World of Disney*, so it made no sense to them to keep the older generations' high expectations as if the world had not changed. In 1994, journalist Piper Lowell explained why:

> It's not that we're whiny. We're cynical and isolated. I, for one,
> had a hard time trusting anything: Love is forever (my parents
> divorced when I was four). Uncle Sam is your friend (if you're
> American, and sometimes not even then). Technology will solve
> the world's problems (just turn off the TV, dear, and take your
> Prozac). And Richard Nixon is not a crook.[5]

To Traditionalists, Xers epitomized everything that was accelerating the world's decline. But that was a misperception. Xers weren't slackers; they were rewiring the world they inherited with new technology and new expectations. If life was like *Donkey Kong*, then let the new game begin. But first, grab a Snapple because we'll be doing this a long time.

Because Gen Xers see themselves as realists, "Get real" was a commonly heard phrase that meant quit spinning things, quit trying to force a happy ending, quit producing the sentimental, simplistic sitcoms of the Boomer era. The entertainment industry picked up this change in thinking, and the word *real* began popping up in movies, music, and television show titles. While the Boomers tried to fix society so it was fair, Xers learned that life isn't fair, and so they lampooned it. They watched shows like *The Simpsons* and created a new way to get their news with *The Daily Show* and *The Colbert Report*. Gen X parodied and rewired the world they inherited.

They had a powerful effect. As a society, we've been forced to "get real." How many of us are less confident in institutions than we were fifteen years ago? If Gen X is about lowered expectations, tongue-in-cheek comedy, and pervasive technology, then we are all Xers now.

GENERATION X'S FOUR BIGGEST GHOST STORIES
Ghost Story #1: Squished

Numerically, Gen Xers are 25 percent smaller than the huge generations of Boomers that preceded them and Millennials that followed them (see the graph at the beginning of this chapter). Gen Xers being squished between two large generations means marketers and the entertainment industry pay less attention to them. As a small generation, they have less political clout. They will inherit the consequences of previous generations' excesses but will not have the political muscle to outvote them.

Being squished also meant they could forget about working their way up in their organizations quickly because they were stuck behind the Boomers who came into the workforce ahead of them. Boomers moved up twice as fast as Xers in their early years as the postwar economy expanded. But organizations eliminated layers of middle managers just as Xers came along. And even before the Great Recession of 2008 killed their 401(k)s, Boomers never intended to head out the door into a traditional retirement when they turned sixty-five. That means Xers are finding fewer promotions available.

As a result, Xers often move up by leaving organizations—and sometimes returning. We've all heard of people who left a company and then came back five years later to a much higher position, leapfrogging those who loyally stayed behind. I sometimes joke with audiences that Boomers could tell from the two-pack-a-day death rattles in their Traditionalist bosses' chests that they only had to wait a few more years before a new spot would open up for them. But with exercise, healthy eating, and a bit of Botox,

Boomers look good, and that means Xers can no longer tell how old their Boomer bosses really are, so they can't gauge how much longer they have to wait to get their bosses' jobs.

As a result, Xers are like England's Prince Charles, spending much of their careers waiting for long-living bosses to move on. The March 2011 cover of *Philadelphia* magazine shone a spotlight on this with their headline:

Dear Baby Boomers,
   JUST DIE ALREADY.
   (We'll take Philly from here. Thanks.)

XOXO, Generation X.

So I warn Boomer bosses to drive slowly when pulling out of the parking lot in case a desperate Xer has cut their brake lines in one last attempt to break through the "gray ceiling." (We'll look at Xers' frustration with the "gray ceiling" in more detail when we cover the sticking point of loyalty in chapter 14.)

There's an irony at work with Generation X: they were supposed to be big, not squished. The post–World War II Baby Boom of the Traditionalists lasted for twenty years, longer than anyone expected. Yet when the Boomers came to childbearing age themselves, there was no corresponding Baby Boom of their own. Instead, there was a Baby Bust. When all those potential Boomer mothers hit childbearing age, they slammed on the fertility brakes.

In 1957, childbirths hit the all-time high of 4.3 million. Seven years later, just before Baby Boomers hit their prime childbearing years, births dropped below four million and fell the next fifteen years to the lowest levels of fertility in US history, to levels less than half of what mothers twenty years before experienced.[6] The first half of the Baby Boomers (born between 1946 and 1956) had transformed the family. Instead of having two or three children, they had one or two—and often none.

The Traditionalists focused on their Boomer children, but the Boomers didn't do the same with their Xer children. Over a million Americans a year had themselves surgically sterilized during the 1970s.[7] Simply put, children were no longer viewed as the best way to find happiness. One survey found that children had dropped behind automobiles on the list of what made people happy.[8] While Boomer women told pollsters they wanted the same number of children as their mothers, the additional children were postponed by education, later marriage, and career opportunities until it seemed too late to have them.

Boomer women wanted their mothers' families; they didn't want their mothers' limitations. Now children were seen as a threat to fulfilling one's dreams, a sentiment mirrored in the demonic children genre of horror films like *Rosemary's Baby*, *The Exorcist*, and *The Omen*, which were popular throughout the Xers' early years.

So the Xers are squished by virtue of being smaller than the generations on either side, and they are smaller because they were less wanted than the Baby Boomers. Is it any wonder they are more individualistic and pragmatic? They were also less wanted than the generation that followed—the Millennials.

By the time the Millennials came along, society was refocusing on "the baby." As Howe and Strauss point out in *Millennials Go to College*, the 1984 horror movies *Children of the Corn* and *Firestarter* flopped while three years later the surprise hits *Baby Boom* and *Three Men and a Baby* replaced the monster child with the vulnerable tot.[9] While Xers grew up in a time less interested in children, many of them had more children than their parents did, children they made the center of their lives. So in a very real way, the Xers squished themselves by creating a Millennial generation larger than their own—an irony worthy of an Xer sitcom.

Ghost Story #2: Divorce

A steep rise in divorce as well as the surge in working Boomer mothers meant that Generation X grew up in the midst of unprecedented changes in family structure.

The first half of Generation X watched divorce become commonplace during their childhood. Between 1960 and 1982 the rate of divorce nearly tripled and then leveled off.[10] (The past twenty years it has declined, especially in the last ten, as more couples choose not to marry.[11]) That meant the percent of Xers who grew up without both married parents (29 percent) doubled from that of the Boomers (15 percent) and Traditionalists (13 percent). Even with a lower divorce rate, 38 percent of Millennials said their parents weren't married.

The ghost of divorce impacted Xers more than the other generations, even though more Millennials have grown up in single-parent families. Because we have now become used to 50 percent divorce rates, children no longer feel that their families aren't normal if their parents divorce. Society has created sup-

US Divorce Rate, 1960–2007

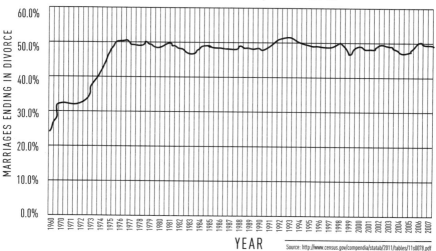

Source: http://www.census.gov/compendia/statab/2011/tables/11s0078.pdf

port systems like child care and after-school programs. We are far too scared of child predators today to place the key around a latchkey child's neck so he can let himself into the house before Mom gets home from work.

In contrast, as the Xers lived through a skyrocketing divorce rate, it felt like something was going wrong. Television reinforced the contrast as young Xers watched the stereotypical 1950s family on television shows like *Father Knows Best* or *Leave It to Beaver* while their single mothers left for evening jobs to make ends meet.

After I made that point in a seminar in Phoenix, an Xer jumped in:

This was so my life. When I was twelve, my dad left us. My mom worked as a secretary, but that wasn't enough, so she sold pretzels in the mall in the evening. To make things worse, my dad took the good car and left us with the second car that barely worked. With 21 percent interest rates, we couldn't afford another one, so we bought the Chilton auto repair manual for our car, and we'd figure out how to fix whatever broke. Nobody helped us, family didn't take care of us, and no government programs saved us. We took care of ourselves. But you know what that proved to me? Life has all kinds of surprises; some of them pleasant, most of them not. But that didn't matter because Mom and I would figure out how to handle whatever came our way.

That's what I mean when I say that *Donkey Kong* is a great metaphor for Generation X. In *Donkey Kong*, you never know when bad things are going to jump out at you, and you succeed or fail on your own.

Divorce also meant that an entire generation grew up with far more diversity and learned to adjust: "At Mom's house we have this set of rules, but when we go to Dad's, there is a different set. I don't pick sides; they both have their good points." But that meant when the Xers got married, figuring out the seating chart at the rehearsal dinner or wedding reception was not so simple: "Hey, we'd better put my stepdad and my mom's current boyfriend at different tables—*really* different. They don't get along." Complicated situations are just a part of life.

The rocket rise of divorce left many Xers feeling alone. More than other generations, they turned to friends to find a family. In between the slapstick, the long-running television show *Friends* told many of the ghost stories that made sense of Xers' lives. The show didn't focus on family, because the characters' parents were distant and dysfunctional. Since their family relationships were unsupportive, the friends turned to each other, just as many Xers had done.

The older generations often couldn't comprehend that Xers' friends were as important to them as their biological family, so it led to conflicts when Xers entered the workforce. When a Boomer boss asked the single Xer if she could stay late to finish up a spreadsheet, this reply was incomprehensible to the boss but totally reasonable to the Xer: "I'm sorry, I can't. I'm meeting friends for dinner." If the Xer had said she had to pick up her child at day care, the Boomer would have understood. A child is family, after all. What the boss didn't understand was that to many Xers, friends *are* family.

At a Kansas City workshop, an Xer pulled me aside and said he didn't think divorce had a serious impact on everyone in his generation. He grew up in rural Kansas and didn't know anyone whose parents were divorced. He could see the divorce ghost story looming over the cities, but not over rural areas.

True, many Xers grew up with both parents. However, the dramatic increase in divorce impacted *all* Gen Xers, even if their parents stayed married. Why? They read about it in stories at school, watched it on TV (as more shows began including divorced couples), and listened to adults whisper about "another couple splitting up." Even if their parents didn't divorce, they probably knew someone whose parents did. If it could happen to their friends, then maybe it *could* happen to them. Life felt more unstable and insecure than it did when the Xers' parents and grandparents were growing up.

Finally, understanding the spike in divorces helps us understand why work ethic has been a big sticking point with Generation X. Just as Boomers reacted against the "put your children first" attitude of the Traditionalists, Xers reacted against "easy divorce" by focusing on their families and their lives outside work. Rebecca Ryan, who founded Next Generation Consulting, discovered through five thousand interviews between 1998 and 2002 that Gen Xers value control over their time more than anything else organizations offer. This need is so important to Xers that she called her first book *Live First, Work Second.* A greater family focus is one reason Xers want more work-life balance. Gen X women who have children are having more kids and working less than Boomer women.[12] Parents spend more time with their children today than even the stay-at-home mothers of the 1950s. That's why Gen X fathers are pushing for more work-life balance—so they, too, can spend more time with their children.[13] Xers want greater family stability for their children than they had.

Ghost Story #3: Downward Mobility

In the 1994 hit movie *Reality Bites,* Winona Ryder's character, who had been the college valedictorian but now can't find a decent job, says to her friends, "I don't have a lawyer. I don't have a dentist. I make $400 a week." Welcome to the downward mobility that ushered the first Gen Xers into adulthood. The confidence in the economy that had inspired the Traditionalists and defined the Boomers went bust for the Xers. Instead, it was now clear to everyone that there was a new reality: lifetime employment and job security were history.

Generation X missed the almost magical economic growth that made the Boomers so optimistic. As hard as it is for us to imagine today, the United States did not face another major recession between the recessions of 1958 and 1973. Even better, between those years, the United States experienced a rapid but sustained growth in which real median household income surged 55 percent[14] as wages rose but inflation didn't. Since 1973, however, the US economy has grown more slowly and has had a nearly stagnant standard of living, increasing by only 10 percent. Making things worse, the mid-1970s and early 1980s saw unusually high inflation and interest rates.[15] The economic boom of the Boomer era was shrinking.

Gen X missed the growth of the economy but arrived just in time for the growth in prices. The huge Boomer generation pushed up housing prices. As a result, only a third of twenty-five- to thirty-year-olds (and half of thirty- to thirty-five-year-olds) owned a home in 1990 despite a decade of economic growth.[16] Ironically, fewer homeowners meant more renters, and that pushed up rent prices by 28 percent.[17]

In addition to being squished for jobs and housing by the larger Boomer generation, Gen Xers saw college expenses quadruple while grants and aid were slashed. Student loans almost doubled between 1977 and 1990, when the Xers went to college.[18] Caught in the aftermath of the 1990 recession, more than 40 percent of the class of 1990 had either no job or one that did not require a college degree.[19] Xers began their adult lives with unprecedented personal debt. They missed the heavy college subsidies and the boom years of the economy, but arrived just in time to use credit cards to cover the higher costs.

The shift from economic optimism to pessimism made generational sticking points inevitable in the workplace. The Gen Xers couldn't see a payoff from the game the Boomers worked so hard to win. Plus, Generation X didn't know how long they would be working at the same places as they watched increasing global competition force companies that could no longer promise lifetime employment to create a new deal with their employees.

In my interviews, Xers have told me why they see the game differently:

- "My boss has a career; I have a job."
- "My parents put off enjoying life until they had achieved their dreams, but where did it get them?"
- "Companies don't last fifty years anymore. I'd love to stay at one place my entire career, but that's not realistic. If my company gets sold or we hit another recession, I may not have a job."
- "It makes no sense to put in thirteen-hour days and relocate seven times when the company won't think twice about laying me off."
- "I don't go to work to find meaning or significance. I don't want to sign my name to another mission statement brought back from an executive retreat up in the mountains somewhere. It's just a job! I do it well, and then I go home to what's most important. Why do the older generations have to make it into something more than that?"

As we saw earlier, the shock of the downturns in the 1970s forced everyone to reevaluate their expectations. Boomers competed harder while the Traditionalists who still owned the companies cheered them on. Both Traditionalists and Baby Boomers were stunned that Generation X wanted to ease up rather than play harder.

I'm generalizing, describing the spirit of the times that shaped the Xers. Even then, not all Xers embraced this shift in thinking. Extensive research conducted by Saatchi & Saatchi in the early 1990s discovered Xers fit into four subcategories, only one of which was as checked out and cynical as Douglas Coupland described in *Generation X: Tales for an Accelerated Culture*. But they got all the press. In contrast, the researchers labeled another of the four categories "traditional materialists" because they played the game as hard as the Boomer yuppies.[20]

The point is that Xers have always wanted to succeed. The Center for Work-Life Policy found recently that three out of four Xers consider themselves ambitious.[21] Even more, 31 percent of Xers earning more than $75,000 a year have an "extreme job" (which demands more than sixty-hour work weeks, short deadlines, and 24/7 access), and 28 percent work an average of ten hours more per week than they did three years ago.[22] So just as most Boomers were not protesters, most Xers were not slackers, although all of them had to decide how they would handle the new expectation that, unlike their parents, nothing would come easy for them.

Ghost Story #4: Parody

Parody creates a poor imitation of something serious in order to make light of it and expose its perceived flaws. Access to information creates parody, as does skepticism—and the Xers have both. They got a downsized American dream, divorced parents, a new deal at work, and a computer to check facts.

Xers are computer/Internet natives, which gave them access to what was going on behind the scenes in a world that was taking itself pretty seriously. (If you carried a typewriter into your college dorm instead of a laptop, you are a digital immigrant, not a native.) For example, these digital natives were the first to gain access to information beyond the news. When Walter Cronkite, called the most trusted man in America, signed off his news broadcast with "That's the way it is," viewers felt confident he was providing objective reporting. Generation X was the first generation to question and verify the backstory behind the news on their computers, so they knew that news is always shaded by someone's perspective. Gen X learned you can't believe everything you are told. So they wanted those in authority to "get real."

Marketers put their tongues squarely in their cheeks to tie in to this "get real" sentiment. For example, when Isuzu wanted to break into the US auto market with a small advertising budget, they aimed at skeptical Xer buyers with parodies of typical high-hype car ads with their "Joe Isuzu" campaign that ran from 1986 to 1990. As Joe Isuzu makes fantastic claims about the cars, the actual facts appear on the screen. In one ad, Joe Isuzu claims, "If I'm lying, may lightning hit my mother." The words "Good luck, Mom!" pop up. Parody became the staple of advertisers trying to reach the tail end of Boomers and the new generation of Xers who were raised on over-the-top hype and were skeptical of all of it. Any brand that took itself too seriously made an easy target.

Generation X expert Rebecca Ryan captures Xers' skeptical attitude like this:

> A generation of Americans who don't talk to strangers and have little faith in institutions, especially employers. In other words, Gen Xers are skeptical. They have a difficult time trusting others, they are obsessively self-reliant, and they don't see themselves as "joiners" of traditional organizations.[23]

Gen Xers are skeptical of organizations. At work they may trust their managers, but they wonder about their companies. Furthermore, associations find that Gen Xers will come to their conferences if they're relevant, but Xers aren't as interested in membership and don't join committees as often or as enthusiastically as Traditionalists and Boomers did. They are also more cautious when choosing a political party. And even if they identify with a party, they may not buy the full platform.

Xer skepticism is most clearly seen in its parodies epitomized in the long-running cartoon shows *The Simpsons* and *South Park*. Jeff Gordinier, in *X Saves the World: How Generation X Got the Shaft but Can Still Keep Everything from Sucking*, thinks that, thanks to the Xers, "we're living through a golden age of political satire."[24] The popularity and growth of comedy news shows on cable channels confirms his observation and stands in contrast to Walter Cronkite's seriousness. Whereas Boomers would have tried to use the microphone to push for change, this audience wants humor. Ben Karlin, who produces Jon Stewart's *The Daily Show* and Stephen Colbert's *The Colbert Report*, told *Rolling Stone*, "The biggest mistake people make is thinking that Jon and Stephen sit down before every show and say, 'OK, how are we going to change the world?' . . . They both really just want to get a laugh."[25] The age of parody expresses the underlying skepticism of a generation.

DONKEY KONG MEETS MIDDLE AGE

Today Xers are moving into middle age and beginning to send their kids off to college. They are trying to survive, noses to the smartphone screen, in a much more volatile global economy.

I recently taught leadership to managers at a large accounting firm. On the way out the door, two Generation Xers said to me, "Xer managers are still squished, you know. All the things we've learned today about how to lead people more effectively make complete sense, but we will run into resistance from a lot of Baby Boomer partners who are old school and want things done their way. But they don't manage the Millennials, who *really* hate the old-school approach, so the old guard doesn't see why things ought to change. That means the Xer managers get caught in the middle and are forced to hold it all together. We've always been squished in the middle."

Gen Xers are the most misunderstood and invisible of the generations, but organizations can't overlook them because these middle-aged Xers will be the leaders organizations desperately need during the next twenty years. They will be the employees with experience and institutional knowledge. They will have the specialized technical skills needed to compete. And they will lead our organizations—and our nation—next.

But in the meantime, despite remaining squished between two massive generations and juggling family and jobs in a downward economy, Gen Xers still retain their sense of humor. They still want organizations to quit spinning the facts and "get real." They still lampoon the world they rewired in the digital revolution. And they still look at life like a video game: you don't have any control over the vines that come your way, but you can always try to land on your feet. Life is *Donkey Kong.*

CHAPTER 7

Millennials: Can We Fix It? *Yes, We Can!*

BORN 1981–2001

📱 Millennials (Born 1981–2001)

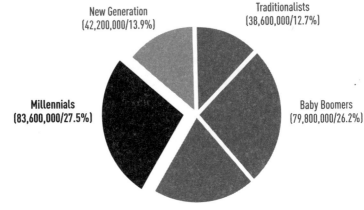

New Generation
(42,200,000/13.9%)

Traditionalists
(38,600,000/12.7%)

Millennials
(83,600,000/27.5%)

Baby Boomers
(79,800,000/26.2%)

Gen Xers
(60,100,000/19.8%)

US Census Bureau
Current population survey, 2010

Names[1]
- Millennials
- Generation Y
- NetGen
- Gen Next

Teen Years
- 2000s through 2010s

Key Events
- Oklahoma City Federal Building bombing (1995)
- Television show rating system established (1997)
- Columbine High School shootings (1999)
- President Clinton and Monica Lewinsky scandal (1998–99)
- New millennium and the Y2K nonevent (2000)
- September 11 World Trade Center attack (2001)
- Department of Homeland Security created (2002)
- Massachusetts becomes first state to legalize gay marriage (2004)
- Dow Jones hits record high (2007)
- The Great Recession begins (2007–9)
- Barack Obama becomes first black president (2009)
- Occupy Wall Street (2011)
- Slowest job recovery after a recession since the Depression (2008–)

Top Television Shows
- *ER* (1995–97, 1998–99)
- *Family Guy* (debuts 1999)
- *Survivor: Australian Outback* (2000–2001)
- *Friends* (2001–2)
- *CSI* (2002–3)
- *American Idol* (2003–11)

Top Music
- "Gangsta's Paradise" (Coolio, 1995)
- "Candle in the Wind" (Elton John, 1997)
- "Can We Fix It?" (*Bob the Builder* theme song, 2000 [UK])
- "Bad Day" (Daniel Powter, 2006)
- "Boom Boom Pow" (The Black Eyed Peas, 2009)
- "Somebody That I Used to Know" (Gotye and Kimbra, 2012)

What Makes Your Generation Unique?
Top five responses Millennials give about themselves:
- Technology use (24 percent)
- Music/pop culture (11 percent)
- Liberal/tolerant (7 percent)
- Smarter (6 percent)
- Clothes (5 percent)[2]

How Millennials See Themselves at Work
Top-ranked terms used to describe coworkers in the same generation:
- Makes personal friends at work
- Sociable
- Thinks out of the box
- Open to new ideas
- Friendly[3]

T he room suddenly got silent. You could have heard a cell connection drop. I had just given forty Baby Boomers, thirty-two Gen Xers, and eight Millennials— all from the hospitality industry—a couple of minutes to answer the question "What do you wish the other generations understood about you?"

The twenty-three-year-old spokeswoman for the Millennials said, "I wish the older generations recognized that not only are we energetic, we're also creative. We have ideas that should be listened to—"

The Boomer manager of the largest hotel cut her off. "What could you possibly know about running a property that I don't know after doing this for twenty years?"

The Millennial spokeswoman politely acknowledged the man's comment and finished reporting the rest of her group's list. A few minutes later, when the groups were working together on something else, I strolled by the Millennials' group and asked what they thought about the manager's comment.

The Millennials' consensus was, "He doesn't get it. I'm glad I don't work at his property."

I asked the original Millennial spokeswoman if she was okay with the exchange. "I'm fine," she said. "We all have relatives who treat us like we're stupid. It never does any good to get into an argument; I find it easier to ignore people who ignore me." The Millennials at the table agreed that they ignore those in the older generations who ignore them.

How good for a business (or a family or a team) can that be?

That hotel manager I described isn't unique. He said what hundreds of Boomers have told me—that Millennials come in expecting to be taken seriously even though they have no "real-world" experience. But here's what will surprise you: Millennials agree with their bosses about their lack of experience. Only 29 percent of Millennials rate their generation as competent in their jobs.[4] They want to gain the real-world experience they know they lack *and* contribute to the team. They don't see why it's either-or.

Because they are the newest generation in the workplace, Millennials get criticized more than the other generations. In a class I taught recently in Canada, a manager complained to me that "this new generation doesn't work worth a dang and quits when it gets hard." His sentiments are echoed around the world. At Foxconn, the largest Chinese high-tech manufacturing firm for American tech companies like Apple, a thirty-year-old manager said that young workers born in the 1990s will "resign the minute they get angry. . . . Very few of them can eat bitterness."[5]

It's obvious that a new generation has arrived, because they have many of us baffled. Ten thousand Millennials a day are joining the workplace,[6] so your organization had better know how they think. These ghost stories have helped thousands of people understand not only the way Millennials think but also why they think differently. Because the Millennials are new and therefore more of a mystery, we'll look at six ghost stories rather than four, as we did for the other three generations.

THE MILLENNIALS' SIX BIGGEST GHOST STORIES
Ghost Story #1: Heavy Parental Involvement
You'll remember that Generation X is the smallest of the four generations because their Boomer parents didn't have a Baby Boom. Instead, they sought fulfillment in ways other than having children. But around 1985, a change was underway. Baby on Board signs showed up in minivan windows as younger Boomers and then older Gen Xers began to have children—a lot of children. The second Baby Boom, or Echo Boom, had begun—and it was bigger than the first.[7]

The Millennials were a "wanted" generation. There were half as many children per family in the second Baby Boom compared to the first, but far more women gave birth. The number of multiple births skyrocketed as fertility became the new growth area in reproductive health care.[8] By 1990, 80 percent of all fathers were in the delivery rooms attending their children's births, up from 27 percent halfway through Gen Xers' birth years.[9] The hands-on dad had arrived! The Millennials think differently because they were raised differently.

An older Generation X manager said to me, "Millennials get bored after nine months on the job, and then they act like their boredom is *my* problem." I said, "It is. You and the Boomers taught them to think that way." Boomers and most Xers remember being told by their parents to go outside and play but to come in when it got dark. How many parents would tell that to their children today? After missing children started showing up on milk cartons and billboards, parents of Millennials couldn't turn their kids loose,[10] so they became their children's activity directors. They arranged playdates and lived in their minivans, driving their kids from one activity to another: soccer, ballet, music lessons, swim team, and so on. And their involvement in their kids' lives didn't end with high school graduation.

Gen X parents sent their young charges off to college but still stayed involved in their lives. According to the Datatel 2006 College Parent Survey, parents today are four times more involved in helping their children succeed in college than their own parents were.[11] No wonder it was the associate vice president of Wake Forest University, Mary Gerardy, who first called them "helicopter parents" because of how they hovered over their children. The parents of the previous generations helped their kids move into their dorm rooms and then left. Today colleges run parent-orientation sessions to get the parents to leave.

Heavily involved parents created the Millennials' expectation that their managers would be more involved, but these parents' impact on the workplace doesn't end there. They stay involved in their children's work lives. Frequently I've had managers say that their Millennial workers' parents write to them to complain that their children didn't get the internship or promotion or good assignment they wanted. But these managers are most shocked when parents ask if they can sit in on their children's interviews. I tell these managers they're learning what college administrators found out over a decade ago when the Millennials started college: their parents are part of the package.

This is not just a case of overprotective parents—Millennials and their parents have a mutual affection and admiration. Almost half of Millennials pick their parents as role models and heroes over celebrities or friends.[12] In 1974, 40 percent of Boomers told Gallup that they would be better off without their parents. In contrast, over 90 percent of Millennials told Gallup that they have a good relationship with their parents.[13] Boomers saw their parents as part of the establishment, while Millennials see their parents as resources to help them get established.

Millennials *want* their parents involved in their lives. Sociologist Reginald Bibby found that 90 percent of Canadian Millennials see their mothers as having a high level of influence on them, and over 80 percent say the same about their fathers.[14] A study by Thom Rainer found that 77 percent of Millennials seek their parents' advice regularly.[15] Millennials believe their parents can offer guidance for navigating the university and the workplace, while many Boomers knew their parents couldn't. Boomers were often the first in their families to go to college. Their Traditionalist parents could show them how to farm or build a house but told them that they didn't know anything about college or the corporate world.

Both my parents were college professors and were constant resources as I went to college—as I am for my kids. All three of my sons are majoring in business, so they call me for ideas for projects and references for their papers or ask my advice on what classes to take. Their professors tell them to use their resources, and I'm one of them. I enjoy helping them and plan to assist them throughout their careers. I'm not coming with them, but you can be sure I will coach them before their job interviews, especially on negotiating compensation—after all, the more they earn, the faster they get off my payroll!

So how should employers deal with Millennials' parents? Engage them! They are hidden resources and potential customers. They have ideas or expertise that will benefit your organization that they will gladly share with their children. Don't roll your eyes when Millennials tell you something their parents said—listen, and grab your pencil if it's good. Send the parents company logo hats and sweatshirts—they'll wear them just like they wore their kids' college-logo wear. Make sure your company's website has information for parents on the recruiting page and a way for parents to ask questions about the company their children may be interviewing with. Millennials consult with their parents about job decisions—so you want those parents to be reassured you will be a good fit for their children.[16]

Ghost Story #2: Fear of Low Self-Esteem

Millennials are confident. Their parents and teachers convinced them they are special, and the Millennials believe it. In one survey, 96 percent of

Millennials agreed or somewhat agreed with this statement: "I can do something great." Not one respondent disagreed strongly.[17]

Their parents communicated with them by dialoguing rather than by dictating. In 2009, the journal *Qualitative Sociology* looked at three hundred advice columns and editorials from issues of *Parents* magazine spanning 1929 to 2006. According to this survey, while Millennial children had less freedom to be outdoors without parental supervision, they had more freedom to disagree with their parents and wear whatever clothes they wanted.[18] Millennials were encouraged to express their feelings.

Millennials were raised not keeping score in organized youth sporting leagues until they were at least nine years old—for fear the losing team would feel bad. Everybody who paid their fee got a participation trophy whether they played or not. Gen Xers put a protective shield around the self-esteem of their children.[19]

A participant in a seminar I led told me about his experience with another parent whose child was on the same youth soccer team: "After our team was beaten soundly in a game, the other child's mother said we should make a 'parent bridge' for the players to run through as they came off the field to get their treats. Mostly joking, I said that as badly as the boys had played, we should just turn our backs and let them get their own treats. The mother was appalled. I asked her, when her son is thirty years old, still living at home, and unable to find a job, if she and her husband will make a bridge, cheer, and give him a juice box for trying his best. I don't think she thought I was funny."

From participation trophies on the soccer field to bouquets of roses after preschool dance recitals, Millennials have been made to feel special. They have their births, baptisms, Bar/Bat Mitzvahs, confirmations, games, and graduations stored on videotapes and DVDs. Considering their twenty years of being the center of attention, why are we surprised when they have the confidence to speak up in meetings even though they have only been on the project a few days?

Ghost Story #3: The Consumer Age

The Millennials were raised as consumers. Their parents could offer them choices previous generations never had. I remember growing up in a town with two hamburger restaurants. It did no good to complain to my parents that I didn't like my fries, because there wasn't another viable option. But today, haven't you seen an SUV leave one fast-food restaurant and go across the street to another just to stop the whining from the backseat?

The Millennials have always had so many options that they need search engines to sort through them all. That's taught them to ask for what they want and look someplace else if you can't give it to them.

The Millennials' consumer approach in the workplace often gets interpreted as an entitlement mentality. When I was doing a presentation for McDonald's, a woman said, "I've been here thirty-six years, and some of these new employees seem so entitled. They ask for things in the first six weeks that I never got until I'd proven myself after six or seven years."

"You know who caused that, don't you?" I asked. Her blank stare said no. "McDonald's did," I continued. The seventy McDonald's employees in the room got quiet. "McDonald's is the company that started giving kids a toy with every Happy Meal. You taught the Millennials to believe they were entitled to a toy!" (For many years, McDonald's has been the largest toy distributor in the world.[20])

I could see that she got it. She came up to me after the session and told me she was excited to go back and talk with her Millennial coworkers.

MONEY MATTERS
Unfortunately, the economic expansion of Millennials' childhood was unsustainable, built as it was on excessive borrowing.[21] Since 2007, when the current market downturn began, many Millennials have had trouble downsizing their expectations and cutting their spending. Sixty percent of twenty- to twenty-nine-year-olds have cashed out their retirement plans. On average, they carry three credit cards, and 20 percent have a debt balance of more than $10,000 (not counting student loans), though many are slowing down.[22] Millennials are graduating from college with an average debt of $26,600 (compared to $14,500 in 1993). But here's the kicker: nearly half of Millennials drop out of college before they earn a degree.[23]

Besides wanting to make money, Millennials also want to make a difference. The Futures Company (what was Yankelovich) calls Millennials "post-materialistic": "Happiness is higher on their agenda than it has been for their immediate predecessors. They don't think money is everything but they aren't ready to give up material comforts in search of happiness and making a difference."[24] The economic downturn is making it harder to get both.

THE TWO HALVES OF THE MILLENNIALS AND THE GREAT RECESSION
The first half of the Millennials grew up in a strong economy with available jobs. The second half of the generation hasn't been so lucky. The first half

could be picky and demanding about jobs because there were plenty available. The second half has struggled in an economy with unemployment at record-high levels.

The "jobless recovery" America is experiencing has impacted Millennials the most, and one in five has returned home to live with their parents.[25] They grew up in an unusual time economists call the Great Moderation because of the steady economic growth with only two mild recessions.[26] Economists expect the global economy to have more volatility even as the United States and Europe grow much more slowly than other parts of the world. Even more challenging, the Millennials will support the huge but long-living Boomer generation, who will continue to draw heavily on underfunded Social Security and health care in their retirement years.[27] The United Nations has predicted that by 2050, there will be only two workers for every pensioner (retiree) rather than four, as there is today.[28] The American dream that every generation will make more than the previous generation is now hitting strong resistance.

The Great Recession has been especially hard on blue-collar jobs, further dampening the prospects for Millennials. The unemployment rate for high school dropouts is 14 percent, but only 4 percent for college graduates. (Twenty-five percent of high school students drop out before graduation.) It takes 20 percent fewer workers to manufacture more (US manufacturing has grown by $800 billion since 1990)[29] due to robotics, automation, and other efficiencies. While there is recent hope for a rebound in manufacturing, the jobs that remain usually require more math and science.[30]

The Great Recession will leave a scar in the psyche of this optimistic generation.[31] It will likely be many years before the economy grows at the pace it did in the 1980s and 1990s. Millennials are facing increasing college costs (more student debt), a difficult job market, and lower wages. Fourteen percent of Millennials who are working full-time say they still rely on financial support from their parents.[32]

Yet despite these discouraging realities, the Pew Research Center found that Millennial optimism is alive and well. In spite of the Great Recession, among the two-thirds of Millennials who say they cannot currently afford the life they want, almost 90 percent of them "expect to earn enough in the future to live the good life." Even before Y2K, September 11, and the 2001 recession crushed the Gen Xers' optimism, they still polled 12 percentage points lower than the now-battered Millennials regarding the future.[33] True to their reputation, Millennials have remained confident no matter what hits them.

Ghost Story #4: September 11, 2001 (9/11)

I asked a group of University of Illinois administrators to name the most important ghosts that shape Millennials. Immediately, a Millennial manager called out, "September 11." I asked him what September 11 changed in his thinking, and he replied, "Everything." When I asked him to narrow it down, he couldn't. He said there was no part of his life that 9/11 didn't impact.

Traditionalists and Baby Boomers believed in delayed gratification—work hard today and get rewarded tomorrow. But there is an entire generation of young adults that has grown up knowing that tomorrow may never arrive. A terrorist or a crazed gunman can turn an office tower, a post office, a school, or a mall into a war zone. Before 9/11, the closest war had come to America in the modern era was Pearl Harbor (1941). But Millennials witnessed the first World Trade Center bombing (1993) and the bombing of the Murrah Federal Building in Oklahoma City (1995). Wars and bombs and battles had previously always been "over there"—across an ocean somewhere. But not anymore. Millennials have grown up with metal detectors, airport searches and scans, bomb-sniffing dogs, and armed SWAT teams in public places because now the enemy is among us—or could be.[34]

September 11, 2001, shaped Millennial culture in at least two major ways. First, Millennials learned to not wait until tomorrow to do something important, because tomorrow may never arrive. For example, Millennials have a higher rate of volunteerism than other generations did at the same age. Second, and related, they have a strong impulse to keep work and life in balance. They see no reason to sacrifice everything today for a future reward that may never come.

Ghost Story #5: Technology Everywhere

Millennials are the first generation to grow up digital, surrounded by technology. Millennials spend more than fifty-three hours a week with media because they use more than one kind at the same time.[35] Boomers learned computers at work, and Xers learned them at home or school. Millennials never had to learn computers—they were built into their earliest toys. For Millennials, a smartphone is a bodily appendage. (Eighty-three percent of Millennials have slept with their cell phones in or by their beds—compared to 68 percent of Xers, 50 percent of Boomers, and 20 percent of Traditionalists.[36]) McCann Worldgroup discovered that half of Millennials would give up their sense of smell to keep their computer or mobile phone.[37]

Millennials love technology for four main reasons:

1. *Technology makes the Millennials important to the older generations.* Most parents of Millennial kids know how valuable their children are when it comes to technology. After spending an unsuccessful hour on the phone with technical support, I can hand my smartphone to my son Max. He has it working in two minutes. "Dad," he'll say, grinning, "it's not a smartphone until you can work all the buttons." Even though he's right, I think, *I brought you into this world, and I can take you out.* But I never would: his technical support is too important to me. Millennials know how valuable they are when it comes to technology. They are the first generation in history to have more experience with the tools that will shape our future than the generations before them.

2. *Technology gave the Millennials freedom.* Traditionalists, Boomers, and most Gen Xers found freedom from their parents outdoors. But the Millennials weren't allowed to play outside alone—life seemed too unpredictable. So their parents made them play indoors, where it was safe. Millennials found freedom from their parents' control on the Internet.

3. *Technology shrank and expanded the Millennials' world.* Millennials are the first generation to be raised in the "global digital village." They know people all over the world as a result of playing online video games and connecting through Facebook and other online venues. The Internet has shrunk the distances but expanded the horizons. The entire world fits on a Millennial's smartphone.

4. *Technology gathers the Millennials into tribes.* Millennials don't have a group of friends; technology has given them a *tribe* of friends. Boomers typically had four to five close friends because that was all you could fit in their instant messaging device—a Chevy. Xers had eight to ten because cell phones allowed them to coordinate where they would meet. But Millennials may have forty or sixty people they think of as close friends, thanks to their phones and laptops.

You may have seen a tribe of Millennials stretched out over five tables at a restaurant, all texting people who aren't there while they talk to each other and listen in on conversations at the other tables. They jump in and out of three or four discussions both verbally and on screen, and no one thinks anything of it. Then suddenly they get up and head to their cars and go someplace else. The tribe has spoken—but their fingers do the talking.

Their phones give them constant contact with their tribe. As one father told me at a seminar, "I used to be irritated when my kids texted during dinner—until they explained how their friends' plans could change three times in thirty minutes, and they can't be that far out of the loop."

Ghost Story #6: Emerging Adulthood

Most of the workplace complaints I hear about Millennials' lack of commit-ment and work ethic can be tied to the dynamics of emerging adulthood.

Remember Stan from chapter 1—the Boomer father whose Millennial son, Brandon, was still living at home and in no rush to find a permanent job, get married, or finish his last year of college? Stan was more worried about Brandon than he needed to be because he didn't understand emerg-ing adulthood.

I told him, "Some Millennials take longer to figure out what they want to do than members of the older two generations did. It's called emerging adulthood, and it's only been talked about for the last ten years or so, but it's not new. It started with you Baby Boomers when four years of college extended your freedoms by delaying when you entered the workforce. The older generations back then complained that you guys were messing around rather than getting serious."

"I've never heard of emerging adulthood," Stan told me. "Brandon pays us rent and never gives us any grief. He's a lot of fun, so it's not that I mind having him home. I'm just worried he's not doing what he needs to do to prepare for the future. He's in no hurry to finish college, and he bounces from one job to the next. I try to talk some sense into him, but my wife tells me I need to back off and give him some time to figure it out. How much more time does he need?"

I replied, "If it's any consolation, I hear this two or three times a week. A lot of families worry about their twentysomethings because they seem to change apartments, towns, friends, love relationships, jobs, and even careers frequently. Society gives them more time than it gave our parents to try out different careers and identities until they find the one they want. Usually it works out fine."

Then Stan asked the question that I often get asked about emerging adulthood: "What's changed so much since I was twenty-five?"

There are a lot of reasons emerging adulthood is more obvious today with the Millennials than it was in earlier generations. But let me keep it simple and give you the biggest one: today, we don't believe a person is an adult until around age twenty-six.[38] Remarkably, twentysomethings agree with that assessment. They think it takes that long to figure out what they want to do so they can settle into a career, commit to a long-term love relationship, and have enough saved up to get their own place.[39] Boomers liked freedom from pressure. They pushed off buying houses until their late twenties. So did Generation Xers. Millennials push it off even further. But they leave college with student loan debt bigger than what the Boomers paid for a condo.

Most of what Stan and other parents worry about usually works itself out. Most Millennials are not lazy; they're just not sure they've found what they want to do, what organization they want to do it with, where they want to live, and who they want to live with.

A couple of days ago I was sitting with a table of Millennials in a class I was leading. They were all well respected and productive, but they articulated the freedom of the twenties this way: "I tell my friends, 'You're not married; you're only twenty-five. This is the time to hike through Europe and Asia for a year. You'll never get this chance again because you'll settle down and have a house and a family. Enjoy the freedom and opportunities while you have them. Do what you really want to do now; don't put it off till later.'"

Most of the worries older generations have in the workplace about Millennials and their work ethic will end up dissipating just as they did for Generation X twenty years ago. With the Millennials, it will just happen a bit later.

GIVE THE MILLENNIALS TIME (AND CUT THEM SOME SLACK)

The Millennials are the least understood generation. When the Millennials first entered the workforce, Gen Xers didn't understand Millennials, Boomers didn't understand Gen Xers or Millennials, and Traditionalists didn't understand any of them. The earlier generations have done fine despite the doubts of their elders—and Millennials will too. Every generation has its own unique ways of doing things. Once the Millennials' children grow up and enter the workforce, all the attention will shift away from Millennials and onto the rising generation of their children. And all the prior generations will be sure that the Millennials' children will spell the downfall of all that's good in the world.

But they'll be wrong. And they'll be missing out.

Like the hospitality manager at the beginning of the chapter who brushed aside the contributions Millennials wanted to make, those who ignore or disparage Millennials won't get much argument from them; they'll be ignored. The Millennials who work for them will pack up the ideas (and with it their enthusiasm) that they so badly wanted to contribute. They'll smile and nod and then go back to texting people who care about what they think. Those managers and organizations will miss out. People ask me if Millennials will spell the end of the world. I'm not worried. I don't think they are magical saviors, nor do I think they'll bring the world down in flames. With the revolution in information tools and technology, they have the possibility to be the most productive generation in history—if those of us who've gone before don't make the situation harder than it needs to be.

PART 2

Sticking Points

*How to Get Four Generations Working Together
in the Twelve Places They Come Apart*

Decoding the Generations

FIRST OFFICER: "Stalling, we're falling. Larry, we're going down, Larry."
Pilot: "I know it."

Those were the last words spoken in the cockpit before Air Florida flight 90 crashed into 14th Street Bridge's northbound span, crushing several cars and falling into the icy Potomac River on January 13, 1982. Because a television news crew who'd been stuck in traffic nearby recorded the devastation and subsequent rescue attempts, millions experienced the horror of seeing the plane slip under the water and the heroism of passengers and bystanders diving in to pull people to safety.

As experts studied the black box recording, they were shocked that the first officer, Roger Alan Pettit, had mentioned repeatedly that the snow was building up on other planes and that the crew ought to check theirs again. But Captain Larry Wheaton dismissed his concerns. Neither pilot had much experience with winter storms, and First Officer Pettit—having been trained in the Air Force to respect his superior officer—made suggestions rather than confronting his captain directly. Consequently, Captain Wheaton was not able to decode the seriousness of his first officer's warnings. As the plane rolled down the slushy runway, Pettit announced that a gauge did not look right, but the captain, again failing to decode the gravity of the situation, ignored his warning.

STICKING POINTS

Half a minute later the plane went down.[1]

As this tragedy illustrates, decoding communication and understanding others can be critical to keeping the mission on track and avoiding needless failure or even tragedy. The same applies to generations. Take these commonly heard statements:

- "I don't expect to be at the same organization for the rest of my career."
- "You can't take people with nose rings seriously at work."
- "Technology is overrated; it's face-to-face communication that has the greatest impact."
- "Just because the boss works long hours doesn't mean we employees have to."
- "If a section of a meeting doesn't apply to you, there is nothing wrong with checking e-mail on your phone."
- "It's not about how many hours you work, as long as you get your work done."
- "People should be in their organizations at least six months to a year before they start trying to change things."
- "There are very few work emergencies worth working late for."

Each of these statements means something different to each generation. Through the ghost stories, we've learned about the four generations in today's workplace and why they are who they are. Those ghost stories provide the understanding we need in order to move into the sticking points themselves. Moving from ghost stories to sticking points is like going from the lunch room or cubicles where individuals can be themselves to the conference room where the four generations have to work together. It's time to look at the twelve sticking points—the twelve areas in the workplace where the generational corners are sharpest and leave a mark when they hit.

My experience has been this: if the four generations will acknowledge the twelve sticking points and work through them as a team, they will find themselves liberated to become a team with a unified vision instead of a group with different agendas. Instead of generational differences holding your team back, those differences will become the fuel that propels your team forward.

But in order to lead through the sticking points, you must be able to decode what the generations mean—and don't mean. In the last four chapters, we've seen how understanding the generations' ghost stories helps us decipher

108

what they mean when they say or do things that seem strange. Awareness is powerful—and it will change your team dynamics and break down stereotypes.

But it's not enough. You need tools and a process for getting the four generations working together in the twelve places they come apart. The following twelve sticking point chapters give you a decoder ring for understanding how the generations approach common workplace problems. They will show you how to lead your team through your generational challenges by applying a five-step process to each of the twelve most common generational differences that get teams stuck.

I've organized the sticking points in alphabetical order and written each as a stand-alone chapter to make it easy for you to jump to the chapter that covers the situation you're facing in your team. Here's what I recommend: when you face a generational challenge, read the sticking point chapter that best matches your situation and then thumb through the rest of the chapters (especially the summaries at the end of each). Thousands of people in my workshops have learned that even if their challenging situation concerns one sticking point, the insights from other sticking points will also help. (For example, in addition to the chapter specifically about dress code, participants find the information about communication, decision making, policies, and respect essential.) Then follow the five-step process for leading through generational sticking points with your team. (You'll want to reread chapter 3 for more detail on the five steps.) Finally, no matter your generational challenge, read the chapters on communication, policies, respect, and work ethic, as these sticking points (and how we handle them) are foundational to the others.

A word about my summaries comparing how the generations see each sticking point: don't expect the people on your team to agree with every generalization I make about their generation. Remember, individuals don't fit into boxes, so no one will feel like every description of their generation applies to them. Furthermore, my generalizations regarding Traditionalists and Boomers emphasize the era when they started working, to give a historical perspective. Remember that many of their attitudes have shifted, just as the technology they use has shifted. The key is to use the generational comparisons in each chapter as the starting point to get your people talking about their own views so they can understand and appreciate one another. As we'll see in the next twelve chapters, great things happen when they do.

Remember: generational sticking points are inevitable, but they don't have to leave us stuck. Use the next twelve chapters as tools to help your team stick together.

CHAPTER 8

Communication

IN SEPTEMBER 2012, Maria Pestrikoff slipped and fell when she flicked a cigarette butt off the edge of her garden in Kodiak, Alaska. Unfortunately, her garden was on a cliff, and because she was texting, she didn't realize how close to the edge she was. She fell sixty feet into rocks ten feet away from the water's edge as the tide was coming in. Fortunately, a friend heard her screams and called for help. Rescuers placed her in a rolled-blanket stretcher and hauled her up the cliff in time to avoid the incoming tide.[1]

Maria's texting mishap was unusual because it involved a sixty-foot drop, but all of us regularly see people texting and walking without looking where they're going. Sometimes they walk right into us, as if they're playing a game of digitally induced bumper cars. It's also a major cause of the jump in teenagers being hit by cars.[2]

Ready or not, communication technologies have changed the way we walk, work, love, and live, and they are changing fast. Four Millennials at NASA illustrated this in the PowerPoint presentation "Generation Y Perspectives."[3] They'd been invited to be part of a "strategic communications

committee" at Johnson Space Center in 2007, and after a couple of meetings, they asked if they could make a presentation to the committee[4] to
address a serious long-term challenge: despite NASA's extensive educational
efforts, 40 percent of Millennials think NASA should go out of existence,
and 39 percent don't think it has accomplished anything of lasting value.
The presenting Millennials used one slide in particular, jammed with 147
Internet logos, to demonstrate what they see as the problem—NASA doesn't
speak their language.

The sticking point of communication has largely revolved around
new technology. Certainly Millennials are not the only generation to use
technology like smartphones and social media, and the older generations
are rapidly adapting and adopting. But web-based, networked technology
(Web 2.0) is a defining experience in their lives. It's a part of their ghost
stories. (Remember, half of Millennials would give up their sense of smell
before their computer or cell phone.)

Mobile phone users in Africa (in millions)	
2005—134	2011—660

Facebook users (in millions)	
2006—10	2011—800

Months to sell the first million units of the PalmPilot	Hours to sell the first million units of the iPhone 4S
18	24

E-books as a percentage of total trade book sales	
2008—0.6%	2011—18%

**US digital music download sales	
2005—$500 million	2010—$2.2 billion

***Number of text messages sent/received per month	
2005—9.8 billion	2010—188 billion

For those of us who have spent most of our careers communicating
through memos or e-mail, mobile technology and access to Web 2.0 is a
nice bonus but not essential. We have trouble understanding how big it is
for Millennials. Cisco did a study in 2011 of 2,200 college students and
young professionals worldwide to see what they wanted from their employers. They found the following:

** Robert Safian, "Generation Flux," *Fast Company*, February 2012, 65–68.
*** USA Today Snapshots, *USA Today*, July 3-4, 2012.

- Fifty-six percent of college students globally would turn down a job offer from an organization that banned access to social media (or they would ignore the policy).
- Two-thirds said they would request information about organizational social media policies in job interviews.
- Eighty-one percent want to choose their own devices or to be allowed to use their own personal devices as well as the ones the company gives them.[5]

If your organization is going to succeed with Millennials, you're going to have to get familiar with the tools that they can't live without.

Toward the end of their presentation, the NASA Millennials summarized their recommendation for communicating with members of their generation: "Touch our lives in ways familiar to us." That's really the point for any of us trying to communicate with four generations at work and in our personal lives. We have to touch each generation—not just Millennials—in ways familiar to them. I was hired by one association whose president said it this way: "Go ahead and make the point that Boomers need to learn to use social media and text more. But can you also tell our younger employees to pick up the phone once in a while? E-mailing doesn't build the same kind of customer relationships, at least not with my generation. We are still the ones making 80 percent of the final buying decisions. I know for a fact the new salespeople would close more deals if they'd speak our language."

The five-step process for leading through generational differences will help you and your team figure out how to speak the other generations' languages.

1. ACKNOWLEDGE

Communication is one of the easier sticking points to get out on the table because people already speak openly about new technology and about the differences in the way the generations communicate—although it gets tricky when one generation insists that another communicate their way and with their rules of etiquette.

When one generation says that another generation's preferred method of communication isn't as effective as theirs, things can get tense. For example, a Boomer manager may ask a Generation X employee to give him the thumb drive with the next day's presentation before the employee goes home for the day, whereas the employee wonders why the boss won't learn to use the company's FTP so she can post the file once her evening's plans are over. In families, grandparents may complain that their grandkids never call, whereas the grandkids wonder why their grandparents won't learn to text. (Haven't we all heard Xers complain about trying to organize a family reunion or a holiday party with one relative who won't use e-mail?)

Differences with communication etiquette get people even more upset. For example, a representative from a large retailer told me it baffles their managers when Millennials text rather than call when they miss work. But younger Xers or Millennials think it's efficient rather than abrupt or impersonal. In families, Millennials may see nothing wrong with texting during a family dinner, whereas their parents view it as rude. These are all questions of etiquette.

Whether it's different views on etiquette or different preferred modes of communication, you have to get these communication tensions out on the table and acknowledge them so you can, well, *communicate* about them.

2. APPRECIATE

What you need to get across is *why* the generations communicate differently, and keep the focus on the common need.

Each generation needs to get the information necessary to do their jobs and to feel like valued members of the team. But the generations' native communication languages are different, heavily impacted by the technology they used while growing up and starting their careers. Understanding why the generations feel more at home with certain forms of communication will help you appreciate rather than aggravate each other.

TRADITIONALISTS

Traditionalists grew up with print media. Because they often didn't have access to other sources of information, they trusted experts telling them the facts. Letters, memos, meetings, and eventually the telephone kept their organizations going. Because many of the early Traditionalists never owned a typewriter, schools taught the Palmer Method of cursive handwriting. Traditionalists did their courting by letter or in person. They often complain that Xers, and especially Millennials, don't know how to sit still and carry on a conversation with eye contact.

BABY BOOMERS

Baby Boomers grew up in the era of television, with entertainers compelling rather than experts telling. The communication was still one way, but it was visual, story-based, and in shorter, more concrete pieces. Boomers did their dating by phone. They often complain that their children and grandchildren don't call them.

GENERATION XERS

Xers grew up with digital communication, the World Wide Web, and e-mail. Unlike the Traditionalists, who didn't have access to multiple sources of information, Generation Xers could (after a long grinding noise) log on to the Internet and double-check what official sources said. Because of the Internet, we all became more aware of spin.

Plus, Gen X began to approach other forums similarly to the way they approached the Internet. For example, a Boomer colleague asked me thirteen years ago what to do to keep people off their BlackBerries during training. I suggested that she be more interesting and relevant. She punched me in the shoulder a little harder than was necessary, but I went on to say that just as not every line on a webpage is interesting or relevant to those reading, so not every part of a meeting is equally interesting or relevant to everyone attending. Maybe, as we skim webpages, her people were skimming her meetings—returning e-mails or accomplishing other tasks while she covered something helpful to other participants but irrelevant to their jobs. "Or maybe you're just too boring," I told her. (She punched me again, harder this time.)

Gen Xers did their dating by phone (and later by cell phone) and instant messaging. They wonder why Traditionalists and Boomers won't just send it in an e-mail.

MILLENNIALS

Millennials grew up with interactive communication. News feeds, blogs, retail sites, and social networking all invite their comments and have created a much more conversational communication experience. As Nick, one of the four Millennials who did the NASA presentation, said in a blog, "One of the main underlying points in the presentation is that our generation wants to be involved in space exploration. We want to be involved in the innovation. We want to be part of the discussion. We expect to participate."[6] Unlike Boomers, they did not grow up in a world of one-way communication.

Older generations who were raised on face-to-face or phone conversations tell me they worry that text messaging is so impersonal and that Millennials will not be able to sustain long-term relationships. Older generations have to remember that people complained that the telephone would ruin relationships as it replaced letter writing.

Millennials complain when their grandparents and parents leave them a voicemail and expect them to call back. They also mutter that their parents and grandparents complain that they're always texting or on their phones.

Because the Millennials are the first generation native to social media and the newest in the workplace, people have more questions about how they prefer to communicate. So let's add some additional insight to what I've laid out about social media earlier in the chapter:

- The University of Maryland (in conjunction with the Salzburg Academy on Media & Global Change) surveyed one thousand students in ten countries on five continents. They found that these Millennials were able to adjust their communication approach to their audience. They called their moms, used Skype to talk to their closest friends, used Facebook to talk to larger groups, and sent e-mails to professors and bosses.[7]
- Older Millennials say they phone, text, and e-mail. Many younger Millennials claim to only phone and text.[8]
- Two-thirds of Millennials selected in-person conversation with coworkers as their top communication method. Only 20 percent prefer e-mail.[9]

3. FLEX

Remember that you determine how much you should flex based on business necessities and generational preferences. A business necessity is anything that will make you lose your foot, customer, money, or funding. Your generational preferences are the forms of communication that make you most comfortable.

No one ever debates that with customers it's a business necessity to flex your communication preferences to match theirs. If your customers are Traditionalists, then you'd better pick up the phone or go meet them in person rather than using e-mail or social media. You'd better have a good handshake, make eye contact, and be able to small talk before you jump into business. But if your customers or potential employees are Millennials, then you'd better learn their tools and use humor (MTV discovered in their 2011 survey that "smart and funny is the new rock 'n' roll"[10]).

That's what one of my clients did after they put their senior managers through the generational workshop. They realized they weren't having as much success recruiting and keeping Millennials, so they pulled together a group of Millennials and asked them what would make the organization better for them. They didn't promise they would implement all their ideas, but they did want to listen.

Their Millennial salespeople gave interesting feedback:

- They felt isolated compared to their time in college or grad school and wanted help connecting more quickly within the organization. They wanted opportunities for networking and peer coaching.
- They needed quicker and more frequent feedback.
- They wanted to learn something new every week, not one or two things a month.

They also asked for technology that would allow them "to serve customers the best way they knew how." They had been speaking on what they called "fossil phones" and hauling crates filled with promotional brochures in the backs of their cars as the organization had been doing for forty years. They wondered why they had to take notes on paper and type them into the customer management software at their office when voice recognition software would allow them to finish right there in their cars before they went to the next customer meeting. If they had tablets, they could show customers only the promotional pieces they needed and then e-mail them on the spot. They told the leadership team that their competitors were beating them in technology and asked if they could at least catch up.

They admitted that they had already installed unapproved software but stressed that they were pushing the boundaries not to rebel but to succeed. They wondered if the sales managers would be willing to see what they had come up with. The leadership team did see and was impressed by the productivity gains. They bought tablets for everyone on the sales team.

The older generations will need to flex with more technology, and sometimes younger generations need to go "old school." Younger team members will need to pull up a chair and ask Boomers about the organization's history and then sit back and listen to their stories. (By the way, oral tradition is the only way you'll learn where the organization's skeletons are buried. No Boomer is going to put political realities in a text message.)

It worked for me. Jim Stewart was a brilliant, old-school Baby Boomer senior consultant, and early in my career I needed to know what he knew. If that meant carrying the boxes as we traveled and letting him communicate his way—listening to him talk (and make fun of me) all evening—that was a small price to pay for the invaluable mentoring I received.

It's a business necessity that the more efficient communication methods ultimately win. But sometimes the old-school communication technology *is* more efficient. We've all seen e-mail conversations cascade out of control. As Gen X–Millennial Cusper Timothy Ferriss, bestselling author of *The 4-Hour Workweek*, pointed out to me, every e-mail you send produces 1.5 responses. Sometimes the best way to catch up on e-mail is to pick up the phone instead.

4. LEVERAGE

Web 2.0 and new communication technology allow us to connect with far more people than ever before. As I said in chapter 7, the Millennials are the first generation in history to be more familiar with the tools of the future than the previous generations. They will apprentice us older generations in the new technologies as much as we will apprentice them. Companies often learn the hard way that they need the younger generations' help. They jump into social media as if it were a normal webpage or, worse, a television or magazine ad, and Millennials and younger Xers mock them mercilessly for trying to turn Facebook into an advertising machine.

To the Xers and Millennials: many of us are eager to learn. We know we've landed in this new world, and like the client I mentioned earlier, we're happy to have you give us the tour. Just remember, we have survived without the newest technology, and many of us have less interest in the latest gadget or software as we get older, so you will have to show us the business case for how it will make our lives better—not just how amazing it is—before we will pony up the money to buy it for everyone.

The point is, every generation has its communication and technology preferences, and those preferences all have strengths and weaknesses. They all make more sense in some situations than others. That's why getting your team talking about this sticking point will leverage the collective wisdom far more effectively.

The older generations may be slower to recognize the upsides of the new technology, but they are especially attuned to the downsides. They can help us avoid some of the perils. For one, they point out that some technology is distracting, if not addicting. While psychologists debate whether people are addicted to their cell phones in the same way they are to alcohol or gambling, we all know people who can't seem to focus their attention or keep off their devices.[11] There's some evidence that technology makes us less productive because of these distractions.[12]

5. RESOLVE

Occasionally, appreciating and flexing are not enough, and the group must select an approach. In those cases, step five is needed. Some communication issues require policy decisions. Here are some common examples.

SHOULD WE ALLOW FACEBOOK?

This is one of the most frequent policy questions I get asked about communication. Managers, whatever you do, don't try to figure out the social media policy yourselves. Read chapter 16 on policies to learn how you can lead rather than manage through this touchy issue. You saw earlier in this chapter how important it is to younger employees around the world to have access to social media. For a few organizations, where security is so important they have blocked all USB ports on computers so no one can sneak files out on a thumb drive, all communication technology, not just social media, is dangerous. But most organizations had better get started in sorting out how they will maintain company secrets, protect people's privacy, and navigate new etiquette questions like "Should I friend my boss?" (54 percent say no) or "Should I friend an employee?" (61 percent say no).[13]

But won't Facebook hurt our productivity? Not for most. The number of organizations that allow Facebook and other social media sites is growing, and while some studies suggest that using Facebook decreases productivity, others show that allowing employees to get on these sites actually *increases* productivity because people work faster in order to make "free time" to check in with friends.[14] If you stop access, they think you're shutting down their "free time" and may slow down because you took the carrot away. So while there are good reasons for some organizations to not allow social sites, productivity is not one of them.

At a birthday party recently a friend asked if he should shut off Facebook access on his company computers. Not only was he concerned about Millennials' multitasking, but he also has Baby Boomers who are no longer getting their work done because they keep checking their Facebook accounts. I suggested that even if he shuts it down on their computers, his employees can still check it on their phones. I asked him, "If they get their work done, do you really care if they're on Facebook?" He replied that he didn't. My advice is simple: set clear work standards, and let workers know that as long as they got all of their work done and to those standards, they can pop over to a personal account. Don't let the few who handle it poorly ruin it for everyone else by prohibiting personal access. Work with the individuals whose productivity drops instead of defaulting to a policy that says no to everyone. Facebook and other Web 2.0 sites are inevitable—if not this year, then soon—so let your people figure out how to stay productive and use these sites appropriately.

One of the big worries older generations have is that if some Millennials share too much of their personal lives on social media, can they be trusted with sensitive information? A Gen Xer who commented appreciatively on the four NASA Millennials' work in the "Generation Y Perspectives" PowerPoint voiced his worry about their focus on more open communication:

> The "establishment" is finding it rather difficult to take the GenY folks into their confidence. GenY folks think that data and information is PUBLIC ACCESS (e.g., music file sharing) but large companies, in fact the entire capitalist system, is built on finding a better idea, KEEPING it a secret until the right time, and making your million before any competitor can find a way to do it better and/or cheaper. GenY seems to have a problem grasping this to some extent.[15]

Controlling sensitive information is a critical issue to resolve before opening up more communication portals.

Finally, people say things online they would not say in person or even in an e-mail. So etiquette guidelines need to be clearly established because what employees say can impact the organization.[16] More than that, this tendency also creates needless tension in the office. During the 2012 campaign season, for example, one in five people unfriended or blocked someone on Facebook because they were sick of their political proselytizing.[17]

All these issues need to be dealt with before you allow social networking sites, so my advice is to organize a cross generational team and hand the issue over to them to work out policies that make sense. They will bring you back a list of online guidelines that will be more effective than anything you could come up with, because you don't know all the Web 2.0 sites that they will. And they won't worry about offending any of the generations because they can explain to their peers the dangers if these sites are not used properly. If older leaders create the social media policy by themselves, no matter how good it is, the negative tweets will start flying the moment it is announced. But if you let your people work it out, they'll figure out how to protect the organization and make Facebook a useful tool and perk.

• • •

The point of this chapter is simple: figure out the language of the other generations and try to speak it. Organizations need to ask the generations to help them shape their messages to better speak each generation's language. And they need to ask the generations to help them shape the medium so they're using the right tools to "touch our lives in ways familiar to us," the simple advice those four NASA employees offered. We can all increase our proficiency with the different communication preferences of the people we work with, live with, or serve.

Communication

 TRADITIONALISTS

BABY BOOMERS

I write a memo, send a letter, listen to a speech, and call a meeting.

I write a memo (with the distribution list alphabetized), pick up the phone, and set up a meeting.

How do I communicate?

What are memos? I send an e-mail or instant message, search online for a summary of the speech, and meet virtually.

I send a text message (vowels are optional) or instant message, replay the speech online, or connect on a social-networking site. You really just left me a voicemail?

GEN XERS

MILLENNIALS

Why I Think That Way

 ### TRADITIONALISTS (BORN BEFORE 1945)
Traditionalists grew up in the "print and radio" era, but phones were commonplace after World War II. They were taught "proper" penmanship and formal writing skills. Their communication was face-to-face.

 ### BABY BOOMERS (BORN 1946-1964)
Boomers went to work in the era of typed, formal memos. They were heavily trained in formal writing skills. They grew up in the broadcast era, watching the world on television, which created higher standards for presentations and put emphasis on the visual. They have always had phones.

 ### GEN XERS (BORN 1965-1980)
Gen Xers grew up in a global world and embraced the new technologies of e-mail and cellular phones.

 ### MILLENNIALS (BORN 1981-2001)
Millennials grew up with smartphones, wireless video games, and text messaging. The world is literally at their fingertips.

CHAPTER 9

Decision Making

AIDEN APPROACHED ME as I packed up after a presentation. He was a Millennial, around twenty-five years old, and was dressed in what's often called "business professional" clothes but with a youthful flair. He asked if I could spare a few minutes. My taxi to the airport was about to arrive, so we walked through the conference center while we talked.

"I didn't want to talk in front of anyone else from my company," he began. "My boss, Tom, tries really hard, and I'm pretty sure he thinks he understands my generation. So I think it would make him feel bad if he knew I had doubts about staying with the company. I want your opinion."

"On whether you should leave?" I asked.

"Yes. Would I be better off somewhere else? I'm feeling stuck. I'm finishing up my master's in international business and have worked on projects with people all over the world. I know firsthand how online collaboration software could help us get projects done more quickly, but I'm not being taken seriously. I've brought ideas to my manager, even to our IT people, but they barely listen before dismissing them. My boss and his generation keep telling me that it takes four or five years for a person to prove himself before people will listen. But I don't know if I can sit through another three years of meetings before they discover I have a brain. Who came up with the idea that only the people who've been around awhile get listened to?"

"I know there are plenty of great ideas you and your younger colleagues could contribute," I said. "Why don't you see if you can stir up some discussion on the topic? That's usually the first step in getting unstuck."

"I guess I could try that," he said without much enthusiasm. When he saw my puzzled look, he blurted out, "Don't get me wrong, I like the people I work with, and I'm learning a lot. But I want to work on the sweet projects and put some ideas out there that people listen to. I don't need to wait three or four more years. I'm talking to another engineering firm right now that seems more Millennial friendly, and I'm not the only one considering moving on. You've been to our company a couple of times now. Do you think I'll have to leave to get listened to?"

I handed my bag to the taxi driver and slid into the backseat. I answered Aiden candidly. "Try having a conversation with Tom. He really wants to create a place where Millennials want to stay. Give him the tool for the decision-making sticking point from our session today and ask how long he thinks it will take to shift the way decisions are made. He probably thinks the division has made more progress than you and the other Millennial engineers do. It will bum him out at first, but he'll take it seriously. I'd give these guys one more shot before you go someplace else. Even if you decide to leave, get the issue on the table and make it better for everyone else."

Aiden's company was stuck, and they were about to lose him. As his story illustrates, the way decisions are made in an organization can be a cause of tension and frustration, but it needn't be. Let's apply the five steps of leading through generational differences to the sticking point of decision making.

1. ACKNOWLEDGE

Maybe you are the manager of a team that doesn't realize there are more decision-making processes available than most teams use. Or maybe you are a team member who is hearing that other employees are getting frustrated and you are wondering what to do. Or maybe you are frustrated yourself. Put the issue on the table and help your team or management see it. Acknowledge the tension that has built around decision making. Aiden didn't have to be in charge to acknowledge a generational sticking point, and neither do you.

2. APPRECIATE

Despite their differences, all generations have common needs that they address in different ways. In decision making, people need to know their ideas are respected and that decisions that impact their work and lives are made fairly by the people most capable to make them.

Here's an overview of what has shaped the different generations' views on decision making that you can use to get your team started in their own conversation.

TRADITIONALISTS

Traditionalists grew up and began their careers in hierarchical organizations where the bosses made the decisions. Sometimes a boss asked a few individuals for their opinions, but he ultimately made the decision and announced it to his subordinates. Because questioning orders was insubordination for Traditionalists in the military, they viewed questioning decisions in their postwar organizations the same way.

Today Traditionalists are much more comfortable questioning decisions, but they still expect people to pay their dues and to defer to those with more experience.

BABY BOOMERS

Baby Boomers pushed their organizations to give people a greater voice. But since that was new to their Traditionalist bosses, Boomers used surveys, quality circles, and process mapping to ease the transition. Boomers did not tell their Traditionalist bosses that they disagreed with their bosses' decisions. Instead, they created committees and teams that would meet for six months, interviewing each employee so everyone was treated fairly. They then summarized all the data, made diagrams and flowcharts, and finally presented it all to the boss. They used their exhaustive research, tools, and processes to convince the boss that things needed to change.

GENERATION XERS

Gen Xers learned from technology and nontraditional families to let the savviest person on the topic make the call. During Xers' childhood, family structures shifted more rapidly than at any other time in Western history. Consequently, many Xers grew up with less emphasis on traditional gender roles and more emphasis on the person with the necessary skills. For example, after Dad moved out, Aunt Susan may have moved in to help with the kids and split the rent. If a Gen X youngster wanted help with his science fair project, he would go to Aunt Susan because she was better at drawing graphs than Mom. Most Boomers grew up with their parents fulfilling traditional gender roles, but many Xers didn't. They learned to get help where they could find it. The explosion of technology that surrounded the Xers as young adults also allowed them to embrace whoever was most qualified to help make a decision.

MILLENNIALS

A 2011 MTV study found that 90 percent of Millennials want senior people in their organization to listen to their ideas and opinions, and 76 percent believe "my boss could learn a lot from me."[1] Whereas the older generations sat in rows and were told to cover their answers when they took tests in school, the Millennials went to school organized in groups and did projects or even took tests as teams. (In my generation, working as a group during a test was called cheating.) So they learned how to make decisions as a group without anyone being in charge. Some of them received conflict-resolution training in fourth grade so they could be peer advisers and help their classmates resolve disputes without involving the teachers.[2]

So when they show up in a situation that uses a top-down decision-making model—either the boss or his inner circle making all the decisions—they get frustrated. They want broader, more inclusive decision-making processes. And if their preferences are ignored, they often disengage—or leave.

3. FLEX

Here are six of the most common ways decisions are made:

1. The boss decides and announces.
2. The boss asks all employees for input and then decides.
3. The boss asks the more tenured employees for input and then decides.
4. The boss and a few employees meet and decide.
5. The savviest person on the topic decides.
6. The team talks it over and comes to a consensus (or at least a clear majority) on a conclusion. If not, the boss or the savviest person decides.

Most teams or organizations have a limited repertoire of overused decision-making processes. Which of these does your team use more often?

Which, if you started using them, would help you flex to accommodate different generational preferences?

One client said the most helpful part of this methodology for their organization was that their managers learned to truly differentiate between their personal preferences and the business necessities. That's critical in decision making because each of us prefers some of those six options more than others. But the business necessity is to match the decision-making process to the problem and the people so that we solve the problem and don't lose the people.

4. LEVERAGE

If we get defensive when another generation raises a sticking point, we lose leverage.

The generational differences over decision making can help your organization become more effective by pushing employees to pick the best decision-making process for each situation rather than staying ingrained in their standbys. Each of the six decision-making approaches has its place, but numbers 2, 5, and 6 better fit a global, information-driven economy. The top-down approaches (numbers 1, 3, and 4) assume that the boss knows the most and therefore knows best. But no single person today can be the master of everything—information is increasing, and technologies are evolving too rapidly. Traditionalists and Boomers grew up in an era when it was possible for the boss or the smartest person in the room to know more than everyone else on a subject, but that is not the case today. Admittedly, the top-down approaches (particularly 1 and 4) may be best in a major crisis when time or confidentiality are critical, but hopefully that's rare. If it's not, your sharp Xers and Millennials will be looking to leave anyway.

Bottom line: retaining Xers and Millennials in your workforce means employing decision-making processes 2, 5, and 6 most often.

5. RESOLVE

Because decision making is more about processes than attitudes, appreciating and flexing are not enough. Your team will need step 5—resolve. You can expand your decision-making processes, and that flexibility will go a long way to help you get unstuck. But you can't bounce between three decision-making processes for each decision; you'll only create complete confusion. Your team will work more effectively after you decide how you will make the decision.

Don't wait. Resolve which decision-making approach best fits the different decisions you'll face *before* they come up. Hundreds of times I have worked with groups who thought they were too busy to talk about the six decision-making processes—until they realized they spent more time in meetings than they did working (a sure sign that people don't agree on the appropriate decision-making process). Then they were eager to get on the same page. Don't make that mistake. Start your team talking through when you should use each of the six most common decision-making options listed above.

If you are the manager, in those rare situations when you need to use the top-down approach (options 1, 3, or 4), explain your reasoning to those under you. There is one thing team members hate more than being left out of the decision-making process: not being told *why* they are being left out. I have heard hundreds of employees complain that they were placed on a team that was asked to research a problem and make recommendations to their managers. The employees invested hours, only to discover at their final presentation that management already had their minds made up (and hoped the team would come to the same conclusion).

Ten years later, the employees who spent all those hours researching still speak with resentment of that waste of their time. It's a classic example of decision-making processes 2 (the boss asks all employees for input and then decides) and 5 (the savviest person on the topic decides) colliding. If their managers had explained up front that they had already made a tentative decision but wanted smart people to give input, they could have made their associates feel respected rather than manipulated. They could have said something like, "Our team has looked at four possible new distribution partners, and we strongly favor the company in Chile. But before we decide, we wanted you five to look it over and make sure we're not missing anything. We'd like you to present your findings and recommendations in three weeks."

When people understand the strengths and weaknesses of the six most common decision processes, they are willing to flex as long as their leaders keep them in the loop. Your team will be far more effective (and more attractive to all generations) if you broaden the decision-making processes you use.

• • •

I knew that Tom, the vice president of engineering at Aiden's company, would take Aiden's frustration seriously, but I didn't know if he would get it. He really did want to create a more attractive environment for Millennials, and he had implemented many improvements. But Tom didn't see how much this sticking point was pulling his team apart, nor did he realize his department relied on three decision-making processes that excluded his younger employees. It's a classic case of what we described in chapter 2: he couldn't fix what he couldn't see. But you see it. More than that, you now understand how the era each generation grew up in influences which of the six decision-making processes each prefers. Just as the sweep of history over the last fifty years has changed our phones, it has also changed how we get work done. Smart organizations updated their metal rotary-dial phones thirty years ago in order to make their organizations more efficient. Smart organizations will update their decision-making processes for the same reason.

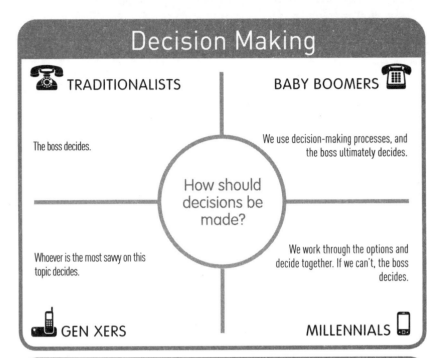

Decision Making

TRADITIONALISTS

The boss decides.

BABY BOOMERS

We use decision-making processes, and the boss ultimately decides.

How should decisions be made?

Whoever is the most savvy on this topic decides.

We work through the options and decide together. If we can't, the boss decides.

GEN XERS

MILLENNIALS

Why I Think That Way

TRADITIONALISTS (BORN BEFORE 1945)
Traditionalists within and outside the military believed questioning orders was insubordination.

BABY BOOMERS (BORN 1946-1964)
Boomers used surveys, quality circles, and process mapping to give criticism to their bosses.

GEN XERS (BORN 1965-1980)
Gen Xers learned from technology and nontraditional families to let the savviest person on the topic make the call.

MILLENNIALS (BORN 1981-2001)
Millennials learned arbitration and group decision-making skills in grade school.

CHAPTER 10

Dress Code

"SIX MONTHS—WE SPENT *six months* debating whether flip-flops are acceptable," Rich, a Baby Boomer operations manager, told the group. "We finally decided associates in the office couldn't wear them, but that didn't solve anything. People then argued over what's a flip-flop and what's a sandal. Human Resources and the executive team spent another six months discussing the ins and outs of footwear. We're *still* talking about it, and no matter what decision we make, somebody's angry."

"I wish we were debating flip-flops versus sandals," said Jennifer, an older Millennial human resource specialist in one of the manufacturing plants. "But we've had quite a stir the last two months around something far more emotional. Some of our younger women have been coming to work in tank tops or camisoles. Their coworkers are complaining that they don't want to see their bra straps or cleavage. Debates around what clothing looks professional are never fun, but when you start dealing with necklines and underwear, people take it personally. They think you're questioning their character."

Brent, a younger production supervisor, chimed in: "You have to have a dress code, but it's a no-win proposition."

I was leading my workshop on the generations for supervisors and managers of a billion-dollar manufacturing company in their state-of-the-art training facility. All the managers agreed that of the twelve generational sticking points, dress code was the most difficult to talk about, especially when it involved propriety rather than professionalism.

And these leaders aren't alone: most managers I've talked to through the years agree wholeheartedly that dress code is the touchiest sticking point.

Every organization has a dress code. Even if they don't put it in writing, every organization defines what clothing is appropriate for safety, professional image, and propriety. Safety issues don't get people wound up. No one's seriously arguing for flip-flops in the warehouse (after all, steel-toed flip-flops defeat the purpose). But because dress is so entwined with a person's identity, professional image and propriety are explosive.

Even acknowledging these dress code sticking points—getting the questions on the table for your team or family to talk about—is hard to do without offending people. If you waltz into a meeting and say, "I've been getting a lot of complaints that people are dressing too casually and showing too much skin," understand that you might be starting the next world war.

1. ACKNOWLEDGE

Any dress code conversation must begin with acknowledging that the four generations give four different answers to the question of which clothes communicate the professional image you want for your organization. But because dress code is such a touchy issue, I recommend that you begin with the common dress needs of all generations (which would usually be discussed in step 2: Appreciate) *before* you put any specifics on the table. Saying something like this might be a good place to start:

> Both clients and employees have questioned whether some clothes people have been wearing lately communicate the professional image we want for our organization. I realize that's tricky because the four generations give four different answers to the question of what clothes look professional. Let's start by remembering that all generations want the same things: to be comfortable, attractive, and taken seriously.

While it's critical with every sticking point to understand and appreciate how the four generations see things differently, you can't even introduce dress code without reminding everyone that we have more in common than we first think.

2. APPRECIATE

As we look at why the generations give different answers to questions about dress code, it helps to remember that each generation is less formal than the one before it. MTV did a study a year ago on Millennials. For one part of the study, they asked people of different generations to draw clothes on stick figures that represented what they wore at work versus what they wore after work. While an older Xer guy changed from his Dockers and tie into shorts and a golf shirt, a Millennial female switched into heels, added bangles to her wrist, and grabbed a clutch purse rather than her work bag. Everything else she marked "same."[1]

I saw each generation becoming more casual at a restaurant that was hosting a wedding rehearsal dinner. I watched the grandfathers enter in sports jackets and ties and the grandmothers in dresses. The parents wore button-down shirts and slacks. Then the wedding party appeared in shorts and flip-flops. Boomers who complain about their kids getting married in flip-flops forget how much they shocked their bosses when they quit wearing the more formal ties and girdles of their parents' generation.

Let your team take their time going through these comparisons so they can create enough trust to talk about their own definitions of appropriate dress. With a subject as touchy as dress code, you'll need to get them talking about the "whys" before the "whats" get them angry.

TRADITIONALISTS

Because most people farmed or labored when the youngest Traditionalists were children, dress clothes were special. Whether silk stockings (or leg makeup during the silk shortage in World War II) or the suit they wore to worship services, formal clothes made a statement that they had good manners and self-respect because they wanted to look their best. My grandmother from the farm never wore a pair of pants, but she did have her work dresses and cotton socks and her going-to-town dresses and hose. She would have died of embarrassment to be seen in public in a work dress. For the young men who served in World War II who had been too poor during the Great Depression to own a suit, their dress uniform became a source of pride. Traditionalists wore formal clothing to all formal and many leisure activities.

BABY BOOMERS

As children, Boomers were dressed up for family photos or friends' birthday parties. But the '60s saw an increased interest in being "natural," so casual clothing made of natural fibers became popular, and blue jeans, formerly laborers' clothing, became their trademark. They wanted to make a statement to their parents and "the Man," and their clothing and hair shouted it. When they joined the workforce, the large Boomer generation faced intense competition for jobs and so complied with the Traditionalists' dress codes. But they dressed casually in their personal lives. Slowly, as their numbers in the workforce grew, they cut a deal with the older generation and brought more of their casual dress into the work dress code.

GENERATION XERS

Generation X grew up taking casual for granted. They introduced men in sandals rather than tennis shoes (women still cringe at the thought of men in socks and Birkenstocks during wintertime), and when they started their own companies, they allowed blue jeans and T-shirts. But in existing organizations, they were so outnumbered that the dress code was not a battle they could win; they chipped away at it instead. Their focus on casual and comfort eventually brought the "Dockers revolution" to men's business casual. Wanting to keep the best talent happy, organizations cut a deal that they could drop the dress slacks and wear khakis instead. Gen X women made sandals common but lost the hose.

MILLENNIALS

Whereas Traditionalists and Boomers grew up seeing one version of respectable formal dress, Millennials saw many different versions of formal dress around the world. Even more, they saw very successful people with very different dress codes. To them clothing makes a statement about personal style, not ability. While Millennials are known for a laid-back, casual style (although there are recent indications of a more formal style reemerging), only 15 percent of Millennials consider casual dress codes highly important, while only half think it even moderately important.[2] They want to be taken seriously. They would prefer casual at work—only 4 percent want business attire compared to 27 percent who would like sneakers and jeans[3]—but most dress up for work. Actually, the higher a Millennial's education level, the less important dress code is to the employee.[4]

3. FLEX

The key to flexing is discerning business necessities from generational preferences. If you know what your business necessities are, it will help you in determining those areas where you can accommodate generational preferences. This is especially true with dress code because each generation believes the others don't get it. The younger generations think that styles have changed; the older generations think that recent styles are too casual or show too much skin.

Remember from chapter 3 that something is a business necessity if you could lose your foot, customer, money, or funding, and everything else is generational preference. Let's apply these criteria to the question of whether flip-flops are appropriate professional wear.

In many occupations an employee could lose a toe or spread germs in sandals of any kind, so it doesn't make sense for employees to wear flip-flops.

Older customers perceive flip-flops as beachwear, not business wear. If you want their business or their funding (if you're a nonprofit), then you'd better dress in a way that makes them feel comfortable. The manufacturer I mentioned at the beginning of this chapter decided not to allow flip-flops because the company gave customer tours of their showroom three or four times a week, and some customers had commented on how casually the younger employees dressed. They didn't want to lose business to a competitor over footwear.

On the other hand, a call center I worked with a couple of years ago allows flip-flops because customers never see their workers' feet. The president is not a big fan of flip-flops, but he is a fan of happy employees, so he didn't let his generational preferences interfere with his business results.

A word of caution here: "client expectations" can be an easy cover-up for generational bias. I recently worked with a huge retail chain that struggled with dress code. Most of their managers were Boomers and older Generation Xers, but two-thirds of their employees were Millennials. Their designers and merchandisers were working around the clock to create "style forward" clothes to attract Millennial shoppers, but their managers insisted the Millennial employees dress like they did. Without realizing it, the managers were imposing their generational preference and claiming it was what their customers wanted.

It's an easy trap to fall into when we start talking about professionalism and propriety. We would make sure that any employee heading off to sell in another country would understand the basic customs and appropriate dress for that place. But we tend to assume that all customers think the way our generation does about dress code. We don't realize that, as I mentioned in chapter 2, customers from different generations are the equivalent of people from different countries.

If you build dress code policies around concrete business reasons rather than what you assume to be common sense, you'll be in good shape.

4. LEVERAGE

The different generations help one another with dress code more than with any other sticking point. They do it in three main ways.

Like people from different countries, the generations need translators who can help decode what clothing means. The older generations can help the younger generations understand that clothing sends a message to other generations, even if that message is unconscious and unintended. This is especially important with propriety issues. One human resources manager clarifies it this way: if you would wear it to a nightclub, don't wear it to work, because you communicate that you'd rather be at a nightclub getting noticed than at work getting things done.

On the other hand, older generations need help to understand when clothes have no message other than what is now the style for an age group. Take tattoos, for example. Only 6 percent of Traditionalists and 15 percent of Baby Boomers have tattoos, so back in their day, tattoos made a big statement. But almost four in ten Millennials and one in three Xers have them,[5] so often there's no message intended other than it's now no big deal. (You know tattoos are no longer symbols of rebellion when parents and children get them at the same time as a bonding experience.)

The younger generations keep the company relevant to younger customers. Even though the manufacturer at the start of this chapter decided to prohibit flip-flops for now, one of their managers pointed out that in the next couple of years, as purchasers get younger, they may need to put some employees in flip-flops so their designers don't look stuffy and out-of-date.

5. RESOLVE

Stop managing and start leading was my advice to the manufacturing company, as it is to you. Stop having Human Resources and the executive team attempt to resolve dress code disagreements for the four generations. They have better things to do with their time, and it doesn't work. No matter what they decide, the employees grumble. Rather, start inviting people from each generation to your dress code committee and let them determine your policy. (See chapter 16 for detailed instructions on using such a team to resolve and communicate dress code policies.)

A bank manager I know came up with one of the most effective approaches I've seen for communicating dress code. If you've ever seen those *Eat This, Not That!* books showing you how to substitute healthier options for high-calorie foods, you'll have the idea. She tired of sending young tellers home to change into more professional clothes, so she placed "wear this, not that" pictures in a booklet. New employees read the booklet in orientation, and the miscommunications and trips home have disappeared.

• • •

It need not take a year to determine if it's a flip-flop or a sandal. There's an easier way to create dress code policy that doesn't cause as much frustration later. What about your team: are you making dress code policies harder than they need to be? Focus on why the generations see dress code differently, and let the generations help one another understand the messages that are being received, even if they never intended to send them. We all need feedback, or we'll never understand how our behavior comes across to others.

Dress Code

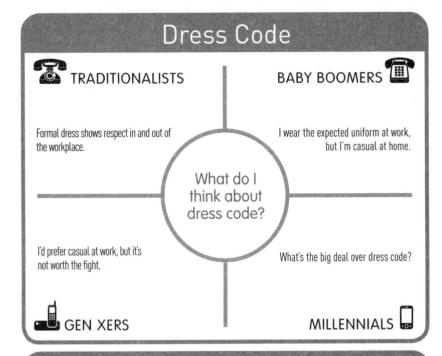

TRADITIONALISTS

Formal dress shows respect in and out of the workplace.

BABY BOOMERS

I wear the expected uniform at work, but I'm casual at home.

What do I think about dress code?

I'd prefer casual at work, but it's not worth the fight.

What's the big deal over dress code?

GEN XERS

MILLENNIALS

Why I Think That Way

TRADITIONALISTS (BORN BEFORE 1945)
Traditionalists wore suits, dresses, or uniforms at work and when going out in their personal lives to show pride in themselves and respect for those in authority.

BABY BOOMERS (BORN 1946-1964)
Boomers were hired by Traditionalists and were expected to dress in suits, dresses, or uniforms, but they brought "casual" to every other situation.

GEN XERS (BORN 1965-1980)
Gen Xers grew up with casual and believe that work is about getting things done, not politics or dress codes.

MILLENNIALS (BORN 1981-2001)
Millennials grew up watching people around the world wear different types of clothes. They think it's contribution, not the uniform, that should matter. But many recognize that unprofessional dress can impact a person's prospects.

CHAPTER 11

Feedback

THEY COULDN'T BELIEVE IT when I told them how much feedback the Millennials wanted. I was facilitating a three-day leadership class, but the twenty middle managers at a large accounting firm kept bringing up the generations. They were especially confused as to how to apply what they were learning about giving effective feedback to their Millennial employees.

When we came to the section of the course where we talked about work-life balance, Bob started a chain reaction. He admitted he felt guilty that he wasn't giving his direct reports, especially the Millennials, enough feedback. But he was so busy taking care of his own work and going to meetings that he had no idea what to do about it.

Two-thirds of the group acknowledged they felt the same guilt and frustration.

Josh jumped in. "This is a big worry for me because I'm afraid that not having time to give my staff feedback will make them leave. And losing staff to another company puts you even further behind."

"That's a big worry," Wendy added. "And I've heard the Millennials need a lot more feedback than we did. Is that true?"

I mentioned that mentoring programs are one of the top two soft bene-fits Millennials look for at an organization.[1] I went on to tell them that less than one in ten Millennials think weekly communication is enough. In fact, 35 percent want it multiple times a day, while 25 percent think once a day is fine.[2]

She shook her head. "You've got to be kidding," she said. "That sounds crazy to me, almost like they're emotionally needy. How much feedback should we give them?"

I replied, "Especially if you're a Boomer, take the amount of feedback you would want, and then double it. Then double it again, and you'll meet the Millennials halfway."

An audible moan came from the room, and Bob said what the others were thinking: "I'm already working way too much. How am I going to find the time to give them all the feedback they want?"

Leading the new generation felt to this group like guaranteed burnout. But it's not just Millennials who want more feedback and mentoring. Future Workplace asked 2,200 employees across industries to rank eight different managerial skills. All generations strongly valued "will give straight feedback."[3] FranklinCovey has one of the world's largest databases of how people view their managers, and one of the three lowest-scoring areas is "provides regular feedback on how well people perform their jobs."

It's no wonder people want more feedback. For three decades, studies have repeatedly shown that mentoring is the most important ingredient for a successful career,[4] and tapping into a network for useful feedback is one of the most powerful predictors of long-term success.[5]

The five-step process for leading through generational sticking points can help your team get a handle on feedback, but it starts with recognizing that the Millennials' desire for more feedback is a generational tension, not a character flaw.

1. ACKNOWLEDGE

Keeping all the generations happy can be tricky, especially if you're a manager in a large organization. You can't control Facebook policies, corporate training programs, or work-from-home options, but you can be great at giving feedback in a way that's meaningful to each generation.

Managers need to acknowledge the sticking point. Admit to your team that you know you don't give them enough feedback, especially for some, but that you are already busy and don't know how to get it all done. Admit that you probably look annoyed when you are in the middle of something and someone wants to talk. Then use the descriptions in the next step to get your team talking about what feedback means to them and how often they would like it.

2. APPRECIATE

Start with the common need. Everyone, regardless of generation, needs to know how they are doing at their job and how they can improve. Then direct your team to focus on the whys, not the whats, of each generation's feelings about feedback. Use these generalizations to get your team started in their own conversation.

TRADITIONALISTS

Traditionalists didn't expect a lot of feedback, and they didn't give it. It's like the saying "No news is good news." Traditionalists were raised with a focus on obedience, not praise. With thousands upon thousands of soldiers in the army, the Traditionalists who went to war only got feedback when they messed up.

BABY BOOMERS

When Boomers entered the workforce, they pushed for formal feedback with fair and consistent processes so everyone would have the same chance for success. Annual performance appraisals were all they could get. These annual appraisals were a big deal because there were so many Boomers jumping for the same promotions that a single negative performance appraisal could stall a person's career.

GENERATION XERS

Because the smaller generation of Gen Xers did not need to compete with one another when entering the workforce as much as the Boomers did, performance appraisals were not life or death for them. Instead, they thought formal performance appraisals were too complicated and after the fact. They wondered, *Who remembers in November all the great things they accomplished in December and January last year?* They also didn't understand why their bosses couldn't just tell them how they were doing on the project while they still had time to fix things instead of waiting for the official appraisal a month after a project was over. They see how real-time feedback is essential to getting work done efficiently. In addition, they talk openly to each other and to those in authority, so they don't know why feedback has to be so complicated.

MILLENNIALS

Boomer parents raised Millennials by listening to them, praising them, and equipping them with problem-solving skills and healthy self-esteem. Millennials received coaching at organized sports, music lessons, clubs, and throughout the college admission process. Plus, since many of the Millennials' parents were familiar with the educational and organizational worlds their children were preparing to enter, these parents could give their children considerably more feedback and mentoring than the previous generations' parents could provide.

Millennials grew up with constant feedback. They (and their parents) could log on and see their grades 24/7. Video games put a live scoreboard on the screen. And with three hundred or more friends at their fingertips through social media, they can ask and get feedback instantly on ideas, homework, or the latest products to buy.

This log-on-and-see-your-score (or grades) generation doesn't understand annual or semiannual performance reviews. Eighty percent of them want your feedback in real time so they can adjust in real time.[6]

3. FLEX

If the older generations think Millennials want too much feedback and Millennials complain they can't get enough, how do you decide how much feedback is reasonable? How much should each generation flex to accommodate the others' generational preferences?

We determine how much to flex by sorting business necessities from generational preferences. It's a business necessity to give people the information they need to do their jobs well. It's also a business necessity to attract the best talent and keep them happy. Today that requires more feedback than many managers prefer to give. The best way to answer the question of how much feedback is enough is to ask the people on your team. You can give more feedback without adding another two hours to your day if you make it better and shorter but more frequent.

- *Better.* Ask your team members what kind of feedback they want to receive. They know their own preferences and can keep you from wasting time on feedback that isn't as helpful to them.
- *Shorter.* Those of us who have been trained through years of annual performance appraisal processes see feedback as a more formal, lengthy, often emotionally charged interaction, so we think we don't have time or energy to give twice as much of it. And we don't.

Thank goodness less formal, shorter feedback is better. Boomers talk too much. Millennials and many Xers don't want the long stories.

- *More frequent.* Think Twitter—how would you say it in 140 characters or less? E-mail your team members (or text them) short, pointed feedback more often. (Or you could just tell them, but that's so old school.)

An additional way managers can ensure their people get more feedback without working around the clock is to request short, pointed feedback from other employees about something specific like a presentation their direct report made or a project he or she led. Let the feedback givers decide whether they want their feedback to be anonymous. The manager can then summarize the feedback and share it with the employee. Some managers have found an even better way of increasing feedback without working late every night. They encourage their teams to ask each other for short, pointed feedback on specific behaviors, competencies, or work products.

You don't need any special tools to get your people better, shorter, more frequent feedback. You can use e-mail, instant messaging, or texting. But over time, social media–like tools will make the process of providing better, shorter, more frequent feedback easier. Work.com, used by Facebook, is one example. It's no surprise that Facebook would want a more informal feedback system, one that felt more natural to their Millennial employees. As Molly Graham, then the head of culture and engagement for Facebook, said, "This is a company designed by millennials for millennials."[7] Work.com (previously named Rypple) allows people to ask for feedback, give feedback, assign badges (it's a social-media thing), thank one another, and see progress on key team and individual goals. It creates a running scoreboard from each individual's feedback that also makes it easier for managers to put together annual or biannual performance appraisals. This system, and others like it, encourages frequent rather than formal feedback. Any technology that makes feedback better, shorter, and more frequent is going to help all generations, even if it feels "Millennial."

One tip for flexing your approach to be more effective with Millennials is to keep it low key. A highly respected surgeon told my dinner party that the resident doctors she supervises (and her teenage son) think she yells at them, something she doesn't believe she does. A recent newspaper column she read, however, made her realize she's not alone. This columnist described work conversations where Millennials felt they had been yelled at even when their bosses hadn't raised their voices or used profanity. The boss just firmly expressed disagreement.[8] Everyone around the table told stories of how their Millennial employees or children have told them to stop yelling when they thought they were acting like Mr. Rogers compared to the lectures they'd received from bosses or parents. Millennials aren't used to being "bossed" as much as the other generations. It wasn't merely in the home that communication styles changed. Sports coaches or teachers that yelled more than they praised drew harsh complaints from parents. Additionally Millennials are used to more affirming forms of negative feedback than the older generations may be used to giving.

Older generations, think TV therapist—counsel, don't yell.

Millennials, we don't mean it personally, so don't take it personally. We don't think we're yelling unless we actually raise our voices.

4. LEVERAGE

All the generations want feedback. If the Millennials' push for greater feedback helps us all get more of the feedback we need, then they, like a lever, will lift everyone's performance.

Your organization can dramatically increase that leverage if your people start asking one another for feedback, because they will be tapping into the wisdom of all the generations. In addition, getting feedback from one another will give your people a broader perspective on how other generations view them than they could get from their bosses alone, and that will make them more aware of how they come across to customers of various generations.

5. RESOLVE

Steps 2 and 3 do the trick with most sticking points, and that's the case with feedback. Of course, organizations should set basic feedback standards for their managers. But you don't need extensive policies that mandate the amount or kind of feedback. They are hard to enforce and sometimes backfire, like the times when your mother made you say you were sorry to your sister even though you didn't mean it. You'll have more success if you train your people to understand generational differences and to give better, shorter, more frequent feedback.

So rather than recommending a specific feedback policy, I will suggest ideas for improving two kinds of feedback—career development and mentoring conversations.

Career Development

If you're going to keep Generation Xers and Millennials engaged, some of your feedback has to be focused on career planning. But in sessions I've led with thousands of managers both on generations and on giving different kinds of feedback, they've told me that they do the worst at career development feedback. Many managers have even told me they try to dodge the topic of career development because they are afraid that when they tell someone they probably won't move up for another seven or eight years, that person will leave for another job.[9]

It has never been harder to know what to tell younger associates. Last Monday I was working with the executive team of a large company that has won awards as a great place to work. Their biggest generational challenge is what to tell their Millennial salespeople who want to know their career path and timetable when there aren't many sales-management positions. These executives were especially frustrated by those who hadn't exceeded their sales targets but still expected to be promoted or get other job opportunities because "it was time."

The Millennials and younger Gen Xers need to understand that their Traditionalist and Baby Boomer bosses may not have liked their hierarchical organizations, but at least they could see their career progression. But today's flatter and constantly restructuring organizations make it far more difficult to tell someone how to advance. Additionally organizations have fewer layers than they did when the Xers entered the workforce, so it's harder to know the next step in the career plan. I've been telling organizations for fifteen years that there's no longer a career ladder—it's a career lattice that zigzags through many projects and lateral moves that provide the experience we need to eventually get where we want to go. But the career ladder sticks in people's minds because it's simple and visual. No wonder managers avoid giving feedback on career development—both they and their employees have a ladder in mind that hasn't existed in most organizations for a long time.

Millennials and Xers, if you want more career development conversations, you must help your supervisors feel comfortable talking about the lattice, not the ladder. Let them know you realize that there is no longer a clear, simple career progression and you don't necessarily expect a promotion; you just want to know what you can learn next, where you can go next, and the possible ways your career might roll out so you don't get bored in the same job. And whatever you do, if you want to talk advancement, first discuss with your manager whether you've exceeded the standards for your current job. You know that in the real world not everyone gets a participation trophy, but nothing communicates that kind of entitlement mentality to the older generations more than those who push for promotions or new opportunities when their bosses think they have not mastered their current jobs.

Mutual Mentoring

Traditional mentoring programs, in which younger employees are assigned to older mentors, never worked well for all participants and can't work today. They didn't always work well for mentees because many mentors didn't commit the time, and the chemistry between the mentor and protégé didn't click for half of them. But today these programs *can't* work. With information changing so quickly, the classic mentor/protégé relationship can't work because it's impossible for one mentor to know enough to provide the protégé with everything he or she needs.

That's why effective mentoring is no longer a mentor/protégé relationship (with all its complicated dynamics)—it's more a mutual mentoring relationship where both people mentor each other. The younger, less experienced employees can mentor their older colleagues in at least two ways. This digital generation is more familiar with the tools of the future than their elders, and they want to help their elders learn. Sixty-five percent of Millennials say, "I should be mentoring older coworkers when it comes to tech and getting things done."[10] But it's not just technology. The second way the younger generation can mutually mentor is to help their older colleagues learn the language and perspective of a different generation.

The world is too complex for the mentor/protégé approach. Today each of us needs a network of mentors both inside and outside the organization, above us on the organizational chart as well as our peers. Peers are especially important because there are not enough managers for all the people who would like a mentor. Even more, we want to learn from our peers. Randstad learned in 2009 that employees were more likely to turn to coworkers, teachers, or professors as role models rather than business leaders, so a network of mentors that includes peers would be more relevant to those who don't aspire to management.[11]

A quick search on the Internet will bring up many ways that organizations are using groups of peers to provide more effective mentoring to more people.[12] Mentors who try to give their protégés everything they need are actually stuck in a time warp where they still see things as they were when they started in the workplace rather than as they are now. But if they help their protégés build a network of resources, they can ensure that their people get more feedback and mentoring without working twenty-four hours a day. That's great news because when I've asked thousands of managers what they find most rewarding, they say mentoring: helping younger and less experienced people grow, develop, and achieve what they didn't believe they were capable of. It would be tragic if some managers never got to experience this thrill because they thought they were too busy.

● ● ●

People want more feedback but aren't getting it. Managers feel guilt rather than excitement, because they struggle to squeeze in time for feedback while they juggle the rest of their workloads. We don't realize that the traditional views of feedback, career development, and mentoring keep the generations stuck.

Feedback is an easy sticking point to work through, so get your team talking about what they want and new ways to provide it. With four generations at work, very few managers are fluent in the language of each generation, so feedback and mentoring leave everyone frustrated when they could be key places the generations stick together. The five-step process helps us through the language-learning conversation that transforms the generational tensions around feedback into a competitive advantage.

Feedback

 TRADITIONALISTS

BABY BOOMERS

If you do anything wrong, the boss will let you know.

Annual performance appraisals and quarterly one-on-one meetings with the boss allow employees to know where they stand.

What do I think about feedback?

People who respect each other don't need a form or a meeting; they just say what they think.

Just put the score on the screen, like a video game, so there's instant feedback.

 GEN XERS

MILLENNIALS

Why I Think That Way

TRADITIONALISTS (BORN BEFORE 1945)
Traditionalists were raised with a focus on obedience, not praise. They learned in the military that "no news is good news."

BABY BOOMERS (BORN 1946-1964)
Boomers' schools focused on standardized tests and grading to cope with the surge of students. When Boomers entered the workforce, they negotiated to get annual standardized performance appraisals.

GEN XERS (BORN 1965-1980)
Gen Xers often consider formal performance appraisals too complicated and untimely. They talk candidly to each other and to those in authority who demonstrate they can handle the honesty. They think real-time feedback is essential to getting the work done efficiently.

MILLENNIALS (BORN 1981-2001)
Millennials were raised by Boomer parents who focused on their self-esteem and used listening and problem solving. Video games also provide them with instantaneous feedback (scores).

CHAPTER 12

Fun at Work

"SINCE WHEN IS WORK supposed to be fun?" some of the Boomer store managers had asked. When a nationwide retailer rolled out the part of its new productivity and results system that allowed its employees to create scoreboards and compete as teams, some of the longtime managers complained it was a distraction and a waste of time. The younger employees, on the other hand—especially the Millennials, who make up over half their workforce—were baffled that their bosses could think work is *not* supposed to be fun. "We'll get a lot more done if we do some joking around and find ways to make it more fun," they said.

This company was caught in a sticking point. The organization had been trying to attract and retain more Millennials. They had heard that they needed to "fun up" the workplace, so they built in time for social interaction, humor, even some play, and it was working. The younger employees liked it. But the older managers didn't. They thought people should finish the work and then play on their own time.

Fun is serious today. You may not have the money to copy the top-notch dining halls, play spaces, and on-site conveniences of Google, Microsoft, and Infosys. You know you can't afford an indoor movie theater or gourmet café. But you'll need to do something because there's no doubt that fun matters to

Millennials. Millennials describe themselves as a generation that makes personal friends at work, is sociable, thinks outside the box, and is friendly,[1] so a workday that's not punctuated with time for relationships and a bit of humor will not engage Millennials' highest values. Nine out of ten Millennials say being able to have fun on the job is a significant factor in picking an employer or choosing to stay, exceeded only by work-life balance and good compensation. For four out of ten, fun on the job is extremely important.[2]

Millennials definitely want fun at work, but so do Gen Xers. Cara, the Xer from chapter 1, almost lost her job for surfing the Internet three hours a day once her work was finished. Her team was stuck around fun as much as work ethic. It bugged other team members that Cara was playing around rather than working.

And it would be a mistake to conclude from the resistance of the store managers above that Boomers don't care about fun. Surprisingly, a study Harris Interactive did in 2004 found that Boomers (as well as older Xers) were least likely to think their workplace is friendly or fun.[3] They want fun, but they aren't finding it.

Fun itself isn't the generational sticking point. All the generations want fun; the sticking point is that they don't agree on how much fun is appropriate. Take "me time" as an example. Seven out of ten Millennials said they need "me time" at work. In comparison, only 39 percent of Boomers agreed.[4] This need for "me time" can come across as an entitlement mentality to older generations in the workplace.

The retailer's director of training and development told me his story because the generational training I offered his store managers helped them get on board with the program. And the retail stores discovered that fun works. The training director told me, "The resistance from the older managers is fading because the managers who jumped into the productivity initiative and made work fun and engaging for their Millennial employees have hit their sales goals."

So how can you "fun up" your work environment without turning people off? And how does your team or organization set policies around fun that keep generational tensions at bay? Using the five-step process for leading through generational differences will help your team navigate this sticking point and create clarity that will help them get back to work—with a smile.

1. ACKNOWLEDGE

The retailer's goal was to become more attractive to Millennials, and they came up with a strong method for accomplishing that. But they weren't able to make progress with the new initiative until they got their managers talking about their frustrations with the "fun" parts of the program. The managers had to acknowledge that they were stuck and didn't see why they had to pander to this new generation.

Maybe you have employees who don't see the need for making work more fun. They don't get why you need to allow Facebook, set up a Ping-Pong table, or plan a silent auction. The trick is to quickly get your people talking about generational differences and not about what's wrong with another generation's values. Here's an example of what you might say: "We've been considering adding foosball and Ping-Pong to the break area so that people can blow off steam and have some fun. But I've heard a few on our team wonder why it's necessary and whether it will interfere with productivity. So I wanted to take a little time to talk about the different ways generations see fun and what we can do to have more fun without irritating other people. This chapter in the *Sticking Points* book summarizes the different views. I don't expect everyone to agree with every detail, but it's a good place to start a conversation of our own."

2. APPRECIATE

Talking about the common needs of the generations before exploring their differences can reduce the emotions and help people listen to one another. You'll need it: a team member watching a colleague play on Facebook while he or she works will definitely get things stirred up. For this sticking point, the common need is that all generations want to enjoy work, feel like they are winning, blow off steam, and make friends, but they don't want to feel taken advantage of by people who are not doing their fair share.

Once you've laid out the common need, use these generalizations[5] to get your team talking about the "whys" behind the differences. (And because fun at work is intertwined with work ethic, you'll want to read chapter 19 as well.)

TRADITIONALISTS

Traditionalists had a stronger separation between work and leisure partly because their work had a clearer separation. Few people would mistake shoveling out animals' stalls for a leisure activity. My grandfather nailed an old, rusted bucket to the side of the barn so his boys could play basketball, but only after they had finished their chores. Just as they were told to finish their vegetables before having pie, they were told to finish their work before playing.

BABY BOOMERS

Unlike Traditionalists, the idealistic Boomers expected more than money from work. They expected to find self-discovery, meaning, and self-fulfillment. Boomers ate up the show *M*A*S*H*, about how a caring but irreverent and humor-loving medical team could achieve far better results than the other hierarchical, rule-bound medical units. It became one of the longest-running television series ever by playing to the growing desire for individuality and self-expression in organizations.

Organizations responded to these shifts in attitude by schooling their managers in employee-oriented management techniques and rolling out employee engagement initiatives to keep the Boomers happy and working hard.

Boomers already think work is fun. Many Boomers don't plan to take a traditional retirement because they can't imagine stopping. One executive told me a couple of weeks ago that his Boomer CEO isn't interested in the generational topic. He can't imagine retiring, so he doesn't see the need for succession planning yet. The executive added, "We joke that the only way he'll hand over the keys is when somebody pries them out of his cold hand after he dies at his desk."

GENERATION XERS

Xers think life is too short to not do something they enjoy, but they don't expect work to be fun, nor do they see work as a primary source of identity or personal satisfaction, as the Boomers do. They frequently say that the Boomers try to make work into something it's not. Xers want to do good work, and they want to do work they enjoy, but it's still work. That's why you have to mix in some fun along the way.

What Xers don't want is preplanned fun that feels forced and makes meetings go longer, keeping them from getting out the door on time. Boomers started meetings with icebreakers like "think of a fruit that best matches your personality" to get fun onto the agenda (and keep it contained and controlled). But Xers grimace at icebreakers because they feel artificial. *Get real*, they think. Fun instead comes from seeing the humor in a situation and enjoying the moment with their colleagues.

MILLENNIALS

For Millennials, especially during emerging adulthood, fun is fuel. MTV asked different generations to send in postcards with what their organizations could do to get the best out of them. Here's MTV's summary of typical responses from the Boomers and Millennials:

Boomer: "Give me my objectives and get out of my way."

Millennial: "I need flexibility, respect . . . and snacks."[6]

Even more, MTV's recent research called "smart and funny" the new rock and roll.[7] Playfulness and humor have been deeply integrated into every aspect of Millennials' lives. As a result, they are used to moving from fun to work and then back again. Adults have always tried to inject fun into things to keep the Millennials engaged. Having grown up with playgrounds in restaurants, educational video games, and over-the-top birthday parties, Millennials are used to having fun baked into whatever they do.

3. FLEX

We determine how much we should flex for generational differences by determining business necessities and generational preferences. If Boomers, Xers, and Millennials wish work were more fun and collegial, it's a business necessity for you to "fun up" your team. Once your team understands why the generations have different views of fun, they can start moving past their stereotypes and determine how to flex so that each generation is productive and happy without irritating the others. With the sticking point of fun, sometimes understanding is all it takes, and then people relax and flex: even if team members don't join the foosball game, they'll quit calling the foosballers "slackers" if their work is getting done. Even though steps 1 and 2 usually do the trick with the sticking point of fun, here's advice for each generation on how to flex to accommodate the different definitions of fun.

First, fun is not a program. Before 2007, when the war for talent was white-hot, some companies created a new position for "fun" directors. These directors would come by and put up balloons at people's cubicles, lead cheers, or plan parties. They were supposed to make things fun so Millennials would stay. I've talked to hundreds of Millennials about fun, and they agree with Generation X—if it's not real, it's not fun. This generation has been to a lot of parties run by professional party planners. They can tell the difference between authentic fun and hype. Quit trying to force fun and instead create an environment where fun happens.

Second, you'll avoid a lot of unnecessary frustration if people will take the hint. Millennials, go ahead and lighten things up in meetings by bouncing from work to fun, but the second time you see a Gen Xer look at her watch or a Boomer's eye twitch because you're bantering and not sticking to the agenda, buckle down and crank out a couple of work items so your elders can relax.

Traditionalists, the third time your boss tells you to "loosen up," remember that for the younger two generations humor is edgier and more sarcastic and may not be your style. Plus, Traditionalists tend to be more private about finances, sex, and their bodily functions than Millennials, so the Millennials' transparency may seem inappropriate. If something the younger generations say really bothers you (or is out of line with the Human Resources policy), of course you should bring it up. But be slow to take offense or roll your eyes.

Xers, you know how to have fun. We know you need to get home, but quit looking at your watches. Really: the work will get done faster if we take a couple of minutes for fun.

Boomers, please, we beg of you: no more icebreakers.

4. LEVERAGE

Leveraging the differences turns a sticking point into the glue that binds the team together. "Funning up" your workplace is not a do-it-yourself project; you have to ask your team what could make things more fun. That's how you add fun for everyone without irritating some. The different generations will tell you what they think is fun without your guessing incorrectly and creating things that seem contrived. Then ask them what's getting in the way of creating an environment where fun happens spontaneously. They'll tell you if you don't get defensive. And they'll surprise you with their practical ideas. There is no formula for fun that works with every group—you have to ask your people and figure it out as a team.

5. RESOLVE

For many of the sticking points, flexing may be enough to get the group unstuck and working together. With the sticking point of fun, it's important to come to a resolution, an agreement as to when people can have fun as long as they get their work done. So don't bring in a Ping-Pong table (or roll out any initiative intended to add fun) without talking about why you think you need it and clarifying the policy for when it's okay to use it. If you don't share your intentions, it may make the generational tensions worse as one generation thinks the other is spending too much time having fun. (See chapter 19 on work ethic for more about breaks or quitting time.)

• • •

All the generations want fun, but they define it differently. The Millennials may value it more highly than other generations, but every generation wants to find enjoyment in their work. There is one question that comes up around the sticking point of fun: Won't the Millennials just grow out of it? Is it worth it trying to fun up the organization in a way that appeals to Millennials?

You could argue that this is déjà vu all over again and that the Xers wanted the same thing when they were in their twenties,[8] but now that many of them have mortgages and kids, they focus more on work-life balance and getting out the door than cubicle-decorating contests or building Play-Doh towers. But that would be missing the point. Your organization shouldn't fun up for Millennials; it should fun up for emerging adulthood. Since people in their twenties, the emerging adulthood stage of life,[9] want more fun activities at work, even when the Millennials get older and settle down, your organization will still have new employees in their twenties who expect more fun. Furthermore, the Millennials won't grow out of it if that means separating work from fun, or personal life from work life. Technology allows them to blend these aspects of their lives. It's a 24/7 work world, and they know they have to take fun when they can get it.

It's worth it to bring more fun to your workplace. It was for the retailer I mentioned at the beginning of this chapter. Those who integrated the new measures and added fun to their processes got better sales results.

Adding fun was also better for Ron, a Boomer managing partner in a one-hundred-person accounting firm who I met at a session in Arizona. Ron couldn't wait to tell me about fun. As soon as the first break began, he came over to share his story. "Throughout the public accounting industry, people complain that the Millennials don't want to put in the hours and that you have to drag them through the tax season kicking and screaming. We haven't had that problem.

"I know from watching my kids at school that this generation is used to stickers and rewards. So we combine rewards and a lot of fun. During tax season, every hour employees put in over the fifty that we require earns them one raffle ticket. At the end of each week, we draw tickets and hand out three or four rewards: tablets, concert tickets, or high-end headphones. The employees are constantly comparing who's done more hours and who has more raffle tickets. They're accountants—they know the firm makes far more money than we ever spend on iPads or concerts—but they don't care because they know we recognize how hard they're working, and it's become a game to them. Then on April 16, we put everyone's raffle tickets back in, draw for two $3,000 TVs, and head for the beach."

"How do you take everyone to the beach on April 16 when there's still another month and a half before the long hours of tax season are over?" I asked, a bit shocked. "Don't you still have to file all the tax returns that received an extension?"

"We close down the whole place," he said with a laugh. "Hey, they work hard for our clients. They can keep up the pace because they know that no matter how heavy the workload is, we are shutting down the office and taking a break. That allows them to catch their breath before we all head back to two more months of long hours. Without the beach day to look forward to, they'd never keep that pace."

"What do the other partners think?" I asked.

Ron admitted, "They just shake their heads and think I'm crazy. They do complain about how much we spend on prizes and the day at the beach. But they can't deny the math."

Now I was excited, so I asked, "Ron, will you tell this story to the class when we get back from break? This is such a perfect illustration of how to bring fun into the workplace."

"Nah," Ron replied with a grin. "There are some competitors in the room. Motivated Millennials are our secret weapon. Let them figure it out on their own."

Figure it out on your own: that's good advice for any team.

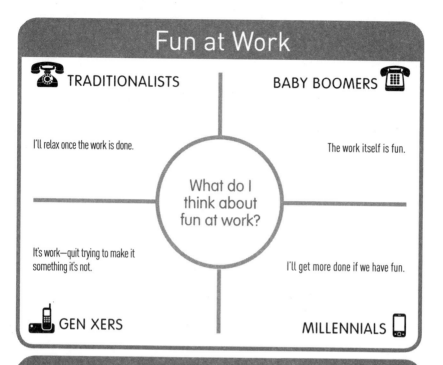

Fun at Work

TRADITIONALISTS

BABY BOOMERS

I'll relax once the work is done.

The work itself is fun.

What do I think about fun at work?

It's work—quit trying to make it something it's not.

I'll get more done if we have fun.

GEN XERS

MILLENNIALS

Why I Think That Way

TRADITIONALISTS (BORN BEFORE 1945)
For Traditionalists, living on the farm or fighting World War II required the work to be finished, or there were immediate consequences.

BABY BOOMERS (BORN 1946-1964)
For early Boomers, postwar optimism assumed life would continue to unveil new, exciting, and engaging opportunities. Work would be no different.

GEN XERS (BORN 1965-1980)
For Gen Xers, fun would be great, as long as they could get their work done and get out on time. Plus, today's organizations can't promise stability and prosperity in the global, technological economy. Work is a place to earn a living first; whatever fun or satisfaction comes along is a bonus.

MILLENNIALS (BORN 1981-2001)
For Millennials, serious things are supposed to be fun. *Sesame Street* made learning fun; school made learning interactive. Video games are a diversion to allow a break while achieving ultimate objectives.

CHAPTER 13

Knowledge Transfer

I WAS SAYING HELLO to everyone who sat in the upper rows of the auditorium when I met René. She told me she worked at the major power utility in the city and wondered if we could talk after the session was over.

After most folks had left, I walked to where she was waiting. We chatted a bit before she began: "I came to the power company three years ago to work in training and development. But I was assigned to a huge project a year ago. It's called the Knowledge Transfer Initiative."

"You don't seem too excited about it," I noticed.

She said, "I am. Sometimes. It's not that I mind the assignment. I don't know how to do it. Our leaders realized that much of the institutional knowledge will walk out the door in the next five years as thousands of Baby Boomers retire, and they want to capture that knowledge in databases so anyone can look up what they need. But it's not working."

I replied, "It's great that they're even thinking about this. Most organizations don't look that far ahead. They will wait until half the Boomers are gone and the situation is an emergency."

"But we can't get the Traditionalists and Boomers to contribute," she said. "They won't write stuff down. We told them why it's important. We've offered them money, we've threatened to write them up, and less than 10 percent have turned in anything, and what little we've got is too incomplete to be much good."

"That's not surprising," I answered. "Most organizations try to get Boomers to write down what they know, but few organizations can get them to do it."

"Why?" she asked in frustration. "Why are they making such a big deal about this?"

I answered her question. "Occasionally it's because they don't care. Or sometimes they want to protect their jobs. But the main reason is that Boomers didn't have knowledge transferred to them that way. They are not the check-the-database generation. Their first instinct is to ask someone when they need to know something. The best way to get Traditionalists and Boomers to transfer knowledge is to quit trying to make them act like Generation Xers."

She tossed up her hands. "So what do we do?"

René is not alone. Thousands of organizations are running into this sticking point, and thousands more will in the future.[1] At least René's company was thinking ahead. Most organizations know knowledge transfer is a challenge but aren't doing much about it. A Boston College Sloan Center on Aging and Work survey of 578 companies found that 59 percent said knowledge transfer was a challenge, but only 34 percent had made projections about retirement rates "to a moderate or great extent," and a quarter had not started. Two out of five had either no or no significant institutional knowledge transfer processes, even though it was one of their top three human resource challenges.[2] Small business owners aren't faring much better. Ninety-six percent of Boomer business owners say it's crucial to have an exit strategy for their companies, but 87 percent don't have one.[3] Randstad found that 80 percent of employers expressed concern, while close to 30 percent were very concerned, about what they would do when the Boomers retire.[4]

And they should be. The Great Recession and the collapse of home values and 401(k)s temporarily postponed their plans, but the number of Boomers retiring will increase until 2030. By then one in five Americans will be over sixty-five, compared to one in eight now.[5] The entire United States will resemble Florida.[6] Not only will your younger employees need the Boomers' knowledge, they will also need to know how to relate to them because in 2030 some younger Boomers will still be working, and the rest will be their customers.

There's no reason your organization can't get a knowledge transfer process going today. The five steps for working through generational sticking points will show you how.

1. ACKNOWLEDGE

Organizations see the need for knowledge transfer, but they're not doing much about it. It won't get better until they acknowledge the sticking point: Boomers and Traditionalists won't write things down, and the younger generations want the knowledge, but they don't want to listen to Boomers' stories the way Boomers listened to Traditionalists'. The knowledge transfer sticking point isn't difficult to see or understand, so get it on the table where your team or organization can face it.

2. APPRECIATE

When putting a sticking point on the table, always start with the common need. It helps tie the generations together before you deal with the differences that can pull them apart. Because knowledge transfer is closely linked to training, communication, and feedback, the common needs of all four sticking points are similar: people need information to do their jobs.

But the generations want to gain and give that information in a way that makes sense to them. We'll never figure out the knowledge transfer process until we appreciate why the Traditionalists and Boomers won't write stuff down.

TRADITIONALISTS

The Traditionalists learned by watching and listening. Because many of the jobs both on the farm and in the factory were hands on, younger workers watched carefully to learn the skills they needed. In 1940, only 24 percent of the population twenty-five and over had completed high school, and 5 percent had bachelor's degrees, so far more learned from on-the-job schooling.[7] As they worked, they learned rules and values by listening to their elders tell stories, often the same ones hundreds of times. Anthropologists refer to this way of transferring knowledge as oral tradition. Many cultures still rely on stories and storytellers to pass on their values and customs to the next generation.

BABY BOOMERS

The Boomers learned by watching and listening as well, even though far more of them finished high school and college and worked with information rather than animals or machinery. Boomers grew up listening to their elders tell stories. Plus, it was a big deal when supervisors invited them to have lunch or go golfing with the other managers. That was their invitation to prove they were smart enough to listen up and get what they needed to know about the unwritten rules and political realities of their organizations. Once Boomers demonstrated that they had mastered the oral traditions, they were deemed ready to advance.

GENERATION XERS
Generation X had knowledge transferred to them through oral tradition and in writing. So they listened to the Traditionalists and Boomers tell stories, but they also took classes and asked peers for help, or they figured things out for themselves. Sometimes they documented what they learned and put it on the Internet so others could find it. They learned to check the Frequently Asked Questions before they called the help desk because it was often faster to find the answer themselves.

MILLENNIALS
At large family meals, the Millennials weren't expected to sit and listen to the adults talk when everyone was done eating, so they didn't grow up with oral stories as their main source of knowledge transfer. Instead, they've grown up watching videos and reading. When they need information, they fire up a search engine and watch a video that explains it, look for online documentation, or post a question, and someone gives them an answer.

Video is the language of this generation. Pew Research Center discovered that a third of Millennials had watched a video online in the past twenty-four hours compared to nearly a quarter of Gen Xers and less than 10 percent of Boomers and Traditionalists.[8] What the older generations often don't realize is that Millennials do learn through oral tradition, but not the oral tradition that requires a live conversation. My son taught himself how to play the ukulele over a weekend using YouTube tutorials. Six weeks later he was playing it in front of four thousand people at church.

Similarly, millions of Millennials aren't meeting with their teachers if they don't understand something; they're jumping online to watch one of over three thousand short videos by Sal Khan, the founder of the nonprofit Khan Academy. His instructional videos on topics like chemistry and algebra receive over six million visitors a month from all over the world.[9] Some schools are even "flipping" their classrooms and sending students home to watch Kahn's videos so they can do the homework at school, where the teacher can give more personalized help.[10] All generations use video—it's now over half the traffic on the Internet[11]—but it's native to the Millennials.

3. FLEX

If something is not a business necessity, it's a generational preference. We need to flex to accommodate as many preferences as possible so everyone does their best work. It's a business necessity that we have the knowledge we need and that we eventually transfer it to the next generation. We'll need to flex the way we ask Boomers and Traditionalists to transfer knowledge. Organizations are planning to do both. In 2011 AARP surveyed one thousand Human Resources directors and asked what steps their organizations plan to take to deal with the loss of knowledge when their older workers retire:

- Sixty-nine percent will invite older workers to stay part-time or return as consultants.
- Forty-six percent will try to get them to stay full-time.
- Fifty-one percent intend to have succession plans for critical positions.
- Fifty-three percent intend to use knowledge-transfer programs[12] (though, as we saw earlier, few have started them).

Organizations won't have to twist the Boomers' arms, because a growing group of workers over sixty-five have no intention of settling into traditional retirement. The Bureau of Labor Statistics has projected that between 2006 and 2016, the percentage of those age sixty-five to seventy-four in the workforce will increase by 83 percent. More surprising, those seventy-five and older will increase 84 percent.[13]

Unfortunately, older workers are the Rodney Dangerfields of our organizations—they can't get no respect. A study by AARP in 2002 found that two-thirds of older workers had witnessed age discrimination. The Sloan Center for Aging and Work found that 40 percent of employers worry about the impact of an aging workforce on their businesses.[14] Human resource professionals value older workers' loyalty and reliability but are concerned about their flexibility, initiative, and understanding of technology.[15] Most disheartening is the study that found older supervisors gave higher evaluations to younger workers, while younger supervisors gave lower scores to older workers.[16] Even older managers show less respect to older workers.

To have the knowledge and workforce you need to win, you will have to replace prejudices with facts. Researchers Bill Novelli and Peter Cappelli report that contrary to stereotypes, in the knowledge economy, workers with more experience perform better, and any negative impacts from aging are negligible.[17] *The Economist* reported in 2011 that studies indicate older workers are better at jobs that require interpersonal skills, as many knowledge-economy jobs do. Conscientiousness rises with age, and older workers have lower levels of absenteeism. Older workers are also more entrepreneurial. Every year since 1996, the Kauffman Foundation has found that Americans aged fifty-five to sixty-four have launched more businesses than those aged twenty to thirty-four.[18] Pew Research found that 54 percent of those over sixty-five say they are "completely satisfied" with their job, compared to only 29 percent of those aged sixty-four and younger.[19]

Keeping older workers and bringing them back part-time will solve one problem while raising another. As one retired Boomer said to a group I was teaching, "If you think Millennials are demanding, you ain't seen nothing yet. I work on *my* terms. I don't need your job, and I don't need your health benefits. So if the work isn't fun, meaningful, or interesting, and if it doesn't fit my schedule, I'm not interested." That's the kind of empowerment only a retirement plan and health insurance makes possible.

BASF, an enormous German chemical company (number 62 on *Fortune*'s Global 500 list in 2012), realized they needed to do both—to keep their older workers and to transfer their knowledge. By 2020, the majority of their German employees will be fifty to sixty-five years old. The situation isn't better for their operations in the United States, where 40 percent of scientists and engineers are over fifty but the pipeline to replace them is shrinking, according to the National Science Foundation. "For the engineers, transferring knowledge to their successors is easier said than done," said CFO Kurt Bock.

BASF began a series of programs in 2006 to keep their scientists and engineers working longer and to facilitate knowledge transfer. They're putting younger and older staff together in teams to leverage the different skill sets. This new organizational structure ensures knowledge transfers naturally between generations. They've also created teaching sessions where longtime workers pass on what they've learned to new employees. Finally, they've changed their compensation plan to reward employee mentoring and to allow protégés to give feedback on how it's going.[20]

4. LEVERAGE

When I was growing up, Reese's Peanut Butter Cups ran the now-classic TV ads which showed two people colliding—one eating a chocolate bar and the other eating from a jar of peanut butter. They would then complain, "You got your peanut butter in my chocolate!" and "You got your chocolate in my peanut butter!" until they discovered that the combination was surprisingly tasty. That set up Hershey's long-running slogan: "Two great tastes that taste great together." It made the point obvious—instead of fighting the differences, leverage them. The same thing applies to knowledge transfer. Xers and Millennials watch videos online; Boomers like to tell stories. This one is a no-brainer.

Instead of chasing your Boomers with pen and paper, invite them to tell stories to a camera for everyone's benefit. If their stories are too long, you can shorten them with inexpensive, easy-to-use video-editing software. (A teenager can show you how simple it is; it might already be on his or her laptop.) If some people freeze in front of the camera, film them from behind while they demonstrate what they know. (Sal Khan insists that a large part of his success is that his videos are unscripted and he never shows his face.[21]) That pulls learners into the demonstration rather than making them feel "lectured to." If you need written documentation, film knowledgeable employees explaining something and have the video transcribed. Transcription services and quick edits are cheaper than paying an employee to hound people who don't want to write.

We are making this harder than it needs to be. We can get knowledge transferred long before the Boomers retire if we flex our approach.

5. RESOLVE

When appreciating and flexing are not enough, the group must select an approach. Knowledge transfer is one of those cases where step 5 is needed.

Your organization must resolve its knowledge transfer policy. Now that you understand each generation's preference regarding knowledge transfer, with some trial and error, you'll find the process that works for you. To get you thinking about how you can use video, here are a couple of stories, one from a small organization and one from a huge one.

I was hosting a webinar on making more time to grow businesses for the managers and owners of independent carpet stores, and I heard of one manager who was showing his employees how to do the same things in their computer system over and over because they only did them once a month and forgot the process. So one morning he brought a video camera on a tripod and filmed himself demonstrating the steps. Now the employees don't ask for help; when they forget, they look up that video and watch it again. It took him three hours and saved him days each year. Because managers wear so many hats in small organizations, video can free up their time to grow their businesses, as well as transfer knowledge to newer employees.

Huge companies can use video (and other web-based technologies like podcasts and online discussions) to speed communication and increase knowledge transfer. That's what BT, a British telecommunications company, calls Dare2Share. In a short video BT made to show how it works, their head of training, Peter Butler, explains that they did a survey of their workforce and learned that "78 percent of the people learn more from each other than they ever do from a formal learning environment."[22]

So they opened the podcast capabilities within Microsoft SharePoint (which they already had) and created a system where employees can make short recordings of demonstrations, interviews, and occasionally animation, and then discuss, comment on, and rate them. They can associate documentation with the videos so people have more detail.[23] The employees have jumped at the chance to record this material because it doesn't take time, training, or preparation.[24] The creators and users tag this content so it's easier to find and rate it according to its quality and applicability.[25]

• • •

Video. That was the answer I gave René when she threw up her hands and asked what she could do to get her knowledge transfer initiative back on track. BT illustrates the power of video to form the basis of an interactive, employee-generated knowledge transfer system that provides a new way to help people connect and stick together.

Are you making knowledge transfer harder than it needs to be? It can be as simple as using your smartphone to record yourself demonstrating how to do something. Better yet, who knows something you'd like to learn? Pop in and record him or her. It won't take more than ten minutes, and you will have the beginnings of a knowledge transfer process.

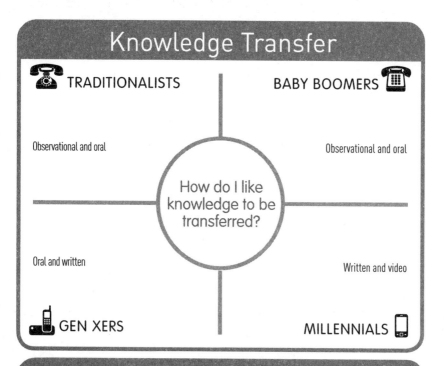

Knowledge Transfer

TRADITIONALISTS

Observational and oral

BABY BOOMERS

Observational and oral

How do I like knowledge to be transferred?

Oral and written

GEN XERS

Written and video

MILLENNIALS

Why I Think That Way

 TRADITIONALISTS (BORN BEFORE 1945)
For Traditionalists, jobs on the farm, in the factory, and in the military were hands on. People learned by watching others perform the tasks. Only a quarter had graduated high school in 1940.

 BABY BOOMERS (BORN 1946-1964)
Boomers who proved they were loyal might get "taken under the wing" of an older associate, but mainly they learned by listening to Traditionalists talk and by figuring it out.

 GEN XERS (BORN 1965-1980)
Gen Xers listened to the Traditionalists or Boomers tell stories, learned in classes, figured it out themselves, or asked a peer. Some documented it and posted it so others could use it.

 MILLENNIALS (BORN 1981-2001)
Millennials go online and use search engines to find documentation, FAQs, or a video showing how to do it, or they post a question and someone gives them an answer.

CHAPTER 14

Loyalty

HAVING GROWN UP with very little, my father-in-law, Bob Irvine, was always grateful that his employer provided him and his family a middle-class lifestyle. He proved his gratitude in 1967 when Chicago got buried by a legendary blizzard. Bob walked most of the three miles to the steel mill until someone driving a privately owned snowplow gave him a ride to the front gate. He slept four nights at the plant, making steel with the few who made it in. Like many in his generation, his motto was "Don't complain; do what it takes." He believed "If you take care of the farm, the farm will take care of you." Even as he watched the slow decline of the steel mill where he worked for forty years, he never said a bad word about the management. He was a company man.

Six months before he planned to retire, Bob was diagnosed with mesothelioma, lung cancer from asbestos exposure. I told him I could help him register for an asbestos settlement. He was adamant that he would agree to participate only if he would not have to sue the steel mill itself, because they had fed his family for forty years. I was stunned. He was loyal to the place where he got sick. He died five months later.

Fast-forward eight years. Tracey and I walked through her organization's plant in hard hats and safety glasses. The plant was growing rapidly and had expanded from two to five production lines in only three years. She was showing me what they were working on now.

"Wow," I shouted over the noise. "I'm even more impressed by how much you've developed Human Resources, now that I see everything else going on here."

She laughed and said, "We do a lot of fifty- to sixty-hour weeks. But I don't mind the hours when I can see results. I'm getting to build the Human Resources department from the ground up, plus determine who we hire. I love making an impact."

"I'd love for people who say Generation X is not dedicated to hear this," I quipped. "But don't you worry about burning out?"

"We won't have to work this hard for much longer. And if we do, I'll find a different job. I love making a difference, but I'm not crazy enough to work this many hours forever."

"So you're dedicated but not loyal," I said. "The older generations don't think Xers are loyal, either."

"Well, they're wrong," she said. "I'm completely dedicated and loyal to every organization I work at for the entire time I find the job interesting and know I'm making a difference. But when that's no longer the case, then I find a new place and give *them* my complete loyalty."

Tracey's definition of loyalty is very different from my father-in-law's. And Tracey is not alone. Many others in her generation share her definition of loyalty. No wonder Boomer supervisors often ask, "Why doesn't anyone stick around for thirty years anymore?" Good question. It's related to another that the two younger generations ask: "Do the older generations think we'll wait until they retire?"

Getting unstuck around loyalty has two parts. First, we need to quit stereotyping and name-calling. To do that, we have to help the generations get a clear definition of loyalty that fits current economic and work realities. If we don't, older generations will always think younger generations have a moral defect because they're not as loyal as the older generations, and the younger generations will think the older generations don't understand the new economy. Because this is foundational, we'll spend more time in this chapter on step 2 of the five-step process so we can understand why the generations see loyalty differently. Second, we must shift our energy away from criticizing other generations' definitions of loyalty and toward discovering ways to make our organizations better so all generations want to stay longer.

1. ACKNOWLEDGE

Start by acknowledging that loyalty has a different meaning today because the world is changing, as we'll see below. The sticking point of loyalty stirs up strong feelings, but teams can work through them if they understand these new realities and talk to one another about why they see organizations differently. That takes us to step 2.

2. APPRECIATE

Step 2 in the five-step process of leading through generational sticking points starts with appreciating the common needs of the generations. It can get tense talking about this sticking point because many see the decline in loyalty as a symptom of a decline in values. You'll want to find common ground by focusing on common needs: security and opportunity.

All generations value job security. The statistics have remained largely unchanged since 1989, when the US economy was growing; almost two out of every three of us would choose a job that offers better security over one that offers higher pay but is unstable.[1] However, loyalty is heavily impacted by a person's age and stage in life. The older we get, the less likely we are to move or leave an organization. Regardless, none of us want to feel stagnant or bored; we all need opportunities to do new things even if we're not seeking a promotion.

You will want to get your team talking about their definitions of loyalty as well as why they think people should stay and under what conditions they should leave. If you keep reminding them of the common needs for security and opportunity and focus your team on the whys rather than the whats, you'll reduce the emotion and increase the understanding while discussing loyalty.

TRADITIONALISTS

If Traditionalists switched jobs, they were often considered hard to get along with. A list of jobs on a résumé could get a Traditionalist blacklisted.

Today, the Bureau of Labor Statistics defines "long tenured" employees as people who have worked three years or longer at the same employer. Organizations have canceled the "deal" that kept the Traditionalists loyal:

1. Pensions that required years of vesting bought the Traditionalists' loyalty because anyone who left lost most if not all of their retirement savings.

2. "Seniority" systems promised that early in your career you would do the "junk jobs" and make less money, but your loyalty would be rewarded with better jobs and better pay.

Bill Novelli and Peter Cappelli mention two other ways companies after World War II bought the Traditionalists' loyalty:

1. In the 1950s, Sears, Roebuck pioneered mandatory retirement at sixty-five to keep employees in their thirties and forties loyal. It ensured they would know when they might receive their next promotion, because they knew when each management position would turn over.[2]
2. Until 1967, age discrimination was legal. In 1965, the US Department of Labor discovered that 60 percent of larger companies had policies that prohibited hiring anyone over forty-five.[3]

It was true: if the Traditionalists took care of the farm, the farm took care of them. Organizations gave the Traditionalists clear career paths, security, and more money to stay. Of course Traditionalists were loyal.

BABY BOOMERS
- Thirty-one percent expect to switch careers.
- Sixteen percent expect to switch employers.[4]

By the time the second half of the Baby Boomers had entered the work-force, the four deals that kept the Traditionalists loyal were breaking down. Organizations could not make the same promises because they had fewer jobs and more project-oriented work in the knowledge-based economy.

The younger half of the Baby Boomers held an average of 11.3 jobs between the ages of eighteen and forty-four, according to the Bureau of Labor Statistics, but they held half those jobs before they were twenty-four.[5] (Boomers were not as loyal as they remember.[6])

Boomers could leave, especially for a significant promotion, but usu-ally their careers did better if they stayed put and worked their way up the career path. Today, 84 percent of Boomers don't expect to switch employers. This discrepancy between job fluctuations earlier in life and stability later illustrates that loyalty is more of an age/stage matter that gets blamed on generational differences. Older people often have more to lose if they leave, so the costs of changing jobs are higher. Now that Boomers are in a more established life stage, it's easy for them to forget that their loyalty is less about values and more about the costs and benefits of changing jobs later in life. Emerging adulthood and early adulthood are more transient life stages, so it's easy to label colleagues in those stages disloyal.

GENERATION XERS
- Fifty-five percent expect to switch careers.
- Thirty-eight percent expect to switch employers.[7]

Three new realities have forced Generation X (and now Millennials) to redefine loyalty:

1. *Jobs are fading.* The shift from stable jobs to project-based work that hit the Boomers has intensified, and these new jobs don't encourage loyalty. Douglas Alden Warshaw in a cover story for *Fortune* magazine describes this shift: "Steady progression up the corporate ladder? Yeah, right. We're living in a project-based economy, one moving from full-time employment with benefits to part-time employment with project-based assignments."[8]

2. *The deal is off.* My father-in-law believed that if you took care of the company, the company would take care of you. But most of us don't believe that anymore. Organizations aren't sure they'll need you in four years, let alone until your retirement. Randstad's 2009 *World of Work* survey discovered that 57 percent of workers describe themselves as loyal to their employers, but only 25 percent think their companies are loyal to them. (Surprisingly, this number has not been affected by the Great Recession. The percentage is unchanged since 2005, the height of the economy.)[9]

   Gen Xers get criticized for showing less loyalty than the Boomers and Traditionalists, but they know that pensions and seniority are gone, Baby Boomers aren't retiring, and whole industries like manufacturing, telecommunications, and print media are redefining themselves, so security comes from having the savvy to handle whatever comes their way. They are ready to move on to the next best thing or to learn something new; they don't intend to be the last person standing when the music stops. Xers don't expect the company to take care of them; they know they have to take care of themselves. To many Traditionalists and Boomers, this comes across as self-centered and disloyal. To Xers, it's a matter of survival.

3. *All dressed up and nowhere to go.* Another reason the definition of loyalty has changed for Gen Xers is that they are jammed up behind the huge generation of Boomers, many of whom got their first promotion when they were young and aren't planning to retire at sixty-five. The Center for Work-Life Policy found that 66 percent of Xers are eager to be promoted, but 49 percent feel stalled at work.[10] In 2011, Mercer found that 37 percent of them were "seriously considering leaving" compared to 42 percent of Millennials (who have the reputation as the least loyal) and 26 percent of Boomers.[11]

In addition, companies are less loyal when handing out promotions. They don't hire from within as much today. Bill Novelli and Peter Cappelli show how significantly this has changed. They report that Taleo, an employment software firm, studied their large clients: two-thirds of hires were outsiders. (In the '50s and '60s, only 10 percent of hires came from the outside.) In addition, a recent study found that 68 percent of executives came from different organizations than the ones they now serve.[12]

Because Boomers got promoted earlier, more often, and from within, they often did better staying with their organizations. But Xers frequently get ahead by leaving. Many of us know Xers who left organizations and then came back later, leapfrogging in the organization chart those who stayed put.

MILLENNIALS
- Sixty-six percent expect to switch careers.
- Almost six out of ten employed Millennials have already switched careers at least once.
- One-third believe they have found their careers.
- Fifty-seven percent expect to switch employers.
- Sixty-one percent of those who see their current job as a stepping-stone expect to switch employers.
- Seventy-five percent of those who consider their job just a way to pay the bills expect to switch employers.
- But only one-third of those who have found their career expect to switch employers.[13]

Millennials don't know a world where loyalty pays. We have been telling them since third grade that they will be the first generation to have five careers in their lifetimes, three of which don't exist yet. Their favorite sports team's star athlete jumped to another team for more money. So they don't see anything wrong with trying different organizations until they find the right one where they can move ahead (over 84 percent of Millennials say career success is important to them[14]) and make a difference.

The key distinctives of the new life stage emerging adulthood are change and choices. Many Millennials can rely on their parents for financial help or for a place to move back to. They aren't in the same hurry Traditionalists and Boomers were. Because they've heard that their generation may live into their nineties, instead of thinking that life's too short to do a job that's not their passion, they think life's too long to grind it out for a paycheck.

For the earlier generations, this can seem unfathomably irresponsible. So much of the dismay of parents who spent more putting their kids through college than any other generation in history is that their kids are keeping their options open throughout much of their twenties. This may help explain why Mercer's What's Working survey found that Millennials "are more satisfied with their organisations and their jobs and are more likely to recommend their organisation as a good place to work, but they are also much more likely to seriously consider leaving their organisation at the present time."[15]

Organizations made a deal with the Traditionalists that if they were loyal, they'd be taken care of throughout their careers. Gen X negotiated a new deal: "You keep me happy, and I'll stay." But the Millennials baffle organizations because they are rewriting the deal: "Just because I'm happy doesn't mean this is what I want to do or where I want to work for the rest of my life." Organizations will get themselves into trouble if they expect Millennials to act like Baby Boomers in a much more rapidly changing world. The Millennials know you can't promise stability and that this is just the first of many jobs they will hold in the course of their careers. Millennials don't expect stability; your organization shouldn't either.

Before we move on, we need to debunk a popular myth that's all over the Internet as well as in countless books and newspaper articles: Millennials care more about meaning than they do about money. This is not true: the vast majority of surveys show that Millennials rank base pay as the most important factor in selecting and staying in a job, just as the other three generations do.[16] They want meaningful work, but they want a well-paying job and career advancement more. It shouldn't surprise us that a generation loaded with record-setting levels of college debt—struggling in the aftermath of the Great Recession but brought up with vacations to Disney World, tablets more expensive than their parents' first car, and big-screen TVs—wants to "make bank."

Even more surprising, Randstad discovered in their 2008 World of Work survey that the Millennials valued an entire list of intangible benefits (satisfying work, pleasant work environment, liking the people they work with, challenging work, and flexible hours) less than the other three generations.[17] Don't misunderstand: they are motivated by meaningful work and will leave if the job is soulless or the culture discouraging, but the Millennials will leave even faster for more money and opportunities to advance, despite what you may have heard.

3. FLEX

Is it true that if you don't give the younger generations what they want, they just leave? Except for the third who have found their life's work, the answer is yes. So does that mean you should give them what they want? That depends on how big of a business necessity they are (see page 34).

Your organization will flex its approach to accommodate the younger generations when it costs too much not to. You will adjust retirement-age Boomers' workloads to accommodate them when it costs too much to lose them. But why wait until the business necessity is costing you dearly? The point is, you can start flexing to accommodate different generations now and create a competitive advantage. The best way to learn what to flex is to leverage each generation by asking them what to change.

4. LEVERAGE

Help the people on your team move from criticizing those who leave to looking for ways to make things more attractive so all generations will want to stay. That would turn the sticking point of loyalty from a problem to a competitive advantage.

A word of advice: don't try to do this yourself. Around the world there are managers and Human Resources staff trying to improve employee retention themselves. Sometimes they do surveys, which provide some insight, but often they're guessing when they could be asking. Don't miss an opportunity to leverage the insight the different generations can bring. Gather a group of people from different generations, give them the five-step process, and turn them loose to talk to their peers. You'll be amazed what they bring back. (See chapter 16 on policies for more detail on how to make these multigenerational committees work.)

5. RESOLVE

Occasionally, appreciating and flexing are not enough, and the group must select an approach. Loyalty is one case where step 5 is needed.

Since your organization can't offer employees the same deal that made the Traditionalists so loyal, what can your organization do? Here are five ideas.

1. Remember that loyalty is the by-product of everything you do in your organization. There isn't a simple formula to keep people around longer. This whole book is about how to make your organization more appealing to all generations.

2. Gather a cross-generational group and let them bring you ideas. (I just said that, but it bears repeating.)

3. Quit measuring yourself by Boomer-era standards. You are going to have more turnover, especially with people who are in their twenties.

4. Millennials say they would like to find a job they could stay at for their entire careers but also tell pollsters they will leave when it gets boring. When people from older generations complain to me that Millennials get bored easily and want a different job every nine to fifteen months, I suggest that video games get boring if you play the same level long after you've mastered all its challenges. To many Millennials, doing the same job for three years is like playing the same level of *Sonic the Hedgehog* again and again. Many of them don't want to leave their organizations as much as they want to play a different game or at least move to a different level. You might not have new positions for them, but you can change up their jobs or invite them to help on a project team so they're not playing the same game every day. Project-based jobs are the easiest places to keep people working on many different things, but with a little creativity, most jobs can become more interesting.

   I told a financial-processing center that was struggling with Millennial boredom that they should try job sharing. When they told me they already did that, I told them I was referring to job sharing between full-time employees, not just part-time ones. I told the managers that by having employees train others on their current jobs while learning a new job themselves, the company isn't left empty-handed if employees leave, and bored employees have an incentive to cross-train.

5. Make sure employees know what opportunities you have internally, because new jobs are only a screen away. One of the big differences with the younger generations is how easily they can find out about job opportunities. Traditionalists and Boomers had to look for jobs in the newspaper or hear of something through the grapevine. But today your associates can search international databases from their phones (right there in a boring staff meeting). So make it at least as easy for them to know about opportunities in your organization. For example, financial software company FactSet Research Systems holds career fairs for employees. Similarly, Marriott uses technology to enable employees to register for the kinds of jobs they would be interested in and notifies them when those jobs are available.[18]

• • •

The five-step process will help your team move from stereotyping the generations to appreciating that they define loyalty differently. When your people see that life stage impacts loyalty more than values and that changes in the economy have undercut the traditional definition of loyalty, they will quit sniping at one another and will figure out how to make the organization more attractive. The changing definition of loyalty will make some of them sad—it would have bothered my father-in-law. But the five-step process will transform loyalty so that it truly is a point at which your team sticks together in order to look for ways to keep talented people of all generations around.

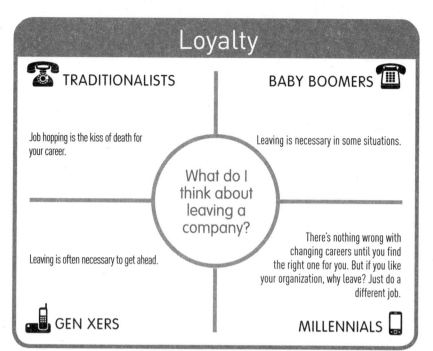

Loyalty

TRADITIONALISTS

Job hopping is the kiss of death for your career.

BABY BOOMERS

Leaving is necessary in some situations.

What do I think about leaving a company?

Leaving is often necessary to get ahead.

There's nothing wrong with changing careers until you find the right one for you. But if you like your organization, why leave? Just do a different job.

GEN XERS

MILLENNIALS

Why I Think That Way

TRADITIONALISTS (BORN BEFORE 1945)
Traditionalists couldn't quit the farm or their platoon. Leaving an organization often got them blacklisted. Pensions and seniority made it better to stay.

BABY BOOMERS (BORN 1946-1964)
Leaving looked bad for Boomers, but it didn't get them blacklisted. Most Boomers got farther by staying and working their way up.

GEN XERS (BORN 1965-1980)
Due to the reduction of middle management, Gen Xers often got farther by going to a different organization. Movement on the résumé was a positive, not a negative.

MILLENNIALS (BORN 1981-2001)
Technology is changing so quickly that many of the Millennials' jobs may not exist in ten years. They think, *Life's too long. If the job isn't your passion, you don't like the culture, or there's not much opportunity to get ahead or make a difference, you owe it to yourself to find something else.*

CHAPTER 15

Meetings

VICTORIA KING, chief nursing officer at Memorial Hermann-Texas Medical Center in Houston, sat in a meeting, watching her Gen X nursing directors disengage, when it clicked: she loved meetings; these younger nurses didn't. Her older nursing directors hated it when the younger ones sent texts or typed on their iPads during meetings. The younger directors couldn't understand what the big deal was since they weren't goofing around; they were doing other work. And Victoria knew they heard everything because they could repeat it back. She also knew her team had to figure out how to keep all the generations engaged in their meetings. Her medical system had not started teaching our generational workshops yet, so she studied about generational differences on her own.

She told me, "We talked a lot about it, and I tried to educate them on generational differences. I wanted the older nurses to understand that the younger generations weren't going anywhere and that this was something we were going to have to deal with. After months of discussion and a lot of give-and-take, we adopted a different approach to meetings that works a lot better for everyone."

Most organizations can relate. The sticking point of meetings—right behind work ethic, communication, respect, and loyalty—is one that comes up most often. It popped to the top of the list again a couple of months ago at the end of one of my speeches for leaders from a huge medical services company. I let them pick any two of the twelve sticking points to explore in depth, and they jumped on how to keep all four generations engaged in meetings. It's a popular pick because the four generations disagree about how meetings should be run, how long they need to be, and when we should use e-mail instead of meeting at all. Meetings frustrate all the generations. In fact, 49 percent of all employees think meetings are a waste of time.[1]

Let's walk through how you can lead your team through the sticking point of meetings using the five-step process, and then I'll give you the advice I gave these leaders and report what Victoria King's team did to make her meetings more engaging for all generations.

1. ACKNOWLEDGE

Not every manager handles this sticking point as well as Victoria King did. A Boomer sales manager in Dallas told me that she outlawed cell phones in meetings when she discovered attendees were texting their complaints about her meeting management to one another *during her meetings*. She instituted a new policy that her sales reps must put their phones on a table by the door as they entered the room for their weekly meeting. She said they now roll their eyes at one another during her meetings. "That's text messaging with body language," I told her. "Instead of trying to avoid their criticism, why not acknowledge there's a problem and let them help you make the meetings better?" If you'll follow Victoria's example and put this sticking point on your next meeting's agenda, your team can make meetings work for you.

Meetings get sticky because each generation thinks the others make them last longer than necessary. Boomer managers were taught to run meetings in structured, linear ways with techniques for squelching topics not on the agenda (all of us older folks have seen the "parking lot" list in action). They often don't know what to do when the Millennials bounce from topic to topic. (Millennials have a popular word for that nonlinear bouncing: *random*.) Additionally, Boomers often do what one friend calls the "death march," where each person reports on his or her work while everyone else listens—or pretends to listen. Xers and Millennials wonder why these reports can't be summarized and e-mailed to everyone instead of a long recitation in the meeting.[2] If you don't get these differences on the table and talk about them, frustration and resentment will build on your team.

2. APPRECIATE

The common need in meetings is simple: everyone needs to communicate and feel connected as a team. You can't resolve this sticking point until each generation on your team understands why the other generations answer the question differently about how meetings should go.

TRADITIONALISTS

Because most decisions were made behind closed doors, Traditionalists did not need as many meetings. Since the boss did most of the talking, not paying attention was seen as disrespect or disagreement.

Today, Traditionalists dislike the authoritarian management style *more than the other generations*;[3] they want to collaborate. Although many Traditionalists use e-mail, most tell me they prefer face-to-face communication.

BABY BOOMERS

Originally Boomers pushed for more meetings as a way to break into the "good old boys'" network. In the pre-Internet days, meetings provided access to information, so attendees not only gained visibility but also were in the know. Full attention was expected.

Boomers use meetings for different reasons today: keeping teams bonded and getting work done. While they complain about too many meetings, they are still more likely than the younger two generations to want to meet in person and more often. (Not being able to grab people for an emergency meeting is a common objection Boomers raise for not allowing people to work from home.) But Boomers also use e-mail and online tools to coordinate people around the world.

GENERATION XERS

Generation Xers think most work can be done online, yet they do value face-to-face meetings. In my interviews with Xers, I found that they highly value meetings as *supplements* to e-mail and online collaboration tools, not as replacements for them. If a meeting is the best option, then Xers are happy to meet—but only if it's the best option. For example, they can't stand the weekly "death march" I described earlier; they think those updates could be done in writing. When parts of the meeting don't pertain to them, Xers think it's efficient, not rude, to send e-mails or read through other papers as long as they don't disturb others.

MILLENNIALS

Millennials have always worked in teams and groups, so they don't dislike all meetings, only boring meetings. Whether the meetings are live or virtual, they communicate constantly as a way to stay connected. To them, texting or e-mailing during a meeting (even to others in the same meeting) or bringing up a funny video or a topic not on the agenda is not rude—it's part of connecting, engaging. Especially if the meeting is boring, the generation raised on *The Magic School Bus* and *Barney & Friends* may interrupt to bring some humor or interactivity to your linear agenda.

Millennials may do meetings differently, but they are able to get things done their way. In chapter 7, I described five tables of Millennials at a restaurant texting people who weren't there or who were at other tables, all while listening to the people at their table and jumping in and out of the conversations at other tables. Such interweaving of communication is common to them. It's how they maintain relationships with so many people. Without any discernible external cue, the five tables of Millennials at the restaurant suddenly rose—as one—and went to their cars, having decided to go someplace else. (Parents of teenagers know to keep their phones close by in case their children text that the group is headed to their home and will be there in twenty minutes.)

Boomer teenagers would have needed a president, vice president, secretary, and treasurer; three meetings; a clipboard; and a megaphone to get thirty people organized and off to the next location. This generation does it from their phones.

3. FLEX

Remember: flexing is what transforms sticking points from issues that break teams or families apart into the glue that holds them together.

I gave the executive team at the medical services company I mentioned this advice about keeping the Millennials engaged in meetings:

1. STOP THE "DEATH MARCH."

Drop verbal reports and have team members write summaries instead. Meetings, especially weekly staff meetings, can get stuck in a report rut. Listening to individuals drone on for several minutes is an invitation to boredom and disengagement. You can read in thirty seconds what it takes a person four minutes to say in a meeting. Giving verbal reports is a generational half step, a holdover from a prior generation when there weren't other electronic communication options and face time was deemed essential to get ahead. Younger generations think it's ineffective.

2. DON'T EXPECT MILLENNIALS TO BE LINEAR.

Romper Room was linear; *Where in the World Is Carmen Sandiego?* was not. Books are linear; the Internet is not. Millennials think like webpages—full of hypertext links that lead from one topic to another. Millennials think more circularly. Linear thinking does not guarantee results, and "random" is not the enemy of achieving goals. As long as the meeting leader establishes the objectives up front, relax when the conversation seems to wander a bit.

But the younger generations must flex as well. You'll remember from chapter 3 that when Mary's Millennials realized working on their computers during her weekly staff meetings frustrated her and the other older team members, they volunteered to put them away. Even more important than their willingness to adjust for the Boomers was a mutual understanding and appreciation that grew out of the conversation they provoked. The newest generation can help their teams by questioning policies and practices that don't make sense to them. It's very easy for people who have been running meetings for decades to get stuck in a rut. We need a new generation to ask if the old ways still work.

Xers can also adapt to the older generations by showing patience (and even joining in) when the Boomers bond by chatting. Xers who manage Boomers and Traditionalists need to be careful that they don't seem rushed or uninterested when their older employees talk longer than their younger employees. They are connecting, not merely communicating.

4. LEVERAGE

How do we leverage generational differences so they make our meetings powerful forums for building tighter teams rather than weekly reinforcements of our generational stereotypes?

Each generation can improve meetings. Traditionalists are often a stabilizing force because they've faced many of the challenges that make people emotional in meetings. Their wisdom and experience can calm a team by bringing the long view to the week's crises. One of the reasons older workers outperform the younger generations is that they've learned when to say "whatever." Boomers bring process and remind us of the value of face-to-face. Xers help us get to the point. And Millennials will make meetings a lot more fun if we let them. (Meetings are great opportunities to add fun to a team. You might want to read chapter 12 on having fun at work.)

5. RESOLVE

Flexing cannot solve all the issues that get multigenerational meetings stuck. Understanding different opinions about meetings will help your people flex your meetings, pulling in different generational preferences so everyone feels more comfortable, but you will still have questions to answer that the generations won't agree on: Will we chat at the beginning? How many excursions will we take from the agenda? Will we allow people to use tablets? Can people show up late? Are the meetings more about building relationships or cranking out work? No matter what the team decides, one generation isn't going to prefer it. How do you resolve those remaining questions without any generations feeling like they lost or gave in?

By going through the first four steps, Victoria King's team at Memorial Hermann-Texas Medical Center figured out how to keep both her Boomers and her Xers engaged in her meetings. Here are some things her team came up with that might be helpful to your team as they resolve what to change.

Victoria told me that what felt like relationship-building time to the Boomers seemed less necessary to the Xers, so the team shortened the meetings. Victoria compensated by spending more one-on-one time with her Boomers.

She began texting her Gen X directors when she was considering certain changes, to get their input electronically rather than around the meeting room table as they had done before. Many changes were finalized without a face-to-face meeting, and when a meeting was necessary, people had already done the preliminary thinking online so they could get to the meat of the discussion much more quickly. Finally, they started and ended their meetings on time.

Victoria wrapped up her list of how she made their meetings more effective for everyone by saying, "Basically, there was a lot of give-and-take before we settled on what works, and I'm sure we'll make changes and improvements in the future. But for now, it's working."

One more thing: the Xers agreed to put away their iPads. I asked Victoria if the Xers felt like they had lost, but she said they didn't. When the Xers understood how much their using the iPads bothered the Boomers, they agreed to put them away, even though they still didn't think they were a big deal.

I asked Victoria what she says to people who want to know what techniques she used to get her team sticking together. She emphasized, "There's not a list of techniques; it's about understanding. Once you and your team understand your generational differences, you'll figure out what to do.

Even if you give another department all your 'techniques,' unless their team understands generational differences, none of your techniques will work for them. Half the battle is educating the team that the other generations are different, and it's okay."

That is the point of *Sticking Points*. Once you understand generational differences and come to appreciate that all the generations have the same needs but try to meet those needs in different ways, you stop trying to change the other generations and start looking for ideas that will help everyone work better together.

There's an old joke that says, "The meetings will continue until we figure out why nothing is getting done." That applies double to the meetings themselves. So why don't you ask the people on your team what will make meetings more effective? Maybe it's time for you to put meetings on the agenda.

Meetings

TRADITIONALISTS

We met infrequently, and the boss did most of the talking.

BABY BOOMERS

Meetings were how we got information, and they created political opportunities for everyone.

What do I think about meetings?

If meetings are not relevant and do not keep moving, I will multitask. We could do some of this electronically.

Meetings are okay, but don't bore me. Make it interactive, or I may interrupt.

GEN XERS

MILLENNIALS

Why I Think That Way

TRADITIONALISTS (BORN BEFORE 1945)
Traditionalists met less often and used meetings for announcements. Most decisions were made behind closed doors. If Traditionalists were not paying attention, they were in trouble.

BABY BOOMERS (BORN 1946-1964)
Boomers pushed for more meetings to create equal opportunities for everyone. Not paying attention was rude, a sign of disrespect. Today, meetings are how they keep the team together and get critical work done.

GEN XERS (BORN 1965-1980)
Gen Xers use meetings to supplement e-mail and other online collaboration tools. They don't think it's rude to send e-mail when parts of the meeting don't pertain to them.

MILLENNIALS (BORN 1981-2001)
Millennials have always had meetings and worked in teams. It's how they stay connected and make decisions. If they text in the meeting or bring up something not on the agenda, they're not being rude.

CHAPTER 16

Policies

I WAS LEADING a generational workshop for a roomful of managers and a few of their executives. I was explaining that with four generations in the workplace today you can't cut a deal anymore—you have to lead rather than manage (see pages 24–25), when I noticed that three Boomers at the front table had their heads together, frowning and whispering.

These men—the senior executives—straightened up, and one of them raised his hand. He began, "We're confused. It seems to us that you're saying leaders don't create policies. The executive team here has been working on the dress code for nine months, and we're sure that when we announce it, half the employees will feel it's too conservative. Are you saying that if we create the dress code, we're managing rather than leading?"

I replied, "That's exactly what I'm saying. But let's back up. Why is the executive team sure that half the employees will feel it's too conservative?"

"Because the young employees see how casually the supervisors in the warehouse dress and wonder why they have to wear dress clothes in the offices," he replied. "Haydn, it's like you just said—there's no way to make four generations happy with any one dress code, or any other policy for that matter."

I agreed. "You've made my point. I've not seen a dress code developed by an executive team that didn't make a four-generation workforce feel that there were winners and losers. That's why I'm suggesting the typical processes for creating policies make things harder than they need to be. With four generations, having the executive team manage the dress code—or any other policies regarding generational sticking points—puts everyone in a no-win situation."

He asked, "What other process can you use in a large organization?"

"I'm not recommending that you use this process to create all policies, but at least for policies around generational sticking points, you can let representatives from each of the four generations wrestle with the business challenges and then recommend policies."

His face clouded, and he shook his head slightly as he said, "It sounds to some of us like you're saying we should 'turn the asylum over to the inmates,' as the saying goes. What if this committee you recommend comes up with something we know will be a disaster?"

I smiled. "That's a common fear until leaders have seen this approach work a couple of times. But once you do, believe me, you won't go back to developing the policy from the top down and then trying to manage the fallout once you announce it."

He leaned back, crossed his arms, and said, "I think this process you're calling leadership is naive. There's no way we would ever turn over something as touchy as the dress code to the employees to figure out."

Most executives, like the one in my session, have only created policies from the top down, so they default into management and struggle to cut a deal with four generations. But they wish there was a better way to create policies, because this typical top-down approach isn't getting the same results it used to. Information is too pervasive, the environment changes too quickly, and employees who make seven decisions about how they want their morning coffee don't get it when they come to work and are told what they have to do and how they have to do it.

The five-step process for leading through generational sticking points is the better way because you can't manage four generations. This process is the road map I promised in chapter 3 that guides your cross-generational team to successful policy creation and implementation. At the end, I give a few tips on helping employees understand and follow policies as well.

1. ACKNOWLEDGE

We've already acknowledged the generational differences around policies: many think you would be "turning the asylum over to the inmates" if you allowed employees to figure out the appropriate policies for generational sticking points. They call it naive because they think the employees will not take into account all the business realities and consequently create ineffective or—worse—harmful policies. But in reality, it's naive to think executives can come up with policies that make all the generations happy. Step 2 will show us why.

2. APPRECIATE

TRADITIONALISTS

The move from the Industrial Age to the information and service age has changed the game. Traditionalists and Boomers came to work in the first age and have lived through the transformation to the second. Almost 20 percent of men were veterans of World War II,[1] and those who weren't had been heavily engaged in the war effort. Top-down management dominated. Many Traditionalists had been raised in hierarchical families in rural communities. Managers directed large organizations the same way they had been managed at home and in both world wars. And it worked. Top-down management built large, successful organizations.[2]

BABY BOOMERS

Boomers were the last generation to start working in the Industrial Age. But Boomers discovered that policy was their tool for breaking through the "good old boys'" network and creating greater fairness and opportunities for themselves. They pushed for personnel departments with job postings for internal jobs, formal interviews, and annual performance appraisals. Boomers didn't expect to get an answer from Traditionalists when they asked why their organizations or families did things a certain way. At home they heard "because I said so," and at work the equivalent was "it's policy."

GENERATION XERS

Generation X is pragmatic. When they entered the workforce, they desired less top-down control, but there were too few of them and they were not in upper management, so organizations continued to manage rather than lead. Xers roll their eyes to each other when policy is dictated to them by managers. They will argue for a while, but if they don't see much hope for change, they'll let it go and figure out how to accomplish what needs to be done despite the policies. The pragmatic Xers have seen policies become ludicrous when rigidly applied in situations where they don't make sense, so they know rules are made to be broken and it's easier to ask for forgiveness than permission.

MILLENNIALS

Millennials like to understand the purpose for the work they do and the reasons behind rules, policies, and procedures. Millennials have grown up with terrorists, school shootings, and metal detectors. They know that there is usually a good reason for each policy, but they'll believe it when they see it. Therefore, if you tell people you have a particular policy to make things safe or fair, but the executives don't follow it or some supervisors don't enforce it in their departments, your Millennials won't take it seriously.

Unlike the Xers who try to figure a way around policies, Millennials just ignore them. I call this generation "Millennials" because they prefer that name to "Generation Y." But I think it's also accurate to call them "Generation *Why?*" They don't fuss, they don't chant, they don't picket like the Boomers did. They just keep asking why. They grew up questioning and negotiating rules with their parents. They knew their parents wanted what was best for them, so they were willing to take the rules seriously if their parents gave good reasons for the rules and enforced them consistently.

At work, they will attempt to observe policies whenever they can out of respect for the boss, but they see policies as guidelines and not rules until the boss can provide reasons that make sense to them. They won't fight, but they also won't follow the policy if the boss can't.

3. FLEX

Understanding how the generations think about policies makes it clear why I said earlier that it's naive to think any group of managers can create a policy and roll it out without a lot of push back. You can't manage generational differences using top-down policies today with four generations—you have to lead. Unless people believe that their generational preferences were fully considered, they'll feel like their generation lost while the executives pushed their preferences through as organizational necessities.

What I'm recommending is a different approach to policy creation that bakes in step 3, Flex, because it brings representatives of each generation to the table, who will sort out generational preferences from the organizational necessities, guaranteeing that each generation gets heard. Traditional top-down policy processes don't take the time to understand why the generations feel strongly or to sort through the different ways we can flex to accommodate those preferences. Instead, they rush to a solution that's simple enough to keep short and uncomplicated. Yet policies for four generations are anything but simple. Without meaning to, these processes skip steps 2, 3, and 4 and go quickly to step 5, Resolve. It's no wonder they create problems.

Once the concept makes sense to them, managers frequently ask, "What would it look like, step-by-step, to hand over sticking point policy development to our people?"

Here's the process I recommend:

1. Find representatives who are respected by colleagues of their generation.
2. Tell them you're not promising to agree with every detail of their recommendations, but that you do have complete confidence that by leveraging their generational differences, they can come up with something better than you could.
3. Lay out the business challenges. Tell them if there's something regulations prohibit, what customers have complained about, or that the budget is limited. If you let them wrestle with the business challenges that you and the other executives would have wrestled with, they won't come back with impractical recommendations.
4. Give them this book and let them work through the five-step process (detailed in chapter 3). Here's a brief summary of what they should do:

- Determine which additional sticking point chapters relate to your sticking point, and read those as well.
- Listen to one another talk about how their generation sees the sticking point until they develop genuine understanding and appreciation for the various generational preferences.
- Sort out business necessities from generational preferences.
- Using business necessities as a guide, determine how much can be flexed to accommodate generational preferences.
- On the issues where flexing resolves most but not all of the issues, work out an agreement for what the policy should say and how the organization can explain it to their people.

It really is that simple. I've discovered from conversations with managers and executives that they worry they'll feel obligated to approve even senseless recommendations or risk discouraging the committee after all the work they've put in. Tell the group up front that you may not agree with everything they come up with but that you will review it with them to make sure they didn't miss anything. But it won't happen if you wait to weigh in until they have brought their final recommendations and then send them back to work on it again. That makes committees crazy because you didn't give them the information they needed earlier, making the project drag on.

4. LEVERAGE

A policy task force made up of representatives from all four generations has great leverage. They can create a policy more demanding than anything management could attempt to roll out, because each generation in the organization will know that their own viewpoint and preferences were thoroughly discussed. It's a myth that Xers and Millennials expect to have everything go their way; but they do expect to have their viewpoints and preferences taken seriously because that's how they define respect. A multi-generational task force has automatic credibility because of its generational diversity (which your executive team probably doesn't have).

This task force will come up with better policies than your executive team could because each member of the task force already knows how their generation thinks about each sticking point. Your executives would need to spend hours in interviews and focus groups to understand all those nuances. They don't have that kind of time, and so the policies they create and the way they explain them will miss important pieces.

The leverage from the task force's generational differences really shows in the credibility this group brings to the rollout of the policy. A Boomer manager will have much more trouble explaining to a Millennial why the dress code prohibits flip-flops in the office than the Millennial representative from the committee. Cross-generational team members have more credibility with the colleagues from their own generation who don't like parts of the policy than your executives would.

A sticking point task force has automatic credibility, will create better policies, and can roll them out with more buy-in, less push back, and greater clarity. You couldn't get that trying to manage it top-down; that's the leverage of leading rather than managing generational differences.

5. RESOLVE

Because policies resolve generational sticking points and clarify how the organization will move forward, everything we've covered in this chapter is really about step 5, resolving sticking points. At a team level, you will need to create policies for eight of the twelve sticking points, but for feedback, respect, training, and work ethic, flexing is usually enough. At an organizational level, policies are needed to clarify what's okay and why. Without them, organizations get even more stuck because their employees see the inconsistencies that result when each department makes its own policies.

POLICY IS NOT A REASON; PEOPLE ARE

Because Millennials feel comfortable questioning policies and see them as guidelines rather than rules (if they don't buy the reason for them), I'm always asked, "How do we get the Millennials to follow our policies?"

I was speaking with five hundred managers of premier golf resorts from around the world. They asked, "What do we do to get the Millennials to stay out of flip-flops and keep their shoes on when they're handing out golf carts and bags?"

"What have you tried?" I asked.

"We've restated our policy," some Boomers said.

"What else did you do?" I asked.

"Well, we made PowerPoints of the policies. And we even animated them."

I said, "This is a generational collision. For Traditionalists and Boomers, policy is a reason. For the other two generations, it's an invitation to ask more questions. Boomers were the last generation to respond to policy. Millennials respond to people. Show them how it impacts people. Why don't you want them to wear flip-flops?"

"Because it's not safe. A golf cart could roll over their foot. Some customers come back pretty drunk, and there's no telling where they're going to drive," they said.

"So the tennis shoes you require them to wear offer significantly more protection than flip-flops when thousand-pound golf carts roll over them? Really?"

"Okay, safety is not the real reason," they admitted. "The real reason is our older members don't like it. They complain about it."

"Do they complain to your Millennials?" I asked.

"No. They complain to the managers or the older employees, who tell us how these young kids are ruining our business."

I asked, "Why don't you explain to them that they can't wear flip-flops because it bothers some of your guests?"

"Well, we do. We tell them it's going to hurt the business."

"They don't care about the business," I said. "This is a part-time job for them. You care about the business because it's your career; your pay depends on it."

"Well, they ought to care about the business. It pays their bills too."

"No," I replied. "Your customers don't pay their bills. These Millennials can get another minimum-wage job tomorrow. You're the ones who need these customers to pay your bills. So quit talking about money and focus on the people behind the policies."

I went on to tell them that they were neglecting two key things:

1. They hadn't translated the generational differences so that the Millennials understood *why* their wearing flip-flops bothered the Traditionalist customers. The younger employees didn't know that Traditionalists felt disrespected when they saw what to them is the lowest form of footwear. If the golf resort managers had explained that just like people from a different country, the Traditionalists had a different view of flip-flops than the younger generations, most of their Millennials would've gotten it.
2. They had not related the policy to their Millennials' values. The younger employees saw everyone their age in flip-flops, so they thought the golf resorts had an out-of-date policy. The managers will get better results if they explain that even if the Millennials don't agree with the Traditionalists that flip-flops are unacceptable, they can still show older customers the respect they would want shown to their grandparents.

This is what I mean by focusing on the people, not the policy. If you do this, Generation Why?—the Millennials—as well as every other generation, will adopt policies more easily.

If you continue to manage policy development around generational sticking points from the top down, you will stay stuck. What a waste. Policies can be powerful ways to pull the generations together if you let a cross-generational group lead through the five-step process.

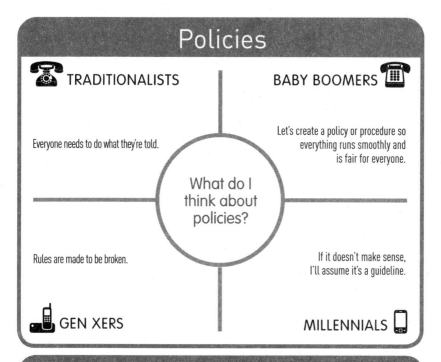

Policies

TRADITIONALISTS

Everyone needs to do what they're told.

BABY BOOMERS

Let's create a policy or procedure so everything runs smoothly and is fair for everyone.

What do I think about policies?

Rules are made to be broken.

If it doesn't make sense, I'll assume it's a guideline.

GEN XERS

MILLENNIALS

Why I Think That Way

TRADITIONALISTS (BORN BEFORE 1945)
Traditionalists grew up thinking, *If I take care of the farm, the farm will take care of me.* Because they were new to the city, they turned to experts and leaders for guidance.

BABY BOOMERS (BORN 1946-1964)
Boomers pushed for new laws enforced equally so the country could realize the promises of democracy.

GEN XERS (BORN 1965-1980)
Gen Xers realized that life can't be managed with rules or policies, and one size doesn't fit all.

MILLENNIALS (BORN 1981-2001)
Parents of Millennials made rules, but their children were allowed to question them if the rules didn't make sense and negotiate them if they didn't fit all situations.

CHAPTER 17

Respect

IN EARLY NOVEMBER 2007, Joakim Noah played his first professional basketball game with the Chicago Bulls. When asked about his team's loss to the Clippers, Noah, a Millennial, spoke openly about his concerns that the Bulls weren't playing as a team and weren't focused on winning.

The next day, the media asked Scott Skiles, then the Bulls' coach, his thoughts about Noah's comments. Skiles replied, "If I had just played my first pro game, I'd probably keep my mouth shut, to be honest with you. It's obvious we're not playing to our ability. . . . But it probably should be somebody else speaking for the group."[1]

The press told Joakim Noah what his coach had said, and he seemed shaken, promising to keep his mouth shut. Skiles's comments and Noah's response made national headlines. Skiles spoke out later in frustration. "That's the kind of thing that makes someone like me not really like most (media), to be honest. I said it in a very lighthearted manner, just taking a little jab at the rookie. So now I had to call Joakim this morning. I wanted to make it perfectly clear with him that I want him to say whatever he wants to say. I love his personality."[2]

It's easy to see why reporters would take Joakim Noah's critical comments as disrespectful. They thought the rookie was young and hadn't earned the right to have an opinion. He hadn't paid his dues. A woman on the staff of an NBA team told me, "Many teams realize the Millennials are different, but most teams don't know how to handle the differences."

But it's not just organizations in the United States that struggle to navigate different generational approaches to respect. "What's wrong with these kids?" the older managers in every group asked me when I spoke in Panama recently. "We would never have been so bold. The young people don't seem to have respect for authority. It's becoming a real problem because our older employees complain a lot about it. Within a few weeks on the job, young employees are questioning how we do things or complaining that they have to do the lowly jobs because they're the newest."

On the other hand, Millennials regularly ask me, "How do we get the older generations to listen to us? They don't take us seriously." The Traditionalists and Boomers who were told by their parents that "children should be seen and not heard" are now working with the Xers and Millennials who were told to "tell me how that makes you feel."

Millennials are redefining respect and causing teams to get stuck around the questions, How long do you have to pay your dues before you can say what you think or put new ideas on the table? How long before you don't have to do the "junk jobs" that no one wants to do?

Let's look at the sticking point of respect within the framework of the five steps for leading through generational differences.

1. ACKNOWLEDGE

Coach Skiles didn't have to put the sticking point of respect on the table; three days of media scrutiny did that for him. Unintentionally, the media spotlighted a clash based on generational differences.

Because respect is so foundational to relationships, it will probably raise the same kind of emotional misunderstandings on your team as it did for the reporters and the Bulls. Acknowledging stereotypes is hard because people don't think their views are stereotypes and don't want to talk openly about them with the generations that frustrate them. They'd much rather make snide comments to people who share their views. Putting on the table that people define respect differently will upset some because they want the "offenders" reprimanded, not acknowledged. That's why moving to step 2 is so critical—it will help decode stereotypes and ease emotions.

2. APPRECIATE

All four generations have a common need—respect—but they meet that need in different ways. The result is a generational sticking point. You won't be able to turn the sticking point into an opportunity without a better understanding of why each generation thinks the way they do.

TRADITIONALISTS

Traditionalists approached new situations by learning the hierarchy and finding their place in it. Today, even the military criticizes the command-and-control leadership style, but after Traditionalists saw its success in World War II, they applied it to all organizations. They expected others to fall in line, prove their loyalty, and do their duty—and by doing so, they would earn respect.

But today, Traditionalists are tired of hierarchical organizations. Traditionalists like the authoritative style less than any other generation (and only 18 percent say it is effective).[3]

BABY BOOMERS

Baby Boomers grew up in smaller families, which raised the expectations for each child. Their Traditionalist parents taught them that education and hard work gave anyone a chance at success. The Boomers rebelled against their parents' authority, the "establishment," and anything that put limits on individual creativity and fulfillment. The Boomers felt much less constrained by social class or hierarchy than previous generations. As a result, they believed anyone could work their way up to a position where they could earn respect.

GENERATION XERS

Xers respect those who have skills and deliver results rather than those who have an official position in the hierarchy. Working in groups on projects in college taught Xers that ability mattered more than position. Their approach to team projects was pragmatic. Let people do what they're good at, and you'll get a lot more done. This no-nonsense approach to respect continued to make sense to them as they left school and entered a struggling economy: listen to the people who deliver results, not the people with the positions.

MILLENNIALS

Millennials were taught that everyone deserves respect and that all people are entitled to express their opinions because they are human beings, not because of their abilities or accomplishments. In previous generations, elementary school teachers managed the classroom hierarchically. But Millennials often resolved conflicts in class meetings run democratically. Even more, Millennials went to school with "zero tolerance" for bullying—bullying being an extreme example of hierarchical "government."

This new view of respect was reinforced at home as well because books instructed parents to listen to their children's opinions and ask about their feelings. Parents were encouraged to use dialogue and explain the reasons behind the rules rather than simply declaring, as their parents had, "because I said so." Millennials also grew up teaching their parents as well as learning from them.

Because of all this, Millennials give respect to those who respect them. Millennials are not naive; they know that younger employees don't have the same knowledge or experience as the older generations. Nor do they think every idea should be acted on. But they believe that everyone should have his or her ideas taken seriously,[4] and they don't believe they should have to wait three years to earn this respect.

3. FLEX

When people appreciate why the generations see a sticking point differently, they naturally want to figure out how to flex so that everyone's common need is met. That's the case with respect.

Get your team to talk about some of the following suggestions for how to flex around respect. But don't stop with my ideas. Ask your team to come up with their own.

1. *Identify their definition of respect, then flex.* Let's go back to Hector's situation, which I left hanging in chapter 1, and see if we can identify ideas that will help us resolve it (see pages 3–4). Hector's team did a great job proposing a plan to their executives, but Rachel should have left her phone in her bag. Like a person visiting another country, Rachel needed to better read the reactions of the other generations and flex her personal preferences. Rachel didn't have enough of a relationship with the head of operations for her to know that Rachel meant no disrespect. If Rachel had left her phone alone, her team would have been hard at work on the new product line instead of stuck in political limbo.

2. *Don't take it personally.* Continuing with Hector's story, if the head of operations had known that the generations have four different views of respect, she would not have taken Rachel's texting personally. One simple rule will keep your team working together when stereotypes threaten to pull them apart: they didn't mean it personally, so don't take it personally.

Because the head of operations didn't separate her personal preference from the business necessity, she turned Rachel's texting into a generational battle. Instead, she could have led through the awkward moment. Remember that a business necessity is anything that will make you lose your foot, customer, money, or funding. Is it a business necessity that everyone in a meeting looks at the person speaking? It may be part of your definition of good manners, but it's not a business necessity.

3. *Approachable and respectful works for everyone.* Randstad's annual *World of Work* survey for 2009 discovered that all four generations want their managers to be approachable (92 percent for Boomers, mid-80s for the other three generations) and have an attitude of respect (Traditionalists and Boomers: 91 percent; Gen X: 89 percent; and Millennials: 85 percent).[5]

4. LEVERAGE

Once people understand and appreciate generational differences, you can use that new understanding to produce better results. Leveraging differences changes a sticking point from a liability to an asset because your team uses those differences to come up with better ideas. Here are three suggestions.

Older generations must learn to watch for the half step. Boomer and Gen X parents often brag about their Millennial children but complain about their Millennial employees. It's because at home those parents act true to their own generation, but at work they tend to take a half step back and act like the generation who trained them. They evaluate their Millennial employees by what their bosses required them to do when they started their careers and become resentful when their Millennial employees don't want to do it.

I saw the half step create severe turnover problems when I was working with the nursing management team in a large hospital. One of the directors explained why the average age of nurses is in the forties: "We Boomers ran off most of the Generation X nurses because we thought that if we had to work the night shift and empty the bedpans when we first started, then they ought to have to do the same."

As we talked about how the Xers and Millennials define respect and work ethic differently, it slowly dawned on them that their constant criticism of the younger nurses' dedication when they would not take the night shift or do the worst jobs had pushed the younger nurses out. As a result, the Boomers had actually made their own lives harder because they had to do all the night shifts rather than share them with the Xers. They said, "We were so busy trying to make it fair that we made it worse. We need to figure out how to keep the Millennials; we can't make the same mistake."

Ironically, people are usually better at avoiding the half step at home because they dialogue with their children more than they do with younger employees. Parents want their children to have it easier than they did, but at work older managers feel it's unfair if younger workers don't have to pay their dues the way they did. You can avoid the half-step trap by focusing on business necessities, not generational preferences.

The younger generations must learn to find the reason behind the policy or procedure. Younger people, you may get frustrated when older generations don't listen to your ideas, but proving that you understand how your current organization works earns respect. As silly as some policies or systems seem, there is usually a reason for them. Uncover that reason before you suggest changes, or the people who have been working there will ignore you. They don't mean any disrespect; they think your ideas are naive. This especially applies when the reasons are political (and touchy). One of the complaints I hear about the Millennials is that they have no patience for working through the political realities in an organization. Do not undercut your credibility. Discover how things work before suggesting changes.

Also, remember that change sounds easy but is hard on people, and leaders can't push too many changes, or their people stop responding.[6] Plus, there are always people emotionally invested in the past systems because they worked so hard on them. Additionally, training and implementation—and the temporary lost productivity during the changeover to new systems—can be *very* expensive. Respect for overall practicality and impact on profitability will earn younger associates a hearing from older workers.

Finally, leverage comes when team members who treat one another with respect extend that same respect to customers. Discussing generational differences among team members will result in better understanding of generational differences in customers. Who better to help you decode what a different generation wants more than one of your employees of that generation? Better customer service and more sales—who can complain about that?

5. RESOLVE

Often the first four steps of acknowledging, appreciating, flexing, and leveraging differences are enough to transform a team from stuck to sticking together, and that's the case with respect. Because respect concerns foundational attitudes, you can't create a policy demanding that people show respect. But you *can* create an understanding atmosphere that enables it. That's what Scott Skiles did with his astute handling of the reporters' feeding frenzy. Once the different generational interpretations of respect had been decoded, it became obvious to everyone that there was no story.

• • •

Respect is a foundational sticking point in that many of the other sticking points—work ethic, communication, decision making, dress code, meetings—intensify or become much stickier if you and your colleagues don't understand how to navigate through differing definitions of respect. So what will you do to help your team show respect? It doesn't matter if you are the manager for a team or project or are simply an associate. It doesn't take big things to make a real difference when it comes to respect.

One of my favorite examples of that is Lonnie, a plant manager I worked with who turned three average factories into top producers and is working on his fourth. This new factory had been stalled in their quality goals for a decade, and people were discouraged and unmotivated with the quality program, even in small things like keeping their work areas clean. "Let someone else do it; I'm too busy," they would say. Lonnie didn't lecture them to pick up trash. Instead, for the first year, he walked the factory floor three days a week, picking up trash and chatting with team members. After six months, the managers began cleaning up, and soon after that the team members did too. When this plant manager showed respect for every part of the quality program and took the time to pick up their trash, everyone realized that cleaning up was important and that no one was above the "junk jobs." Of course, there's more to improving quality than the big boss picking up trash, but Lonnie discovered with each plant he turned around that his willingness to clean up was the key first step to getting the team on board. Respect is foundational.

There are hundreds of ways, large and small, to lead your team through the sticking point of respect. Get your team talking about the ones that will work for them.

Respect

TRADITIONALISTS

I will figure out the hierarchy and find my place.

BABY BOOMERS

I can work my way up to a position that gets respect.

What do I think about respect?

I will give you respect if you prove to me you deserve it.

I will give respect to those who "get it" and will take me seriously.

GEN XERS

MILLENNIALS

Why I Think That Way

TRADITIONALISTS (BORN BEFORE 1945)
Traditionalists came from hierarchical families, fought in a hierarchical military, and got jobs in hierarchical organizations.

BABY BOOMERS (BORN 1946-1964)
Boomers were taught that hard work and education could give anyone a chance.

GEN XERS (BORN 1965-1980)
Gen Xers learned to assess a leader's skills rather than assume position equals competency.

MILLENNIALS (BORN 1981-2001)
Millennials grew up learning from—but also teaching—their parents.

CHAPTER 18

Training

AFTER SPEAKING IN DALLAS, I was waiting to jump in a taxi for the airport when a woman who had been in the session asked if she could share my cab to the airport. After we got situated on our respective sides, I learned she was heading back to a city in a different state, so I asked if she had flown in just for the seminar. She nodded yes and explained she was the director of a medical center with nine hundred employees.

She asked, "Do you mind talking on the way to the airport, or do you need the next half hour for downtime?"

"I don't mind," I replied.

She explained that for the last two years, the long-tenured nurses had been complaining that the new nurses didn't have the same high standards and needed training in quality. She said, "The training is not going well. The Millennial nurses complain that it's boring and impractical, and some of them sleep through it. The older nurses tell the Millennials they ought to be grateful the organization is investing in the training. The older nurses had to go through quality training in the '90s, so they say the Millennials need to quit acting so entitled."

"Have you seen the training?" I asked.

"Parts of it. We dug up the quality training program we did back in the late '80s. I sat through an hour and a half of the full-day workshop. I had planned to stay the entire morning, but it was too boring," she said sheepishly.

"I think you found your answer."

"I've never thought training in quality was the answer. I don't think our Millennial nurses have lower quality standards. Their clinical outcomes are just as good as our experienced nurses'. The experienced nurses don't like the Millennials' informal style and their unwillingness to defer to those who have more seniority."

"So why did you offer the training?"

"I figured unless we trained the Millennials in quality, my longer-term nurses would keep bringing it up."

"What are you thinking after the session this morning?" I asked.

"I was pretty sure before we started the training that this was a generational issue, not a quality issue," she said. "Your session confirmed it. We've trained half the nurses in total quality, and the generational tensions are worse because the older nurses see the training as proof that the younger nurses are not reliable or responsible. I realized this morning that we need to finish the training and then go to work on the generational differences. Do you have any ideas for how to make this training work for all four generations?"

That's the question many organizations are asking because they know training that works will help them win the best talent and win in the marketplace. Slightly more than half of employers offer education and development to attract younger employees, while a third do so to keep their older employees.[1]

Employees of all generations want more training. Randstad found in 2011 that 74 percent of younger employees want more skills. Half of Millennial workers wish they had more hard skills, while 40 percent want soft skills (interpersonal skills, time management, change management, etc.). Sixty percent would take a company-sponsored training course.[2]

Contrary to the stereotypes that older generations are resistant to change, Randstad found that 56 percent of older workers said they want more skills.[3] Another study found that 71 percent expected to focus more on "learning a new skill or hobby" over the next five to ten years, while two-thirds planned on "taking courses to learn something new."[4] But most organizations have a blind spot when it comes to training older workers. Sadly, employees over fifty-five receive about a third of the hours of formal training that younger workers do.[5]

Both organizations and individuals have one thing in common—they will both have to learn to survive.

1. ACKNOWLEDGE

The generational sticking point around training has two parts. As we've seen, all generations want more skills and more training. They say, "The world's changing—how will you help me keep up?" That's the sticking point for the organizations that don't make training a priority or whose training isn't very effective.

We also get stuck around training because it's getting harder to offer training that all generations think works. So organizations ask, "How do you make training work for four generations?"

There's always a lot of mumbling and side conversations about training. Start talking openly about these issues in your organization—both the desire for training opportunities and the need for training that's effective and engaging to different generations.

2. APPRECIATE

Once the training sticking point is on the table, help your team rally around the common need. All generations need to learn new things in order to sharpen their skills and keep work (and life) from getting stale. A little history will help your team understand how the generations learned as they grew up and then started in the workplace. It provides insight into why training that works for one generation won't work for another.

TRADITIONALISTS

Early Traditionalists in rural areas had a radio, a monthly regional newspaper, a few books if they could afford them, and often a family Bible (which in my family served as a filing system for all important papers). Compared to the farm, libraries, newspapers, colleges, and companies provided later Traditionalists access to vast amounts of information. Their organizations taught Traditionalists what they needed to know, and Traditionalists valued the opinions of experts.

Many Traditionalists still value experts and titles, though today they check multiple sources for information and know that experts often disagree.

Traditionalists still have a high tolerance for lectures. They grew up learning from books, using memorization and lectures in more formal and structured classrooms where the teacher's word was law. (My grandmother Emily—born in 1908—regularly told us her family had two rules regarding education: "The teacher is always right, even when she's wrong" and "Whatever punishment you get at school, you'll get double at home.")

BABY BOOMERS

Whereas Traditionalists grew up listening to experts telling, the Boomers grew up with television and entertainers compelling. Boomers learned at school to sit still through lectures—no matter how boring—but TV made them less tolerant toward poor communicators. They value compelling stories and motivating speakers. They loved group discussions—which offered a break from lectures and allowed each individual to express themselves. When they came to the workplace, they learned to abide by ground rules (to encourage fairness), to role-play, and to build towers out of cardboard and do trust falls ("Fall backward, and we'll catch you"). And of course they discussed.

Few organizations trained all their employees. Instead, they used training to reward those Boomers with a bright future. They'd send off twenty high potentials to a weeklong training program that was often ghastly by today's standards. But even though the training was boring and impractical, Boomers got the ultimate reward—certificates, which they had framed on their way home so they could hang them on their walls as trophies in their highly competitive world.

GENERATION XERS

Xers expect the future to continue throwing them new challenges, like a video game that gets more difficult at each level. They think keeping current—more than receiving exceptional performance appraisals or even promotions—is the only job security. If they aren't learning new skills or software or building a résumé, they're falling behind. Therefore, they believe that organizations that don't provide opportunities to learn are robbing them of their future security, just as if the organizations were raiding the Traditionalists' pension funds. When organizations wondered why they should train people who might leave, Xers replied, "I won't *need* to go if you train me well enough that I could leave."

The way Xers learn was shaped by the fast pace and visual impact of *Sesame Street*, the Internet, and group projects. They do not have anywhere close to the tolerance of Traditionalists and Boomers for lectures. They don't see training as a reward for a few but as essential for all. They want learning to be practical and fast paced with a good dose of tongue-in-cheek humor. While Traditionalists may give the benefit of the doubt, Xers won't believe a trainer just because he or she has a title. Xers don't hesitate to question authority. They don't hesitate to give feedback, wanted or not.

Training has never been more important for Generation X. There are fewer Xers than Boomers, so organizations will compete for the best Xer talent to fill the spots Boomers will vacate when they retire. In the typical organization, well over half of the leaders could retire in the next six years. Succession planning and preparing Gen Xers for leadership can't be pushed off in this market downturn as it was in the last.

MILLENNIALS

Interaction. In a word, that's what Millennials want. They have moved around and learned through activities since they were in preschool, and they communicate through video and visual media far more than the other generations. PowerPoint presentations and manuals aren't enough. Entertainment has been woven into every aspect of their lives, so boring is the kiss of death. They want to contribute to the knowledge rather than passively memorize information. They expect to work in groups. They network out of the classroom and expect to network in the classroom as well. They know learning can be engaging as well as practical, so they have little patience if it's not. They value action and results more than knowledge accumulation. Consequently, they are frustrated by busywork or the training exercises (popular during the Boomer era) that take a lot of time but provide little practical value.

Millennials respect session leaders who are prepared, organized, and have real-world experience, but leaders should not get defensive when questioned. Millennials know instructors don't know everything, and they don't expect them to, because they can instantly find six experts online who disagree.

Millennials have always learned, they know they have no future if they don't learn, and they want to learn. A group of Millennial employees told one of my clients that they didn't want to learn two new things a month—they wanted to learn two new things a week.

3. FLEX

It's a business necessity to make training work for all four generations. That requires organizations to offer content in forms that suit the different generations best.

The business necessity is that your people gain the skills they need. They can do that from a book, a classroom, a video, a webinar, an online or computer-based self-paced curriculum, a study group, an online learning community, a mentoring relationship, an educational video game, or just a search on the Internet. While no organization has unlimited money, even small ones can offer four or five different approaches to learn the same content. The age-old debate of whether to offer training in the classroom or online is silly. Offer both and let your people choose which method works best for them. As long as you verify their proficiency, you've achieved your business necessity. Offer as many learning options as you can deliver with quality.

4. LEVERAGE

If we're not careful, we can assume that other people learn best the way we do. For example, if our learning style is visual, we'll make sure there are plenty of graphics and diagrams in our presentations. The people who are visual will love it; the kinesthetic learners, who like to move around, will be praying for a fire drill. The same thing applies with generational preferences. Everyone communicates better with their own generation, so instructional designers can miss half their audience if they don't leverage the input of other generations when developing training programs.

5. RESOLVE

When it comes to the sticking point of training, flexing to accommodate different generational learning preferences is usually enough. Rarely is step 5 needed. That's illustrated by the medical center director who raised the question at the beginning of this chapter: "Do you have any ideas for how to make this training work for all four generations?"

I gave her a simple answer to her question: without spending a lot of money, the medical center could offer the same content in three different ways. First, they could offer live classroom training as they had been doing. They could also offer an online version combining video clips recorded during a live workshop, online content and exercises, and then proficiency tests to prove mastery. Finally, the medical center could offer self-directed study of the course manuals with proficiency tests but allow participants to e-mail the trainers with questions.

She thought those options were great for the next time they did the training. But since half the organization had already gone through the classroom training, she wondered if there was a way to improve the program so that all four generations could get something out of it. I said I couldn't know for sure what to recommend until I saw the actual course material and interviewed some of the previous participants. I told her I would need five days to do the interviews and rework the course so it worked for the Millennial nurses. She nodded, calculating in her head what that would cost.

Then I gave her another option. She could buy five fifty-dollar gift cards to popular restaurants and meet with five Millennial nurses who'd already attended the classroom training. In about two hours, they could tell her exactly what to change to make it valuable for them, and she could thank them with the gift cards. (I told her I strongly recommended the first option because I have children to put through college, but either would work.)

We make training the different generations harder than it needs to be. Your organization will make real progress if you ask each generation how to make training better and then deliver it in the way your people want to learn. Asking your people how to make your training more effective works whether you are looking for ideas to enhance and supplement traditional classroom training, as the medical center was, or are radically rethinking your approach, as UPS did a decade ago.

UPS DELIVERS TO THE DIGITAL GENERATION

In 2003 UPS realized they had a problem. The weeklong classroom training for new drivers that had worked for decades failed the Millennials. Thirty percent of new drivers resigned their first year despite some of the best pay and benefits in the industry.[6] After the training, drivers were taking three to six times longer to achieve acceptable performance, and accidents and injuries were on the rise. Peggy Emmart, corporate schools coordinator, explained that the job had changed but the training hadn't: "While in the early '90s our [drivers] may have needed to concentrate on eight key tasks each day, they now routinely perform 30 to 40 major tasks within the same timeframe."[7]

So UPS looked for a better way to train Xers and Millennials. Stephen Jones, a former driver himself, headed the project, fully expecting to have a training center filled with video game–like simulators. But he hired a former professor of instructional technology, Skip Atkinson, to review the literature on training Millennials and do focus groups with UPS's Millennial employees to verify if computer-based training was the way to go. To their surprise, without exception their Millennials asked for hands-on learning. Atkinson explains, "We found out very quickly that a lot of the studies out there [that advocated computer-based training] had been done with a very select audience—college-bound, usually white, in affluent suburbs, able to afford these electronic toys—and that had nothing to do with the part-time loaders coming up through the organization at UPS."[8]

UPS did create a few computer-based simulations to prepare drivers to spot hazards on the road or sales opportunities with customers, but they are a small part of the reinvention of their weeklong training (which they call "Integrad"). Instead, new recruits get what they asked for—the opportunity to practice what they will be doing every day on the job.

They start with the primary task of a driver's day—getting the correct packages off the truck by following a twelve-step process within 15 seconds every time.[9] UPS built a transparent delivery truck filled with weighted packages. Trainees don't play computer games to learn how to find packages; they practice in a real truck while an instructor with years of on-the-job experience coaches them until they get it right.[10]

First-year drivers have the most slip-and-fall injuries because they are not used to carrying packages on ice or snow. Now rookies at UPS are strapped into a harness that slides along an overhead beam as they carry a package while wearing Teflon cleats. Instructors spray a thick coating of furniture polish on the track, guaranteeing the rookies' feet will slip, so their bodies learn how to adjust the next time they hit real-world ice.[11] As a result, slipping accidents have dropped.

Even more dangerous than falling is going up and down the steps carrying packages hundreds of times a day. Doing it incorrectly will ruin employees' ankles over the long term, but it didn't work to tell that to young (and invincible) drivers. They had to show them. Now drivers must master the "three points of contact" rule in a special "on/off car": hand on the handrail, left foot on the bottom step, right foot on the ground. UPS installed sensors at each point that measure the force with which the drivers' feet hit the ground, and put the score on a screen. A chart on the wall makes it easy to calculate how quickly an employee's ankles will give out unless they improve.[12] The time it took to reach proficiency dropped dramatically.

The facilities manager at the original Integrad training site in Landover, Maryland, has seen the impact of the new measures: "Managers now don't want somebody who didn't go to Integrad. . . . I was proud of the old type of training I used to do. But the people who graduated from that program don't hold a candle even to the people who are disqualified from here."[13] That's great news for UPS, who needs to hire twenty-five thousand drivers between 2010 and 2015 to replace retiring Boomers.[14]

Your organization may not have the money to build simulators, or your work processes may change too quickly to make live or even computer-based simulators cost effective. But you can use what UPS learned to meet the needs of the digital generation. Let me suggest four lessons:

1. Don't complain that the younger generations don't have what it takes. UPS didn't waste their time complaining; they changed their training to better prepare everyone for the new demands the job places on drivers.
2. Don't assume you know what your people need, even after reading all the research. Ask them how they want to learn.
3. Create hands-on practice opportunities. It doesn't matter what generation your employees are or what learning style they have: learning will stick better if they spend more time practicing in the actual situation.
4. Be clear on what you want employees to be able to do when they're done, and then give them challenges of increasing difficulty until they can do it. The biggest problem with most training is not the method but that we dump all the content on the learner at once without ongoing assessment and support. (See chapter 11 on feedback.)

Your organization, like every other, will increase the time, energy, and money they spend on training not only to attract and retain all four generations but also for your own survival. According to the Gartner Group, the United States spent $65.7 billion last year on educational technology alone.[15] But organizations want training that works—training that creates proficiency, delivers measurable results, and that the four generations find engaging and valuable. So they, like you, will continue changing and adapting their training to break through this generational sticking point. That way, training helps employees stick with the organization and provides the shared knowledge that helps teams stick together. That's the kind of sticking point we need.

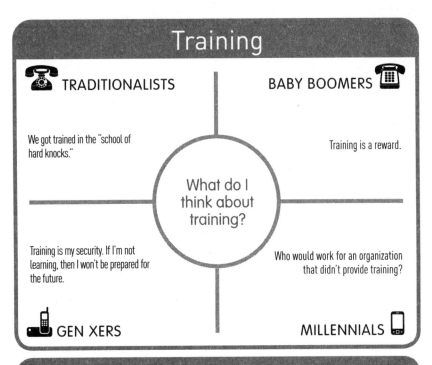

Training

What do I think about training?

TRADITIONALISTS

We got trained in the "school of hard knocks."

BABY BOOMERS

Training is a reward.

GEN XERS

Training is my security. If I'm not learning, then I won't be prepared for the future.

MILLENNIALS

Who would work for an organization that didn't provide training?

Why I Think That Way

TRADITIONALISTS (BORN BEFORE 1945)
For Traditionalists, information was available through libraries, newspapers, colleges, and companies.

BABY BOOMERS (BORN 1946-1964)
For high-potential Boomers, ongoing training was a reward. They were accustomed to lectures and memorization, so they could pull the useful parts out of ineffective training.

GEN XERS (BORN 1965-1980)
Staying current is the only job security for tomorrow. Gen Xers believe that organizations that don't provide opportunities to learn are robbing them of their future.

MILLENNIALS (BORN 1981-2001)
Millennials know that other parts of the world have higher educational standards and knowledge is doubling rapidly, so organizations that cut learning in tough times are too dangerous to work for.

CHAPTER 19

Work Ethic

REMEMBER CINDY FROM CHAPTER 1 (see page 1)? She had a Generation X computer tech named Cara who surfed the Internet three hours a day when she finished her work. Cindy had planned to fire Cara, but during my presentation, she got a nagging feeling that maybe their tensions were generational rather than performance related. Cara had the largest workload and the highest customer satisfaction scores of anyone on her team, but Cindy worried that Cara was setting a bad example for the rest of the team.

I've asked hundreds of groups what Cindy should do with Cara, and it typically leads to a big debate. To some it seems ludicrous that you would fire your best performer because she gets work done quickly. But to others it's obvious that if she's at work, she should be asking for things to do because she's not paid to surf the Internet; she's paid to add value to the organization.

In my experience, tensions around work ethic come up more than any other sticking point. When Boomers like Cindy started their careers, everyone knew the answers—even if they didn't like them—to these common work ethic questions:

QUESTION: If the boss works long hours, does that mean his employees have to as well?

ANSWER: Yes.

QUESTION: Why does it matter how many hours you work if you get your work done?

ANSWER: Because we pay you for a full day, and you can find other things to do.

QUESTION: Do you have to come in to the office, or can you work from someplace else?

ANSWER: That's too stupid of a question to even dignify with an answer.

But today managers, team members, and parents who assume the younger generations will give the same answers are surprised and frustrated when they don't. And the younger generations wonder what's wrong with these people. They think, *I cranked out twice as much work in college and still had time for my life. Why do I have to put in more hours if my work is done?* Worse, Boomers who didn't like the old answers are now pushing back as well. (Their rejection of the old answers will only intensify after they retire and come back to work part-time; so we ain't seen nothing yet.) What your team needs is the five-step process to lead through the sticking point of work ethic.

1. ACKNOWLEDGE

The first step is to acknowledge the generational sticking point. The truth is that with four generations in the workplace, there are vastly different definitions of what it means to have a good work ethic. Don't avoid the tensions; get your team talking about these questions:

- Does it matter how many hours you work if you get your work done?
- Do you have to come in to the office, or can you work from someplace else?

Let these questions hang in the air for a couple of moments. These questions can sometimes produce an awkward silence, and that's okay. Many people try to talk their way out of awkward silences. Don't. Just let people think for a minute. Then suggest that the team spend some time understanding the generational differences around work ethic.

2. APPRECIATE

When you're addressing generational sticking points, it is critical to find the common need. For the sticking point of work ethic, the common need is fairness and balance. We all want everyone to do their fair share so no one feels taken advantage of. In addition, we all need to balance the many roles we have in life. Although the generations see work-life balance differently, Randstad's *Workmonitor Global* survey found in 2010 that *all* of them want more of it.[1]

The simplest way to summarize how the generations see work differently is to compare work to a meal. The older two generations see work as the steak and everything else in life as the vegetables, salad, and dessert. The younger two generations see life as a waffle. Work is one quadrant of the waffle, and everything else—friendships, family, volunteer work, religious organizations, night classes, or even weekend drumming in a rock band—make up the other three squares. So please, boss, keep your work syrup off the other three squares of my waffle.

Unless the older generations understand the reason why the Xers and Millennials see work ethic differently, they will continue criticizing the "slackers." In the same way, the younger generations must understand the different world the Traditionalists and Boomers grew up in.

TRADITIONALISTS

The closest to the farm of all generations, the Traditionalists are the most confident that hard work pays off. Farm life provided Traditionalists with instant results that proved this: if they didn't milk the cows, there would be no milk for breakfast. Pew Research Center discovered that 74 percent of us believe that the Traditionalists have the best work ethic of any generation.[2]

Traditionalists, often by organizing into unions, pushed for five-day work weeks, consistent shift hours, and the same pay for the same job. The five-day work week spread to other service jobs until five days a week rather than six became the standard. Because of these changes, in many jobs, Traditionalists after World War II worked fewer hours than they did on the farm.

BABY BOOMERS

Traditionalists may be seen as having the best work ethic, but ironically, they didn't work the most hours. The Boomers took that prize. Because of the Baby Boom, Boomers had to compete with each other to get a job or get ahead. One of the simplest ways to differentiate themselves was to come in before and then stay later than their bosses. In one of my workshops a woman who had worked for AT&T at their corporate office in the 1970s told the group that her first week on the job, a longtime employee showed her the ropes. She told her, "If you want to do well here, you'll want to come in before Reggie arrives, and you'll want to leave after Reggie has gone home. You don't want people to think you're a nine-to-fiver; they have to see you at your desk." She told the group that all 150 people in her department would sit at their desks looking busy with their bags packed and under their feet, waiting until someone gave the all clear that Reggie had pulled out of the parking lot. At that time, 150 employees left simultaneously, causing a nice traffic jam.

If it took staying late to get ahead, then Boomers stayed late. Plus, Boomers pursued self-actualization at work. Traditionalists had jobs; Boomers had careers. Boomers expected work to provide excitement and achievement, so they kept work at the center of their lives and put in long hours.

GENERATION XERS

Gen Xers don't expect work to provide significance and excitement to the same degree that Boomers do. Xers have had many jobs (and bosses) they've not liked, but they've needed the money.

Generation X survived the downward mobility of multiple recessions and have downsized their expectations. They want to get ahead—they are more ambitious than the Boomers are today—but they're also desperate for work-life balance because of their incredibly high expectations for themselves as parents. Younger Boomers may have been helicopter parents, but schools have learned, and now universities are learning, that many Xers are lawnmower parents—they'll mow down anything in the way of their kids with a team of lawyers, psychologists, doctors, and college-entrance coaches.[3]

Xers know they will work some evenings and weekends to get through a work crisis, so they feel it's only fair to make some personal calls or do some personal web surfing during office hours. What they can't abide is when the crisis was caused by poor planning or political shenanigans. One Xer I interviewed said it well: "If it's a legitimate crisis, I'll work Thursday night. But if it's been sitting in your inbox for the last week and you are just tossing it to me at 4:00, then I've got plans. If it's your mistake, then it's your late night. I don't see why I should miss volleyball so you can go home to dinner just because you're the boss."

MILLENNIALS

Millennials have high expectations. Eighty-four percent of Millennials want to succeed.[4] They are the first generation to have as many women (65 percent) as men (68 percent) who want jobs with added responsibility. They are also the first generation in which mothers of young children want to advance as much as their female peers without kids.[5] Before they go on vacation, Millennials are more likely than the other generations to ask for an in-person meeting to make sure nothing falls through the cracks while they're gone.[6]

But Millennials are the only generation that doesn't cite "work ethic" as one of their principal distinctives,[7] nor do they rate themselves as work-centric as the Traditionalists and Boomers do. They are not as intense about work as other generations expect because of a combination of values and life stage. They saw their Boomer parents spend fifty weeks a year working like crazy and then trying to make up for it in a two-week, over-the-top vacation. Even more, their parents have told them not to do what they did; it's not worth it. So they have different values that, short of a massive economic depression, will stay with them the rest of their lives. And because they're in school longer and marry later, they don't yet have the same financial pressures as Generation Xers who are now in their child-rearing years.

Even during the Great Recession, Millennials have less financial pressure to do whatever it takes to succeed at work because Millennials don't face the same stigma moving back in with their parents.[8] I ask Boomer men under what conditions they would have moved back home with their parents. The most common answer? Death. (Alfred Hitchcock made a movie in 1960 about a boy who lived with his mother too long—*Psycho*.)

Millennials have grown up in the global, electronic age where work never stops, so they wonder what the point of rigid office hours is as long as the work gets done. Recently, when I asked a group of executives what differences they've noticed as they lead multiple generations, one told me, "When a Boomer is running late, he or she calls me on my cell phone, gives me a long explanation of what went wrong, apologizes profusely, and promises it will never happen again. But the Millennials walk in twenty minutes late without even a word of explanation and carrying a Starbucks." He's right: overall the Millennials see work hours as more porous than the previous generations. But in their minds that does not make them less hardworking because they know they can make it up later.

They don't see a forty-hour work world with the thick boundaries between work and personal life that the Traditionalists and Boomers had. They know they can log on tonight and get more done in a half hour than they could in two hours in their cubicle with all the interruptions and Boomer chatter. So they leave at 5:00 to meet up with friends or head to the gym, and then get back online at 9:00 and finish up.

The most important thing to remember is that Millennials want it all— they want to succeed, but they prioritize friends and family higher than anything else.[9] Whether the Millennials can have both success and work-life balance, as well as money and meaning, is yet to be seen. They're not the first generation to want it all. But their desire for both/and rather than either/or is not a stage; it's integral to their value system.

3. FLEX

The key criteria for how much to flex for generational differences is to determine if you are dealing with business necessities or generational preferences. Focusing on results rather than hours places the emphasis on business necessities. Would a business owner rather have an employee who works every minute of an eight-hour day but doesn't accomplish much, or someone who takes "me time" throughout the day but develops the idea for a new product or lands a new customer?

Admittedly, if you work in a store or a factory, it's a business necessity to be there when the doors are open. And if you're in a project-oriented job and you're not getting your projects done on time, then you'd better put in more hours, whether that means coming in earlier or working on the weekends (or it's time to find another job). However, hours worked is not a valid measure for many jobs in today's information-driven, global, 24/7 economy. Focus on the outputs, not the hours.

But that means if an employee—no matter what the generation and no matter how much you like him or her—doesn't deliver results, you need to address performance. That's hard for many managers. It's easier to hold people accountable for hours than for results. After Yahoo's CEO Marissa Mayer made international news by pulling her employees back into the office to get "all hands on deck," Richard Branson of Virgin Airlines laid out very helpful advice on his blog for making flexible schedules work: "If you provide the right technology to keep in touch, maintain regular communication and get the right balance between remote and office working, people will be motivated to work responsibly, quickly and with high quality."[10]

In a similar way, I have worked with hundreds of organizations whose executive teams worry that flexible work arrangements like telecommuting or working from home will drop productivity and kill communication. It's reassuring to managers to see their people working and to know that they can pull them into a room for emergency meetings if there's a crisis.

Personally, I have trouble relating to their fears because I have spent all but two years of my career working from home. Most of us who have done it know how much more you can get done without the interruptions. We also know from experience what years of research have borne out: that we work *more* hours because we just slip in for a minute to check e-mail and don't come out for another hour.[11] (Because of that, a minister I know in New York had the door to his home office walled off and a new door added so he had to go outside the house to get into his office.)

I tell executives to offer flexible working arrangements, but not because of the reasons they've heard. It's time for some myth busting. Flexible work arrangements are often touted (along with meaningful work and paid time to volunteer) as the holy grail of attracting Millennials, and executives believe it. PricewaterhouseCoopers discovered in their twelfth annual CEO survey that 61 percent of CEOs believe they are experiencing challenges recruiting and integrating Millennials. They see flexible working arrangements as one of their top recruitment strategies.[12]

But flexible working arrangements like telecommuting and working from home are not as important to Millennials as we've been told. Millennials love flexible schedules but are lukewarm toward telecommuting and working from home unless the commute is excessive. Flexibility in schedule is preferred by over 80 percent of Millennials and is extremely important to almost 40 percent when considering an employer,[13] but telecommuting is only extremely important to 11 percent of Millennials. Instead, the vast majority prefer the structure and mentoring opportunities of a workplace.[14] Furthermore, numerous surveys in the last five years have discovered that working from a coffee shop has never been among the highest things most Millennials look for in a job—things like good pay, strong benefits, a stable company, respectful managers, interesting work, and a flexible schedule. Even more, flexible work arrangements have continued dropping in importance for Millennials until by 2008—and here's the kicker—*they valued them less than the other generations.*[15]

So do you have to come in to the office, or can you work from someplace else? Your organization should offer flexible working arrangements where people can work from home or the library or the beach as long as they get their work done and are available for meetings when needed. But you shouldn't offer it thinking it's the secret weapon for attracting Millennials; you should offer it to attract all generations.

Can flexible hours be abused? Of course. Some of the two hundred employees at Yahoo! who worked from home full-time had started their own businesses and had little accountability or productivity.[16] Flexible arrangements, like any good working relationship, require consistent communication and clear accountability for results.[17]

We can help our teams create more flexible answers to the questions around work ethic if we can understand why other generations define it differently than we do and keep our generational preferences from dominating the discussion.

4. LEVERAGE

Your team will work best when you leverage the strengths of the four generations. Each generation helps balance the extremes of culturally induced workaholism and messing around on Facebook two hours a day. Together they will help each other get more done while having more fun doing it:

- Traditionalists know that there is no trophy until you put in the hard work.
- Boomers know that good processes save time and prevent errors.
- Xers can show us how to cut to the chase.
- Millennials can figure out where the shortcuts are.

We need all these generations working together and sharing their insights in order to make the most productive, well-rounded teams.

5. RESOLVE

When it comes to work ethic, flexing is usually enough to get the team unstuck, unless you are in a service or manufacturing job and can't leave early. Then step 5 is needed. You'll need to resolve the questions so that everyone understands what can flex and what can't.

But once people understand that the results, not the hours, matter in most jobs today, they can appreciate rather than irritate one another. That's what Cindy's team needed. They certainly didn't need to create a new set of policies with ever more complex rules to keep Cara boxed up.

• • •

Work ethic is the most common sticking point you'll encounter in the workplace, but it doesn't have to leave you stuck. Here's one example of what can happen when the generations help each other figure out how to get things done and balance their lives in our 24/7 world.

After three days in my training class, Steve, a remarried Boomer with three elementary-school-age children, finally blurted out, "I've been here twenty-five years, and this company is not treating us fairly anymore. Ever since we started supporting people all over the world two years ago, I'm on the phone with Asia until 11:30 three nights a week. And then I have to be in at 8:00. I'm tired all the time. The last year and a half has been the worst of my career, but nobody in management seems to care."

The world had changed for Steve and his organization, but the way his company measured work ethic had not changed. But that's where generational differences provided the leverage he and others on his team needed. Stephanie, a Generation X manager, quietly asked Steve why he came in at 8:00 if he was working until 11:30.

"Because the workday starts at 8:30 here," he replied. "It always has. My boss has never told me I could come in later."

Jeff, another Generation X manager, jumped in and said, "When I work in the evenings supporting Asia, I don't come in until 10:00 the next day unless there's a critical meeting. My boss has never said a word about it. She understands that we don't have 8:30 to 5:00 jobs anymore."

Steve just stared at them. "You mean you don't come in until 10:00, *and* you've never been questioned? Then why am I still working the full day and hating my job?"

"Because you're a Baby Boomer," the three of them said simultaneously.

Steve laughed and announced to his coworkers, "From now on, I'm a Gen Xer. I'm coming in tomorrow at 10:00." Steve got unstuck, and the whole team felt rejuvenated and reconnected. Leveraging differences helps us get the four generations working together in the places they come apart.

Work Ethic

TRADITIONALISTS

I work 9 to 5 and stay late with overtime.

What do I think about work?

BABY BOOMERS

I work 8 to 6 and then take it home.

I try to get it all done at work; I'll take it home if I have to.

It's a 24/7 world, so I'm leaving at 5:00. I can log on tonight.

GEN XERS

MILLENNIALS

Why I Think That Way

 TRADITIONALISTS (BORN BEFORE 1945)
Most Traditionalists worked in industrial jobs until the latter half of their careers.

 BABY BOOMERS (BORN 1946-1964)
Boomers expected work to provide excitement and achievement, and they had to differentiate themselves, so many worked long hours.

 GEN XERS (BORN 1965-1980)
Gen Xers don't expect work to provide significance and excitement. They know they will work some evenings and weekends and feel it's only fair to make some personal calls or do some personal web surfing during office hours.

 MILLENNIALS (BORN 1981-2001)
Millennials have grown up in the global, electronic age, where work never stops, and sometimes they don't see the point of rigid office hours. They take breaks for life, fun, and other interests when convenient, even during the workday, and sometimes work after office hours.

CONCLUSION

Sticking Together

AS SEVERAL TOP-LEVEL managers from Cactus Feeders left my session, they realized the market for new employees had shifted. Vice President of Employee Development Kevin Hazelwood told me, "One thing has haunted us since you talked. We would have been happy to hire Traditionalists forever. But we realized from the presentation that in ten years, our company will be Millennials, so we need to learn to work with them now."

Cactus Feeders is the largest independently owned cattle-feeding company in the world. This employee-owned company cares for over one million animals a year on nine feed yards. They realized that for Millennials, a job in agriculture—especially production agriculture—is not one to brag about to their friends, no matter how impressive the company is.

Cactus Feeders changed things so the company would be a better place to work for the younger generations. First, they learned that just making more money didn't motivate the younger Xers or Millennials. So Chairman/CEO Mike Engler and the board started exploring what their company purpose was beyond making money and providing jobs. They knew the world would be twice as hungry in twenty years as the growing middle class around the world demanded more protein. So they came to the conclusion that their purpose was to "feed a hungry world." Of course, in order to do that, they had to make money. Their people responded. They were surprised how willing the mid-level managers were to talk about the company's bigger purpose and how readily the employees embraced it. But what surprised them most was that all the generations came together around this common purpose. It wasn't just the younger Xers and the Millennials who wanted a purpose more than making money.

Cactus Feeders didn't stop there. When they determined that their purpose is to feed the world, they looked for ways to make a more meaningful contribution. They discovered that 67 percent of kids in their school districts were on reduced or subsidized lunch, and 20 to 30 percent of students in the twenty counties around where they operated were food insecure. CEO Engler put $50,000 into the Cactus Feeder Hunger Fund to feed kids and asked the rest of the organization to match it. Having a compelling purpose that translates into making a difference in people's lives has made everyone excited about what they do.

Finally, they realized that younger associates get their identity, their value, and their sense of belonging from the groups they associate with rather than from the institutions they serve or roles they play. Kevin explained this insight: "My father was an army guy; he counted on institutions for his value and sense of belonging. We Gen Xers insisted on being individuals, but we found our value and sense of belonging in the roles we chose. But the Millennials' identities come from their choices and the groups they belong to who shape and validate those choices. Unless we can make them proud to tell their groups that they work here, we'll struggle to recruit or keep them."

So Cactus Feeders set up two kinds of groups where their new managers can connect and help each other—developmental groups for learning and functional groups for idea sharing and support. They believe it's not enough to call someone a manager or give someone a role, even in a company that's employee owned.

Until they understood, Cactus Feeders fought generational changes. Now they believe they are positioned to take advantage of the generations' differences. They're adamant that they don't have it all figured out. But Kevin told me, "We used to say, 'What's wrong with that kid?' But now when I hear a supervisor say that, I think, *This guy just doesn't know what motivates them.* If you figure that out, the kid will work his butt off."

Cactus Feeders certainly demonstrates that when we don't get generational differences, we will react to the small things, ignore the big things, and propose the wrong things. But they also show how quickly we can figure out practical ways to change our business once we understand why the generations see things differently.

With four generations in the workplace and five at home, sticking points are inevitable, but getting stuck is avoidable. When Cactus Feeders quit trying to manage the generational differences and started leading, they put the five-step process to work and turned the corner. What they came up with works better for everyone, not just the younger generations they were trying to accommodate.

YOU CAN DO IT

Sticking points are inevitable, but the same generational conflicts that get teams stuck can cause teams to stick together. You've learned how to spot generational sticking points and what to do about them, and you can do it. You can turn stuck to sticking together with your teams, organizations, and families.

And you can also use the five-step process when you're stuck around generational differences with individuals. Who don't you get along with? Are generational differences playing a part in the tension? The most powerful impact of learning about generational sticking points for most people is that they realize those differences play a part in the frustrations they have with coworkers or family members.

If you're seeing generational sticking points in your relationships, put the five-step process to work. Take a moment and acknowledge that you're stuck. Figure out what needs the other person is trying to meet and why he or she sees things that way. That will give you some ideas about how you can flex to better accommodate the other person's generational preferences. Instead of getting irritated, look for ways to leverage generational strengths rather than getting stuck around the differences. Then you can figure out how you're going to resolve the tension, how you will do things differently.

Notice I've said nothing yet about talking to the other person. Use the five steps on your own first, then try talking to the other person. You have a new understanding of the whys behind generational differences, so you can bring up the topic in a much less judgmental and much more productive way. Remember these two things, and you've got this:

- Don't take it personally; the other person doesn't mean it personally.
- Speak the other person's generational language.

You already knew more about how to speak other generations' languages than you realize. This book has merely helped you tap into it.

So call your mom. She'll appreciate a text, but she really wants to talk to you.

Or quit complaining that your kids never call. Send them a text message about something funny that happened to you today. Get the chat going.

I bet you they'll text back.

Acknowledgments

I'D LIKE TO THANK

- Sean Covey for asking me to write a book and personally demonstrating that it was possible despite a demanding job.
- FranklinCovey for their willingness to allow me to speak and consult on my own as My Generational Coach while working for them full-time. When they talk win-win, they mean it. I appreciate your partnership as my licensed provider for workshops. What a great group of people to work with. I especially want to thank Scott Miller, Catherine Nelson, Debra Lund, and Adam Merrill.
- My agent, Sealy Yates, and everyone who work so hard at Yates & Yates.
- William Kruidenier and Tim Stafford, who each helped write and edit parts of the book. Both offered invaluable advice.
- Jon Farrar and Jonathan Schindler, my hardworking editors. I've read hundreds of authors who say that their books are much better because of the hard work of the editors. I now know what they're talking about.
- My favorite Millennials: Bart, Josh, Max, and Katy. I'm proud of you.
- Laurie. Always been in love with you; always will be. I can't wait to watch hand in hand another couple of generations grow up.
- All the people who said thanks on their way out the door for getting it right about their generation and all the people who asked me to write this book.
- All those who want to create teams that leverage the generations instead of griping about their irritations. Your questions, excitement, and laughter fill this book and my work. May your tribe increase.

Appendix: Frequently Asked Questions

I HAD JUST MET two instructors in the faculty lounge at a conference center during our lunch break. As we chatted, I mentioned that I research generations. Both instructors said they didn't think much of the field. One said she thought the similarities among the generations were greater than the differences. The other said she agreed that we had four generations for the first time in history, but she thought each generation acted the same way when they entered the workforce. The opinions my lunchmates expressed about the validity of generational research represent two of the most frequently asked questions I hear. I've included my answers to those, as well as a few others, below.

1. AREN'T GENERATIONS MORE ALIKE THAN THEY ARE DIFFERENT?

Yes, the generations are more alike than they are different. Many surveys indicate there are fewer differences than what some of the generational literature or trainings say. Sometimes people emphasize any difference too much, generational or otherwise. However, Pew Research Center discovered that 79 percent of the public sees a generation gap, defined as "major differences . . . in the point of view of younger and older adults." That's five percentage points higher than when Gallup asked the question in 1969![1] These studies seem contradictory at first glance, but they're not.

The hardest part of generational research is sorting through the studies that seem to say contradictory things until you can see clear patterns and sort out the different nuances between the generations. My experience is that a person has to spend a minimum of four hundred hours reading through the best of the research in order to discern these patterns. Most of us don't have four hundred hours to dedicate to this topic, so my goal in this book is to guide you through the nuances by summarizing and simplifying the hundreds of subtle distinctions found in multiple surveys and studies.

Ultimately, we don't need sociologists to tell us that a seventy-five-year-old votes, works, or buys differently than a thirty-five-year-old. We see it for ourselves at family reunions or meetings at work. The significant gap between Traditionalists and Millennials has shone prominently in the last two US presidential elections—Traditionalists have voted overwhelmingly Republican and Millennials Democratic. Pew Research Center discovered that we see more generational differences today, but we're almost equally divided on whether we think they cause more problems than they did in the '60s, the era famous for its generational gap (and use of tie-dye). When asked, 31 percent see more, 38 percent less, and 25 percent the same amount of generational conflict than in the '60s and '70s.[2]

Those statistics mean that most of us see the differences but don't see these generational gaps causing major problems in our organizations or families, just sticking points.[3] That's great news. It means what I've said throughout the book: generational tensions are inevitable; generational problems are preventable.

So yes, the generations are more alike than different, but using that as a reason to ignore generational differences won't help you deal with sticking points that sidetrack your team. And the same applies to your sales and marketing efforts. It's inevitable that your salespeople will struggle connecting with all the generations, because most people can relate well to two of the generations but not four. That's why marketers spend millions of dollars to pinpoint generational differences. How are you helping your salespeople relate and sell to all generations? How are you preparing your employees to satisfy five generations of customers?

In summary, generations *are* more alike than different. But we still see the differences as strongly as we did in the late '60s, when they dominated the news. The good news is that we think they cause minor problems rather than crises today. That's why good leadership will work with everyone because people from all generations have the same basic needs. When people, regardless of generation, are treated like whole people and not managed like things, they will volunteer their best.[4] Understanding generational differences enhances your effectiveness by allowing you to flex your approach to make each generation more productive.

2. ISN'T A LOT OF WHAT GETS CALLED "GENERATIONAL DIFFERENCES" JUST ABOUT LIFE STAGES?

There are many characteristics and behaviors that can be attributed to specific stages in life, regardless of generation. Fathers of four-year-olds have much in common even if one is an older Millennial and the other is a younger Boomer on a second marriage. The new life stage of emerging adulthood is another example. When people complain that Millennials are postponing adulthood and stretching the time they spend experimenting with different careers and identities, they forget that the same was said about the Baby Boomers and Xers when they were in their twenties.

But the experiences and values shaped by the different eras do impact how people experience a life stage. Boomers spent more money than Traditionalists did at each stage in life because they didn't experience the trauma of the Depression. They went through the same life cycle milestones, but with a greater optimism about money. But those high, optimistic expectations have also created another significant uniqueness. Pew Social Trends reported the Baby Boomers are more pessimistic about their own lives and about the direction of the nation than other generations. While middle age is the most demanding and stressful time in life for most people, Pew reports that the Boomers have felt less overall life satisfaction than the other generations throughout their lives.[5] Why? The Boomers have higher expectations than the other generations and therefore are more likely to feel that life (or their country) has missed the mark.

Another major challenge of age-cohort research (the technical name for generational studies) is separating what is unique about a generation from what everyone experiences at that age. Admittedly, generational research is not an exact science, and it's impossible to completely separate which behaviors are caused by life stage from which are generational differences, especially when people are in their teens. But over time, enough data comes in from surveys, voting patterns, and purchases to see enough differences emerge and confidently identify a new generation. (That's why we don't know the start date or name of the newest generation. They aren't old enough to have enough data to pinpoint.)

3. HOW WIDELY DO THE GENERATIONAL GENERALIZATIONS APPLY IN DIFFERENT REGIONS OF THE UNITED STATES?

Generational differences are only one lens we can use to understand how people are influenced and shaped. Their culture, family values, age, religious affiliations, access to media, education, and socioeconomic status all shape their thinking. In general, the closer people are to farming, the more conservative they are, and the more they are a blend of their own and the previous generation. We've already seen this effect in chapter 6 where the man in Kansas questioned the impact of divorce on Gen X because no one he knew in his rural community had gone through one. While every part of the United States and Canada felt the impact of increasing divorce, he and his friends didn't feel it as directly because their community had more conservative values. You can also see it in political issues. In every election season in the United States, news outlets regularly explain that younger people in the South and Midwest are more conservative than those on the coasts, even though they are more liberal than the older generations there. As a rule of thumb, the coasts are more likely to match these generational generalizations whereas people in the South and center tend to have more characteristics of the preceding generation.

4. TO WHAT EXTENT DO THESE GENERATIONAL GENERALIZATIONS APPLY IN OTHER COUNTRIES?

While the generational generalizations I make in this book are primarily pulled from research in the United States and Canada, there are a number of factors that had a similar impact on many other parts of the world as well. Countries with these factors tend to have generational trends similar to what is observed in the United States and Canada:

- **Industrial Revolution.** The Industrial Revolution caused the rural-to-urban migration in countries outside the United States and Canada as well. Urban environments create greater discontinuity with the past and greater openness to new ideas. Many of these generational differences become more pronounced in cities.
- **World War II.** If the country participated in the war, then its citizens most likely had their own "baby boom," although they may have had it later. For example, many European countries had it six or seven years later than the United States and Canada because of the time it took to rebuild after the war.
- **Access to Western television, music, and the Internet.** The more experiences people share, especially when they are young, the more common characteristics they have, even if they live in different parts of the world.

Millennials are the first global generation; they share many characteristics worldwide because the Internet has made the world smaller. The Futures Company's extensive research found four different subgroups of Millennials worldwide.[6] Not all Millennials are the same, but their characteristics are spread throughout the world.

Understanding a person's culture, family values, age, religious affiliations, access to media, education, and socioeconomic status will help you understand how to adjust the generalizations in this book. For example, a Generation X woman whose parents emigrated from India told her team that she and most other first-generation Indians she knew had Boomer and Traditionalist characteristics. She described a family structure based on more traditional male and female roles than many Western Gen Xers embrace. In adjusting these generalizations for another country, it's essential to know the history of that country. In Panama, Generation X is more optimistic than the Boomers because the Gen Xers were the first generation who were told they would do better than their parents as the economy boomed.

5. IS THIS BOOK DESCRIBING ALL MILLENNIALS OR ONLY MIDDLE-CLASS MILLENNIALS IN PROFESSIONAL JOBS?

That depends on which part of the book you're reading and on the research I'm citing. Some surveys, like those from Gallup or the Pew Research Center, encompass all members of a generation, whereas others, especially those about attitudes at work, focus on those with jobs, especially professional jobs.

As you can tell from my stories, I get to speak to and interview everyone from executives to forklift drivers. But most of my work is with organizations, so my research includes far fewer interviews with those who are unemployed or retired.

That's why I say that it depends on which part of the book you're reading. Chapters 4 through 7 on the generational ghost stories cite more studies done on the full population, whereas the sticking point chapters cite more studies that focus on professionals. Even then, those chapters have many references to studies that look at both white- and blue-collar workers and occasionally those without employment.

Finally, I'm the first to acknowledge that this focus on generational differences at work does not tell the whole story. As the United States becomes more ethnically diverse, generational research into specific groups increases. For example, Hispanics use smartphones more than the rest of Americans.[7]

The Pew Hispanic Center researches how Hispanics in the United States are similar to and different from the general population. While there are commonalities, cultural distinctives add nuances to generational generalizations. There's neither room nor adequate research yet to cover those nuances in each sticking point chapter.

Not only does diversity add more to the story than this book can tell, but my focus on the workplace leaves out those of each generation who live in poverty. The Great Recession has pushed one in five children into poverty.[8] The Millennials (and the new unnamed generation of post-Millennials) in poverty have less in common with their designer-dressed college-bound peers carrying the latest electronic toys and far more in common with the Gen Xer in chapter 6 who spent his weekends helping his mother repair the car after his father left. A quick search of the Internet will reveal many books and resources that explore this segment's important story.

This illustrates that no one book can tell the whole story for a generation of over eighty million. Even more, it is a reminder that we must lead rather than manage people. No matter our roles in life or our positions in our organizations, we must listen for understanding rather than jump to conclusions. We've all got stories that we're just aching to tell, and we'll never stick together unless we listen.

Notes

CHAPTER 1: STICKING TOGETHER OR COMING APART

1. I make Gen X longer because I put more focus on their attitudes, whereas others make the generation shorter because they emphasize when the birthrate picked back up.

2. For a short summary of the impact of changing demographics and life expectancies on the economy and labor market, see "European Demography: Working-Age Shift," *The Economist*, January 26, 2013, http://www.economist.com/news/finance -and-economics/21570752-growth-will-suffer-workers-dwindle-working-age-shift; Barbara Beck, "The Slow Farewell," *The Economist: The World in 2011*, November 22, 2010, 89; Ken Dychtwald, Tamara J. Erickson, and Robert Morison, *Workforce Crisis* (Boston: Harvard Business School Publishing, 2006), 17.

3. John Cassidy, "Meet the 'Missing Millions' Who've Vanished from the Economy," *Fortune*, April 8, 2013, 52.

4. Vanessa Fuhrmans, "Surgeon Shortage Pushes Hospitals to Hire Temps," *Wall Street Journal*, January 13, 2009, http://online.wsj.com/article/SB123179145452274561 .html.

5. Obama's strong showing with Millennials in two elections has led many to think they will vote Democratic for the rest of their lives. See Molly Ball, "A Democratic Age?" *The Atlantic* (April 2013): 16.

6. Ellen McGirt, "How Chris Hughes Helped Launch Facebook and the Barack Obama Campaign," *Fast Company*, April 1, 2009, http://www.fastcompany.com /1207594/how-chris-hughes-helped-launch-facebook-and-the-barack-obama -campaign.

7. Michael Scherer, "Person of the Year: Barack Obama, the President," *Time*, December 19, 2012, http://poy.time.com/2012/12/19/person-of-the-year -barack-obama/.

8. James Dao, "Ads Now Seek Recruits for 'An Army of One,'" *New York Times*, January 10, 2001, http://www.nytimes.com/2001/01/10/us/ads-now-seek -recruits-for-an-army-of-one.html?pagewanted=all&src=pm.

CHAPTER 2: BLUE SCREEN OF DEATH: THE DIFFICULTY OF LEADING FOUR GENERATIONS

1. My father, Dr. Wayne Shaw, denies that this ever happened.
2. Andrew Noymer and Michel Garenne, "The 1918 Influenza Epidemic's Effects on Sex Differentials in Mortality in the United States," *Population and Development Review* 26, no. 3 (September 2000): 569, fig. 2, http://demog.berkeley.edu/~andrew /1918/PDR_1918_flu.pdf.
3. *Time*, Briefing, January 23, 2012, 7.
4. Howard Bahr, interview by Ben Wattenberg, *The First Measured Century*, PBS. The transcript can be found at http://www.pbs.org/fmc/interviews/bahr.htm.
5. If you'd like to know what I told him, see chapter 16 on policies.
6. Stephanie Armour, "Generation Y: They've Arrived at Work with a New Attitude," *USA Today*, November 6, 2005, http://usatoday30.usatoday.com/money/workplace /2005-11-06-gen-y_x.htm.
7. Christina Binkley, "Law without Suits: New Hires Flout Tradition," *Wall Street Journal*, January 31, 2008, http://online.wsj.com/article/SB120175142140831193 .html; Jennifer Smith, "Associate Perk of the Week: 'Persuasive' Ties and Brooks Brothers Suits," *Law Blog* (*WSJ* Blogs), February 23, 2012, http://blogs.wsj.com /law/2012/02/23/associate-perk-of-the-week-persuasive-ties-and-brooks-brothers -suits/.
8. J. Walker Smith and Ann Clurman, *Rocking the Ages: The Yankelovich Report on Generational Marketing* (New York: Harper Business, 1997), XI–XIII.

CHAPTER 3: GETTING UNSTUCK: FIVE STEPS FOR LEADING THROUGH THE TWELVE GENERATIONAL STICKING POINTS

1. Peter Drucker, *The Effective Executive* (New York: Harper and Row, 1966), 75.
2. Peter Capelli and Bill Novelli, *Managing the Older Worker: How to Prepare for the New Organizational Order* (Boston: Harvard Business School Publishing, 2010), 102.
3. Diversity alone doesn't increase performance. It's how we leverage the differences that matters: "Decades of research on the effects of diversity within teams and small groups indicate that diversity can have negative effects as well as positive ones. The empirical research does not support the simple notion that more diverse groups, teams, or business units necessarily perform better. . . . The simplistic business case of the past is simply not supported in our research. . . . *There is virtually no evidence to support the simple assertion that diversity is inevitably either good or bad for business*" (italics added). T. Kochan et al., "The Effects of Diversity on Business Performance," *Human Resource Management* (Spring 2003). These researchers suggest that you must provide training in how to leverage diversity in order to capitalize on it. The five steps outlined in this chapter provide a simple way to do that.

PART 1 INTRODUCTION: TELLING GHOST STORIES

1. "Chicago's Top Five Most Haunted Spots," *CBS Chicago*, October 3, 2011, http:// chicago.cbslocal.com/top-lists/chicago%E2%80%99s-top-five-most-haunted -spots/.

2. Because these are ghost stories rather than detailed descriptions of historical events, the emphasis is on interpretation, especially interpreting one generation to another. The interpretations are a distillation of a lifetime of interest in sociology and history, much of which I lived through personally, as well as interviews and anecdotal data collected through my professional work as a consultant. You'll find endnotes that cite sources for specific facts or interpretations of those facts that are not mine, but most of the historical events are well known and so are without references.

3. J. D. Heiman and Phil Roura, "Tales from the Urban Crypt: Legendary Whoppers about Gotham's Buildings, Subways, Hotels, and Bridges Run Ghastly and Ghostly Gamut," *New York Daily News*, September 13, 1998, http://www.nydailynews.com /tales-urman-crypt-legendary-whoppers-gotham-buildings-subways-hotels-bridges -run-ghastly-ghostly-gamut-article-1.804961.

4. Pew Research Center, *Millennials: A Portrait of Generation Next* (February 24, 2010), 135, http://www.pewsocialtrends.org/files/2010/10/millennials-confident -connected-open-to-change.pdf.

5. Thom S. Rainer and Jess W. Rainer, *The Millennials* (Nashville: B&H, 2011), 144.

6. Arthur Conan Doyle, *Sherlock Holmes: The Complete Novels and Stories* (New York: Bantam, 1986), 1:202.

7. Pew Research Center, *Millennials*, 57.

8. See his classic article "How I Learned to Let My Workers Lead" in *Harvard Business Review* (November 1990).

CHAPTER 4: TRADITIONALISTS: KEEP CALM AND CARRY ON

1. Pew Research Center, *Millennials: A Portrait of Generation Next* (February 24, 2010), 5, http://www.pewsocialtrends.org/files/2010/10/millennials-confident -connected-open-to-change.pdf.

2. Because the Traditionalists cover so many years, some experts divide them into two generations, often called the GIs and the Silents. The differences between the first half and the second half of the Traditionalist generation are much more subtle than the famous gap between Traditionalists and Baby Boomers. So I keep the Traditionalists as a four-decade generation. That the later generations developed more significant differences in half that time illustrates the impact of television and the Internet.

3. Peter F. Drucker, *Managing in the Next Society* (New York: St. Martin's Press, 2002), 235.

4. Benjamin Schwarz, "Life in (and after) Our Great Recession," *The Atlantic* (October 2009): 96, http://www.theatlantic.com/magazine/archive/2009/10/life -in-and-after-our-great-recession/307651/.

5. See my workshops "Leading through the 6 Change Reactions" and "Working through the 6 Change Reactions" at www.mygenerationalcoach.com.

6. Jeffrey Jensen Arnett and Joseph Schwab, *The Clark University Poll of Emerging Adults* (December 2012), 7, http://www.clarku.edu/clarkpoll/pdfs/Clark_Poll _Peer%20Inst.pdf; "Why We're Officially 'Adults' at Age 28," *Yahoo! Lifestyle New Zealand*, October 18, 2012, http://nz.lifestyle.yahoo.com/marie-claire/all -about-you/life/article/-/15150188/why-we-re-officially-adults-at-age-28.

7. For a more in-depth look at emerging adulthood see Jeffrey Jensen Arnett, *Emerging Adulthood: The Winding Road from the Late Teens through the Twenties* (Oxford: Oxford University Press, 2004).

8. Rob Stein and Donna St. George, "Number of Unwed Mothers Has Risen Sharply in the US," *Washington Post*, May 14, 2009, http://articles.washingtonpost.com /2009-05-14/news/36875994_1_unmarried-women-single-women-stephanie-j -ventura. Teen pregnancies are down almost half since 1990: *USA Today Snapshots*, "Fewer Teen Moms," December 8, 2011, 1.

9. "This century's first sexual revolution was in progress [in the 1920s]. . . . The percentage of women born between 1900 and 1909 who had intercourse before marriage doubled from 25 percent to 50 percent! . . . Most of the increased sexuality occurred in stable, affectionate relationships." Ira L. Reiss, *An End to Shame: Shaping Our Next Sexual Revolution* (Amherst, NY: Prometheus Books, 1990), http://www2.hu-berlin.de/sexology/BIB/AETS/b04.htm.

10. Parents or grandparents who are interested in how to instill work ethic and other crucial values in an urban setting will find H. Stephen Glenn and Jane Nelsen's book *Raising Self-Reliant Children in a Self-Indulgent World: Seven Building Blocks for Developing Capable Young People* (Roseville, CA: Prima Publishing, 2000) or Glenn's CD set *Developing Capable Young People* especially helpful.

11. For more detail on the regionalization of the United States in 1900, see Frederick Lewis Allen's classic *The Big Change: America Transforms Itself, 1900–1950* (New York: Harper and Row, 1952), 3–26.

CHAPTER 5: BABY BOOMERS: DO YOUR OWN THING

1. Pew Research Center, *Millennials: A Portrait of Generation Next* (February 24, 2010), 5, http://www.pewsocialtrends.org/files/2010/10/millennials-confident -connected-open-to-change.pdf.

2. Randstad, "Limited Interaction among Generations in the Workplace Indicates New Challenges," news release, May 27, 2008, http://us.randstad.com/content /aboutrandstad/news-and-press-releases/press-releases/2008/20080527001.xml.

3. Steve Gillon, *Boomer Nation: The Largest and Richest Generation Ever and How It Changed America* (New York: Free Press, 2004), 51.

4. During World War II, the only thing left to do was to send women home. Despite decades of emphasis on extended bed rest for postpartum recovery, medical records indicate that women were sent home thirty-six hours after delivery because hospitals needed the beds. Instead, women received nurse visits for the next five days. See Elizabeth Temkin, "Driving Through: Postpartum Care during World War II," *American Journal of Public Health* 89, no. 4 (April 1999): 587–95.

5. J. Walker Smith and Ann Clurman, *Generation Ageless: How Baby Boomers Are Changing the Way We Live Today . . . and They're Just Getting Started* (New York: Collins, 2007), 35.

6. The article pointed to 250,000 swimming pools in the United States.

7. Yuval Rosenberg, "Talking 'bout Our Generation," *Fortune*, June 26, 2006, 106, http://money.cnn.com/magazines/fortune/fortune_archive/2006/06/26/8379997 /index.htm.

8. Cheryl Russell, "A Generation of Free Agents," *The Courier-Journal*, October 24, 1993, 5.

9. Landon Y. Jones, *Great Expectations: America and the Baby Boom Generation* (New York: Coward, McCann & Geoghegan, 1980). This book is often credited with coining the term *Baby Boomer*.

10. Knowledge Networks, *Associated Press—LifeGoesStrong.com Boomers Survey* (March 16, 2011), http://surveys.ap.org/data%5CKnowledgeNetworks%5CAP _Boomers_Survey_Topline_RETIREMENT.pdf.

11. Gillon, *Boomer Nation*, 5.

12. Ibid., 8.

13. Lev Grossman, "The Beast with a Billion Eyes," *Time*, January 3, 2012, 40, http://www.time.com/time/magazine/article/0,9171,2104815,00.html.

14. *Time* columnist James Poniewozik argues that *The Tonight Show* should get rid of Johnny Carson's desk and try something significantly different because the variety of options available is eating ratings. See "Break Up the Desk Set," *Time*, April 22, 2013.

15. For more detail on the drop in test scores and the rise in crime, see Landon Y. Jones, *Great Expectations*, 128–50.

16. Don Tapscott, *Grown Up Digital: How the Net Generation Is Changing Your World* (New York: McGraw-Hill, 2009), 11.

17. Daniel Yankelovich, *The New Morality: A Profile of American Youth in the '70s* (New York: McGraw-Hill, 1974), 6. In 1981 Yankelovich updated this research in a book called *New Rules: Searching for Self-Fulfillment in a World Turned Upside Down* (New York: Random House, 1981).

18. Daniel Yankelovich, interview by Ben Wattenberg, *The First Measured Century*, PBS, January 12, 2007. The transcript can be found at http://www.pbs.org/fmc /interviews/yankelovich.htm. See also research from University of Michigan psychologist Joseph Adelson, "When the Young Teach and the Old Learn," *Time*, August 17, 1970, http://www.time.com/time/magazine/article/0,9171, 909577,00.html.

19. Yankelovich, *The New Morality*, 83–85.

20. Smith and Clurman, *Generation Ageless*, xxv.

21. Molly Grimsley, Mail Call, *Newsweek*, November 28, 2005, 8.

22. Commentator David Brooks focuses on this potential in his final paragraph on the high-income Boomers: "This is a class of people who grew up with the word *potential* hanging around their necks, and in many ways still, their potential is more striking than their accomplishments." David Brooks, *Bobos in Paradise* (New York: Simon & Schuster, 2000), 273.

23. Quoted in Kevin Mattson, *"What the Heck Are You Up to, Mr. President?"* (New York: Bloomsbury, 2009), 2.

24. "Carter's 'Crisis of Confidence' Speech," *American Experience*, http://www.pbs.org /wgbh/americanexperience/features/general-article/carter-crisis-speech/.

25. Marissa Piesman and Marilee Hartley, *The Yuppie Handbook* (New York: Pocket Books, 1984).

CHAPTER 6: GENERATION X: GET REAL

1. Pew Research Center, *Millennials: A Portrait of Generation Next* (February 24, 2010), 5, http://www.pewsocialtrends.org/files/2010/10/millennials-confident-connected-open-to-change.pdf.

2. Randstad, "Limited Interaction among Generations in the Workplace Indicates New Challenges," news release, May 27, 2008, http://us.randstad.com/content/aboutrandstad/news-and-press-releases/press-releases/2008/20080527001.xml.

3. The story of the beginnings of *Donkey Kong* is told in chapter 2 of Jeff Ryan, *Super Mario: How Nintendo Conquered America* (New York: Penguin, 2011), 19–31.

4. The belief that success in life is less what you make of it and more due to external control increased 50 percent between the 1960s and the 2000s. See Jean M. Twenge, *Generation Me* (New York: Free Press, 2006), 139.

5. Piper Lowell, "Out of Desperation," *Sojourners* (November 1994), http://www.sojo.net/magazine/1994/11/out-desperation.

6. The drop in births in the '60s was a product of Baby Boomers having fewer children and the timing of when the Traditionalists had their children. Children that would've typically been born in the '60s came earlier, in the '50s, because Traditionalists had more children earlier in their lives than had been typical. Norman Rider concluded that 55 percent of the fifteen-year Baby Bust was due to timing alone. Landon Y. Jones, *Great Expectations: America and the Baby Boom Generation* (New York: Coward, McCann & Geoghegan, 1980), 195.

7. Geoffrey T. Holtz, *Welcome to the Jungle: The Why Behind "Generation X"* (New York: St. Martin's Press, 1995), 18.

8. Ibid., 20.

9. Neil Howe and William Strauss, *Millennials Go to College* (Ithaca, NY: Paramount Market Publishing, 2007), 28.

10. US Census Bureau, "Table 78. Live Births, Deaths, Marriages, and Divorces: 1960 to 2007," http://www.census.gov/compendia/statab/2011/tables/11s0078.pdf; Karen Sternheimer, "Is Marriage Under Siege?" *Everyday Sociology Blog*, July 28, 2008, http://nortonbooks.typepad.com/everydaysociology/2008/07/is-marriage-und.html.

11. "Divorce Rate Drops to Lowest Since 1970," *USA Today*, May 11, 2007, http://usatoday30.usatoday.com/news/nation/2007-05-11-divorce-decline_N.htm.

12. James P. Vere, "Having It All No Longer: Fertility, Female Labor Supply, and the New Life Choices of Generation X," *Demography* 44, no. 4 (November 2007): 821–28.

13. Stephanie Armour, "As Dads Push for Family Time, Tensions Rise in Workplace," *USA Today*, December 11, 2007.

14. US Department of Commerce, *Money Income of Households, Families, and Persons in the United States: 1985* (issued August 1987).

15. In December 1980, interest rates hit their highest point in the century and remained in the teens throughout the mid-80s.

16. The economy boomed during the childhood of the second half of Gen X—the dot-com era. So some wonder why I say the economy was negative for both halves of Gen X growing up. The boom in the economy during the second half of Generation X held a dark secret. Even though the economy grew rapidly

again during the '80s and '90s, with only a mild recession in 1990, much of that growth went to the top 10 percent of wage earners. Those in the middle- and bottom-income brackets remained almost flat. They kept hearing that the economy was growing and watched the stock market break new records, but the Xers saw the air going out of the American dream for most of the workforce. See Jim Tankersley, "Horatio Alger, RIP," *NationalJournal*, September 25, 2012, http://www.nationaljournal.com/next-economy/analysis-working-hard-is-no -longer-the-ticket-to-achieving-the-american-dream-20120925 and Kirstin Downey, "Sometimes There's Upward Mobility . . . But Usually, in History, There Isn't," *NationalJournal*, September 25, 2012, http://www.nationaljournal .com/next-economy/in-world-history-upward-mobility-has-rarely-happened -20120925.

17. Katherine S. Newman, *Declining Fortunes* (New York: Basic Books, 1994), 53.
18. Paul Rogat Leob, *Generation at the Crossroads: Apathy and Action on the American Campus* (New Brunswick, NJ: Rutgers University Press, 1994), 406.
19. Gary Steinberg, "The Class of '90," *Occupational Outlook Quarterly*, June 22, 1994, 12.
20. Faye Rice, "Making Generational Marketing Come of Age," *Fortune*, June 26, 1995, 114.
21. Sylvia Ann Hewlett and Lauren Leader-Chivée, with Catherine Fredman, Maggie Jackson, and Laura Sherbin, *The X Factor: Tapping into the Strengths of the 33- to 46-Year-Old Generation* (Center for Work-Life Policy, 2011), 9.
22. Ibid., 1, 21.
23. Rebecca Ryan, *Live First, Work Second: Getting inside the Head of the Next Generation* (Madison, WI: Next Generation Consulting, 2007), 112.
24. Jeff Gordinier, *X Saves the World: How Generation X Got the Shaft but Can Still Keep Everything from Sucking* (New York: Viking, 2008), 136.
25. Ibid., 29.

CHAPTER 7: MILLENNIALS: CAN WE FIX IT? *YES, WE CAN!*
1. I call this generation "Millennials" because they strongly prefer that name to the others. In fact, they would rather have no name than be called Generation Y, because they don't want to be compared to Generation X. Neil Howe and William Strauss, *Millennials Rising: The Next Great Generation* (New York: Vintage, 2000), 17. Millennials expert Donald Tapscott coined the term *NetGen*.
2. Pew Research Center, *Millennials: A Portrait of Generation Next* (February 24, 2010), 5, http://www.pewsocialtrends.org/files/2010/10/millennials-confident -connected-open-to-change.pdf.
3. Randstad, "Limited Interaction among Generations in the Workplace Indicates New Challenges," news release, May 27, 2008, http://us.randstad.com/content /aboutrandstad/news-and-press-releases/press-releases/2008/20080527001.xml.
4. Ibid.
5. Reuters, "Worker at Apple-Supplier Foxconn in China: 'We're Humans, We're Not Machines,'" *World News on NBCNews.com*, http://worldnews.msnbc.msn .com/_news/2012/04/06/11052196-worker-at-apple-supplier-foxconn-in-china -were-humans-were-not-machines.

6. Dan Schawbel, "Millennials vs. Baby Boomers: Who Would You Rather Hire?" *Time*, March 29, 2012, http://business.time.com/2012/03/29/millennials-vs -baby-boomers-who-would-you-rather-hire.

7. According to the US Census Bureau, there were over four million births in fourteen of the twenty years from 1989 to 2009. In comparison, the first Baby Boom had four million births per year for only ten years.

8. Sharon Jayson, "Twin Births Have Doubled Since 1980," *USA Today*, January 5, 2012, http://usatoday30.usatoday.com/NEWS/usaedition/2012-01-05-CDC -twins_ST_U.htm.

9. William Strauss and Neil Howe, *Millennials and the Pop Culture* (Great Falls, VA: LifeCourse Associates, 2006), 50.

10. "Etan Patz: Little Lad Still Lost," *Economist*, April 28, 2012, 36, http://www .economist.com/node/21553479.

11. "Parents of Millennial College Students: A Survey Snapshot," Southwestern University, http://southwestern.edu/gateways/parents/orientation/handbook /survey.php.

12. Anna Bahney, "High School Heroes: Mom and Dad," *New York Times*, May 16, 2004, http://www.nytimes.com/2004/05/16/style/high-school-heroes-mom-and -dad.html?pagewanted=all&src=pm.

13. John Leo, "The Good-News Generation," *US News & World Report*, October 26, 2003, http://www.usnews.com/usnews/opinion/articles/031103/3john.htm.

14. Misty Harris, "Teens, Parents Get Along Better," *Calgary Herald*, May 12, 2009, http://www2.canada.com/calgaryherald/news/story.html?id=af2a130a-cc8a-4863 -996b-e6174d7cb629.

15. Thom S. Rainer and Jess W. Rainer, *The Millennials: Connecting to America's Largest Generation* (Nashville: B&H, 2011), 57.

16. Robert Half International and Yahoo! HotJobs, *What Millennial Workers Want: How to Attract and Retain Gen Y Employees* (2008), 2, 8.

17. Rainer and Rainer, *The Millennials*, 16.

18. Sharon Jayson, "Are Kids Today Having a Childhood They'll Remember?" *USA Today*, April 15, 2011, http://usatoday30.usatoday.com/news/health/wellness /story/2011/04/Are-parents-overprotecting-their-kids/46135302/1.

19. It's only fair to point out that what I and others saw as an overemphasis on self-esteem has declined the past ten years. So it will be interesting to see how the youngest third of Millennials and the generation that follows them respond in the workplace.

20. Gus Lubin and Mamta Badkar, "15 Facts about McDonald's That Will Blow Your Mind," *Business Insider*, November 25, 2011, http://www.businessinsider.com /facts-about-mcdonalds-blow-your-mind-2011-11?op=1.

21. Even while real wages stagnated for 95 percent of Americans, the Boomers accelerated their spending by reducing the traditional 7 to 8 percent savings rate to 1 to 2 percent, according to The Bureau of Economic Analysis.

22. Christine Dugas, "Generation Y's Steep Financial Hurdles: Huge Debt, No Savings," *USA Today*, April 23, 2010, http://usatoday30.usatoday.com/money /economy/2010-04-23-1Ageny23_CV_N.htm. Neil Shah, "Young Adults Retreat from Piling Up Debt," *The Wall Street Journal*, March 5, 2013, 1.

23. Ibid. See also "Degrees of Difficulty," *Time*, October 29, 2012, 36.

24. Nicola Ellis, "Unmasking Millennials: The Futures Company on a Misunderstood Generation," Warc (March 2011), 4.

25. Don Peck, "Can the Middle Class Be Saved?" *The Atlantic Monthly* (September 2011), http://www.theatlantic.com/magazine/archive/2011/09/can-the-middle -class-be-saved/8600/.

26. Justin Fox, "A Fun Free Recovery," *Time*, June 29, 2009, 21, http://www.time .com/time/magazine/article/0,9171,1905516,00.html.

27. Allan Sloan, "The Next Great Bailout: Social Security," *Fortune*, July 30, 2009, http://money.cnn.com/2009/07/29/news/economy/fixing_social_security.fortune/. Under the current system, health and pension entitlements will take 17 percent of the United States' GDP: "The American That Works," *The Economist*, March 16, 2013, 13.

28. Barbara Beck, "The Slow Farewell," *The Economist*, November 22, 2010, 89, http://www.economist.com/node/17493402.

29. David Von Drehle, "Yes, We'll Still Make Stuff," *Time*, May 25, 2009, 49, http://www.time.com/time/specials/packages/article/0,28804,1898024 _1898023_1898085,00.html.

30. Charles Fishman, "The Insourcing Boom," *The Atlantic* (December 2012): 44; James Fallows, "Mr. China Comes to America," *The Atlantic* (December 2012): 54; Rana Foroohar, "The Economy's New Rules: Go Glocal," *Time*, August 20, 2012, 26; Special Report: Outsourcing and Offsharing, "Here, There, and Everywhere," *The Economist*, January 19, 2013.

31. Neil Shah, "Young Adults Retreat from Piling Up Debt," *The Wall Street Journal*, March 5, 2013, 1.

32. Pew Research Center, *Millennials* (February 24, 2010), 49.

33. Ibid., 40.

34. The popularity of zombie movies and TV shows reflects these fears.

35. Steven Reinberg, "US Kids Using Media Almost 8 Hours a Day," ABC News online, January 20, 2010, http://abcnews.go.com/Health/Healthday/us-kids -media-hours-day/story?id=9611664. The survey finds few parents set rules as to the use of smartphones and computers.

36. Pew Research Center, *Millennials*, 32.

37. McCann Worldgroup, *The Truth about Youth* (May 2011), 5, http://www.scribd .com/doc/56263899/McCann-Worldgroup-Truth-About-Youth.

38. University of Chicago News Office, "Most Americans think people need to be 26 to be considered grown-up: Seven steps toward adulthood take five years, NORC survey at University of Chicago finds," news release, May 9, 2003, http://www -news.uchicago.edu/releases/03/030509.adulthood.shtml; Pew Research Center, "When Does Adulthood Begin in this Economy?" March 13, 2012, http://www .pewresearch.org/daily-number/when-does-adulthood-begin-in-this-economy.

39. Jeffrey Jensen Arnett and Joseph Schwab, *The Clark University Poll of Emerging Adults* (December 2012), http://www.clarku.edu/clarkpoll/pdfs/Clark_Poll _Peer%20Inst.pdf; "Why We're Officially 'Adults' at Age 28," *Yahoo! Lifestyle New Zealand*, October 18, 2012, http://nz.lifestyle.yahoo.com/marie-claire /all-about-you/life/article/-/15150188/why-we-re-officially-adults-at-age-28.

PART 2 INTRODUCTION: DECODING THE GENERATIONS

1. Chris Kilroy, "Special Report: Air Florida Flight 90," AirDisaster.com, http://
www.airdisaster.com/special/special-af90.shtml; Del Quentin Wilber, "A Crash's
Improbable Impact," *Washington Post*, January 12, 2007, http://www.washington
post.com/wp-dyn/content/article/2007/01/11/AR2007011102220.html.

CHAPTER 8: COMMUNICATION

1. "Texting Woman Falls off Kodiak Cliff, Rescued," *Anchorage Daily News*,
September 26, 2012, http://www.adn.com/2012/09/26/2640951/texting-woman
-falls-off-kodiak.html; Chris Matyszczyk, "Texting Woman Falls off Cliff," *CNET:
Technically Incorrect*, September 27, 2012, http://news.cnet.com/8301-17852_3
-57521443-71/texting-woman-falls-off-cliff.

2. Greg Toppo, "Report: 'Distracted Walking' Endangers Teens," *USA Today*,
August 30, 2012, http://usatoday30.usatoday.com/news/nation/story/2012
-08-30/teen-cellphone-injuries-pedestrian/57414454/1.

3. You can see the presentation at http://www.nasa.gov/pdf/214672main_KPainting
-GenY_rev11.pdf. Nick Skytland, a NASA engineer, said this about it: "This
presentation has been created so that anyone who wants to can take it and use
it. Share this with your management. Share this with your parents. Share it with
people who don't understand why you like to snowboard in the afternoon, work
from 'offsite' on your mac, use Twitter to communicate with your friends, and
expect to be involved in the 'big picture' at work." Nick Skytland, "Generation
Y Perspectives," *OpenNASA*, February 19, 2008, http://www.opennasa.com
/2008/02/19/generation-y-perspectives.

4. Ibid.

5. Julie Bart, "College Grads Say Salary Is Less Important than Facebook Freedom at
Work," Hot Hardware, November 8, 2011, http://www.hothardware.com/News
/College-Grads-Say-Salary-Is-Less-Important-than-FacebookFriendly-Work
-Policies.

6. Nick Skytland, "Generation Y Perspectives."

7. "Media's Effect on This Generation," *Relevant Magazine* (July/August 2011): 16.

8. Read more at Thom S. Rainer and Jess W. Rainer, *The Millennials: Connecting to
America's Largest Generation* (Nashville: B&H, 2011), 193.

9. Robert Half International and Yahoo! HotJobs, *What Millennial Workers Want:
How to Attract and Retain Gen Y Employees* (2008), 12.

10. Thomas Pardee, "Media-Savvy Gen Y Finds Smart and Funny Is 'New Rock 'n'
Roll,'" *AdvertisingAge*, October 11, 2010, http://adage.com/article/news/marketing
-media-savvy-gen-y-transparency-authenticity/146388/.

11. For a succinct overview of the impact of technology on our brains and relationships,
see Sharon Jayson, "Ever-Present Devices Can Push Our Crazy Buttons," *USA
Today*, March 27, 2012, http://usatoday30.usatoday.com/LIFE/usaedition/2012
-03-27-Technology-crazy--iDisorder_CV_U.htm. See also Hanna Rosin, "The
Touch Screen Generation," *The Atlantic* (April 2013): 57.

12. Tim Mullaney, "Tech Distractions for Workers Add Up," *USA Today*, May 18,
2011, http://usatoday30.usatoday.com/tech/news/2011-05-18-social-media
-worker-distractions_n.htm.

13. Andrea Bennett, "Should You Friend Coworkers?" *The Responsibility Project* (blog), Liberty Mutual, May 16, 2011, http://responsibility-project.libertymutual.com /blog/should-you-friend-coworkers-#fbid=7kvliOfrgr-.

14. A study done by research firm Gartner showed that in 2010, 50 percent of large organizations blocked social sites, but by 2014, that number is expected to drop to 30 percent. Sharon Gaudin, "More Companies Are OK with Employees Using Facebook at Work," *Computerworld*, March 26, 2012, http:// www.computerworld.com/s/article/9225558/More_companies_are_OK_with _employees_using_Facebook_at_work.

15. Allen, March 1, 2008, comment on Nick Skytland, "Generation Y Perspectives."

16. For examples, see Rick Hampton, "Age-Old Bad Judgment Lives Long in Digital Age," *USA Today*, March 20, 2013, 1.

17. Lee Rainie and Aaron Smith, "Social Networking Sites and Politics," Pew Internet, March 12, 2012, http://www.pewinternet.org/Reports/2012/Social-networking -and-politics/Main-findings/Social-networking-sites-and-politics.aspx.

CHAPTER 9: DECISION MAKING

1. Nick Shore, "Turning on the 'No-Collar' Workforce," *MediaDailyNews Commentary* (blog), March 15, 2012, http://www.mediapost.com/publications/article/170109 /turning-on-the-no-collar-workforce.html#axzz2LxEEjoco.

2. FranklinCovey's education practice has done amazing work with its *The Leader in Me* program, helping schools empower children to resolve their own challenges. See http://www.franklincovey.com/tc/solutions/education-solutions/elementary -education-solutions--the-leader-in-me.

CHAPTER 10: DRESS CODE

1. Nick Shore, "Turning on the 'No-Collar' Workforce," *MediaDailyNews Commentary* (blog), March 15, 2012, http://www.mediapost.com/publications/article/170109 /turning-on-the-no-collar-workforce.html#axzz2LxEEjoco.

2. Thom S. Rainer and Jess W. Rainer, *The Millennials: Connecting to America's Largest Generation* (Nashville: B&H, 2011), 143.

3. Robert Half International and Yahoo! HotJobs, *What Millennial Workers Want: How to Attract and Retain Gen Y Employees* (2008), 13.

4. Rainer and Rainer, *The Millennials*, 143.

5. Pew Research Center, *Millennials: A Portrait of Generation Next* (February 24, 2010), 57, http://www.pewsocialtrends.org/files/2010/10/millennials-confident -connected-open-to-change.pdf.

CHAPTER 11: FEEDBACK

1. Robert Half International and Yahoo! HotJobs, *What Millennial Workers Want: How to Attract and Retain Gen Y Employees* (2008), 8.

2. Ibid., 10.

3. Jeanne C. Meister and Karie Willyerd, "Mentoring Millennials," *Harvard Business Review* (May 2010): 70, 72, http://hbr.org/2010/05/mentoring-millennials/ar/1.

4. Margaret Heffernan and Saj-Nicole Joni, "Of Protégés and Pitfalls: A Complete Plan for Getting the Mentoring You Need," *Fast Company* (August 2005): 82.

5. Ellen McGirt, "How to Make All Feedback Positive," *Fast Company* (December 2012/January 2013): 64, http://www.fastcompany.com/3002936/how-make-all-feedback-positive.

6. UNC Kenan-Flagler Business School, "Maximizing Millennials: The Who, How and Why of Managing Gen Y," quoted in Tim Willingham, "Maximizing Millennials: Why to Hire Gen Y," *Daily Infographic*, July 6, 2012, http://dailyinfographic.com/maximizing-millennials-why-to-hire-gen-y-infographic.

7. Ellen McGirt, "'Boy CEO' Mark Zuckerberg's Two Smartest Projects Were Growing Facebook and Growing Up," *Fast Company*, March 19, 2012, http://www.fastcompany.com/1822794/boy-ceo-mark-zuckerbergs-two-smartest-projects-were-growing-facebook-and-growing; Thomas Goetz, "How Facebook Uses Feedback Loops: Meet Rypple," *Wired*, June 20, 2011, http://www.wired.com/business/2011/06/facebook-uses-feedback-loops/.

8. Rex Huppke, "Millennials Struggle with Confrontation at Work," *Chicago Tribune*, November 19, 2012, http://articles.chicagotribune.com/2012-11-19/business/ct-biz-1119-work-advice-huppke-20121119_1_millennials-generational-differences-diversity-issue.

9. In chapter 14 on loyalty I describe in more detail what's changed in the workplace that makes career planning harder today and provide ideas for what organizations and teams can do about it.

10. Nick Shore, "Turning on the 'No-Collar' Workforce," *MediaDailyNews Commentary* (blog), March 15, 2012, http://www.mediapost.com/publications/article/170109/turning-on-the-no-collar-workforce.html#axzz2LxEEjoco.

11. Randstad, "Are Companies Prepared for the Looming Manager Shortage?," news release, July 23, 2009, http://us.randstad.com/content/aboutrandstad/news-and-press-releases/press-releases/2009/20092307001b.xml.

12. Jeanne C. Meister and Karie Willyerd give a couple of helpful examples to get you started in their article "Mentoring Millennials"; also see Kathy E. Kram and Monica C. Higgins, "A New Approach to Mentoring," *Wall Street Journal*, September 22, 2008, 10, http://online.wsj.com/article/SB122160063875344843.html.

CHAPTER 12: FUN AT WORK

1. Randstad, "Limited Interaction among Generations in the Workplace Indicates New Challenges," news release, May 27, 2008, http://us.randstad.com/content/aboutrandstad/news-and-press-releases/press-releases/2008/20080527001.xml.

2. Thom S. Rainer and Jess W. Rainer, *The Millennials: Connecting to America's Largest Generation* (Nashville: B&H, 2011), 137.

3. Robert Morison, Tamara Erickson, and Ken Dychtwald, "Managing Middlescence," *Harvard Business Review* (March 2006), http://hbr.org/2006/03/managing-middlescence/ar/1.

4. Nick Shore, "Turning on the 'No-Collar' Workforce," *MediaDailyNews Commentary* (blog), March 15, 2012, http://www.mediapost.com/publications/article/170109/turning-on-the-no-collar-workforce.html#axzz2LxEEjoco.

5. Because fun encompasses so much of what an organization does, it's the most broad reaching of the sticking points. Consequently, I recognize that the generalizations

regarding how the generations see fun require a bit more oversimplification than with other sticking points. When you discuss with your team these descriptions of how each generation sees fun, don't be surprised if they question parts of them.

6. Shore, "Turning on the 'No-Collar' Workforce."

7. Thomas Pardee, "Want to Reach the Millennial Market? Start with Snooki," *AdvertisingAge*, November 30, 2010, http://adage.com/article/special-report -me-conference-2010/mtv-reach-millennial-market-snooki/147370/.

8. In the '90s companies were hiring directors of fun, and Xer managers were proclaiming the coming change in the workplace. In an article typical for 1999, Auren Hoffman, the founder of BridgePath.com, claimed that "companies run by Generation Xers have used fun to create an unprecedented productivity gain. Most Boomer-led companies have yet to incorporate fun into their culture (and probably never will) and are therefore suffering from productivity and ingenuity losses." He goes on to make this contrast: "Boomer companies have coffee and tea, Gen X companies have Tang, beer, and Mountain Dew. At BridgePath.com, we make meetings more bearable by building LEGO structures and making Play-Doh art. Music fills our office and people dress any way they please. Last week, we spent our lunch painting clay pots for other co-workers and planting flower seeds to watch them grow during the next year." Auren Hoffman, "On the Job, Xers Just Want to Have Fun," *San Francisco Chronicle*, September 12, 1999, http://www.sfgate.com/news/article/On-the-Job-Xers-Just-Want-To-Have-Fun -We-spend-2908988.php.

9. For an explanation of emerging adulthood, see pages 102–103.

CHAPTER 13: KNOWLEDGE TRANSFER

1. Of special concern is how organizations replace their managers when they retire. Randstad learned in 2009 that 51 percent of the people with experience to be managers said they're not interested. They don't want the increased pressures, extra hours, and people issues that come with management. Fifty-two percent believe the manager's role needs to be reinvented. Organizations are not doing a good job communicating the positives of managing, and until they do, they will not get the management talent they need to juggle four (and eventually five) generations. Randstad, *Managers of Tomorrow: Setting a New Standard* (2009), 2, 3, http://us.randstad.com/content/aboutrandstad/knowledge-center/employer -resources/World-of-Work-2009-Topic-Report.pdf.

2. "National Study of Business Strategy and Workforce Development," Sloan Center on Aging and Work at Boston College online, http://www.bc.edu/research/aging andwork/projects/businessStrategy.html.

3. *Bloomberg Businessweek*, SmallBiz (August/September 2008): 21.

4. Randstad, *The World of Work 2007*, 25, http://us.randstad.com/content/about randstad/knowledge-center/employer-resources/World-of-Work-2007.pdf.

5. Ibid.

6. The shift in the European Union is even greater. Today one person is supported by 3.5 workers, but that is projected to drop to 1.8 in 2050. That means that one couple will support each retiree. "Too Much, Too Young," *The Economist*, April 7, 2011, http://www.economist.com/node/18502005.

7. Kurt J. Bauman and Nikki L. Graf, *Educational Attainment: 2000* (Washington, DC: US Census Bureau, August 2003), 2, http://www.census.gov/prod/2003pubs/c2kbr-24.pdf.

8. Pew Research Center, *Millennials: A Portrait of Generation Next* (February 24, 2010), 36, http://www.pewsocialtrends.org/files/2010/10/millennials-confident-connected-open-to-change.pdf.

9. Kayla Webley, "Reboot the School," *Time*, July 9, 2012, 38, http://www.time.com/time/magazine/article/0,9171,2118298,00.html.

10. Marco R. della Cava, "Sal Khan Commands a Worldwide Classroom," *USA Today*, May 30, 2012, http://usatoday30.usatoday.com/LIFE/usaedition/2012-05-30-Khan-cover-_CV_U.htm.

11. Lucy Kellaway, "Words Fail Them," *The Economist*, November 22, 2010, 142, http://www.economist.com/node/17493438. Globally, there are expected to be 1.5 billion Internet video users by 2016, up from 792 million Internet video users in 2011; Cisco, "Cisco's VNI Forecast Projects the Internet Will Be Four Times as Large in Four Years," *The Network*, news release, May 30, 2012, http://newsroom.cisco.com/press-release-content?articleId=888280.

12. Rebecca Perron, *Employer Experiences and Expectations: Finding, Training, and Keeping Qualified Workers* (Washington, DC: AARP, 2011), 30, http://assets.aarp.org/rgcenter/econ/finding-training-keeping-qualified-workers.pdf.

13. "Older Workers," United States Department of Labor online, July 2008, http://www.bls.gov/spotlight/2008/older_workers/.

14. "Age Shall Not Wither Them," *The Economist*, April 9, 2011, 78–80, http://www.economist.com/node/18527063.

15. "Hiring Grandpa," *The Economist*, April 7, 2011, 8, http://www.economist.com/node/18474681.

16. G. R. Ferris et al., "The Age Context of Performance Evaluations Decisions," *Psychology and Aging* 6 (1991): 616–26, cited in Peter Cappelli and Bill Novelli, *Managing the Older Worker* (Boston: Harvard Business School Publishing, 2010), 97.

17. Ibid., 27. University of Michigan researchers found that older workers were wiser in how they responded to questions involving conflict directed to Dear Abby: "5 Good Things about Aging," *Consumer Reports on Health* 25 (no. 5): 4.

18. "Age Shall Not Wither Them," 78–80. Companies should start seeing older workers as assets rather than liabilities.

19. Paul Taylor et al., *America's Changing Workforce: Recession Turns a Graying Office Grayer* (Washington, DC: Pew Research Center, September 3, 2009), 17, 21, http://www.pewsocialtrends.org/files/2010/10/americas-changing-workforce.pdf.

20. Mina Kimes, "Keeping Your Senior Staffers," *Fortune*, July 20, 2009, 146, http://money.cnn.com/2009/07/10/news/companies/basf_retaining_senior_engineers.fortune/index.htm.

21. della Cava, "Sal Khan Commands a Worldwide Classroom"; Webley, "Reboot the School," 36–41.

22. "Dare2Share project at BT," YouTube video, 3:33, posted by "edavidove," September 19, 2009, http://www.youtube.com/watch?v=gtVYkEdGtfo. Quote begins at 0:11. For a podcast of the BBC story on Dare2Share as well as Sun

Microsystems' approach, see "Learning Curve," *In Business: Peter Day*, BBC Radio 4, podcast audio, 21:30, August 2, 2009, http://www.bbc.co.uk /programmes/boolszhn.

23. Sundar Balasubramanian, "BT Let's Talk," July 21, 2011, http://letstalk.global services.bt.com/en/2011/07/dont-get-formal/ July 21, 2011; BT Dares to Share— Social Learning Case Study: http://daretoshare.wordpress.com/2009/03/21/bt -dares-to-share-social-learning-case-study/.

24. "Dare2Share project at BT," beginning at 1:13.

25. Eric Davidove and Peter Butler, "Dealing with the 'Capability Recession' at Lower Cost," *Accenture*, April 2009, http://www.accenture.com/us-en/outlook/Pages /outlook-online-2009-effective-social-learning.aspx.

CHAPTER 14: LOYALTY

1. Paul Taylor et al., *America's Changing Workforce: Recession Turns a Graying Office Grayer* (Washington, DC: Pew Research Center, September 3, 2009), 16, http:// www.pewsocialtrends.org/files/2010/10/americas-changing-workforce.pdf.

2. Peter Cappelli and Bill Novelli, *Managing the Older Worker* (Boston: Harvard Business School Publishing, 2010), 47.

3. Ibid., 45.

4. Pew Research Center, *Millennials: A Portrait of Generation Next* (February 24, 2010), 46–47, http://www.pewsocialtrends.org/files/2010/10/millennials -confident-connected-open-to-change.pdf.

5. "Number of Jobs Held and Job Duration for Baby Boomers, 1978–2010," *TED: The Editor's Desk*, Bureau of Labor Statistics online, July 31, 2012, http://www .bls.gov/opub/ted/2012/ted_20120731.htm.

6. Center for Creative Leadership found no statistical differences among Traditionalists, Boomers, and Xers between 26 and 30 years of age. See Jennifer Deal, *Retiring the Generation Gap* (San Francisco: Jossey-Bass, 2007), 128–30.

7. Pew Research Center, *Millennials*, 46–47.

8. Douglas Alden Warshaw, "Pulling Off the Ultimate Career Makeover," *Fortune*, July 4, 2011, 73, http://management.fortune.cnn.com/2011/06/21/pulling-off -the-ultimate-career-makeover/.

9. Randstad, "2009 World of Work—Survive to Thrive," news release, September 1, 2009, http://us.randstad.com/content/aboutrandstad/news-and-press-releases /press-releases/2009/20090109002b.xml.

10. Sylvia Ann Hewlett et al., *The X Factor: Tapping into the Strengths of the 33- to 46-Year-Old Generation* (New York: Center for Talent Innovation, 2011), 17.

11. Mercer, "One in Two US Employees Looking to Leave or Checked Out on the Job, Says What's Working Research," *news release*, June 20, 2011, http://www .mercer.com/press-releases/1418665.

12. Cappelli and Novelli, *Managing the Older Worker*, 52.

13. Pew Research Center, *Millennials*, 46–47.

14. Thom S. Rainer and Jess W. Rainer, *The Millennials: Connecting to America's Largest Generation* (Nashville: B&H, 2011), 130.

15. Chris Johnson et al., "Global Compensation and Benefits: What's Working," Mercer, January 19, 2012, http://www.mercer.com/articles/1445615.

16. Rainer and Rainer, *The Millennials*, 109, 134; Robert Half International and Yahoo! Hot Jobs, *What Millennial Workers Want: How to Attract and Retain Gen Y Employees*, 14, http://www.accountingweb.com/sites/default/files/generationy_robert_half.pdf. Pay leads the way outside the United States as well: "Global Compensation and Benefits: What's Working," Mercer, http://www.mercer.com/articles/1445615. Millennials also prove they are more money oriented than the other generations because they rank "soft" benefits lower than the other generations do: Randstad, "Limited Interaction among Generations in the Workplace Indicates New Challenges," news release, May 27, 2008, http://us.randstad.com/content/about randstad/news-and-press-releases/press-releases/2008/20080527001.xml.

17. Randstad, "Limited Interaction among Generations in the Workplace Indicates New Challenges."

18. Scott Flander, "Millennial Magnets," *Human Resource Executive* online, April 1, 2008, http://www.hreonline.com/HRE/view/story.jhtml?id=84159035.

CHAPTER 15: MEETINGS

1. "Are Most Company Meetings a Waste of Time?" *USA Today*, September 20, 2010.

2. Randstad, one of the largest Human Resources and staffing organizations, found in their annual survey that half of all employees prefer e-mail for routine communication; only 21 percent prefer meetings for this purpose. For important news like organizational changes, the numbers flip: half want to be told in a meeting, and only 21 percent will accept an e-mail. Randstad, *The World of Work 2007*, 20–21, http://us.randstad.com/content/aboutrandstad/knowledge -center/employer-resources/World-of-Work-2007.pdf.

3. Randstad, *The World of Work 2009*, 7.

CHAPTER 16: POLICIES

1. Mark Thompson, "The Other 1%," *Time,* November 21, 2011, 38, http://www.time.com/time/magazine/article/0,9171,2099152,00.html.

2. For an interesting summary of what today's organizations can learn from the armed forces, see "How to Make a Killing," *The Economist*, February 16, 2013, 69, http:// www.economist.com/news/business/21571852-business-has-much-learn-armed -forces-how-make-killing.

CHAPTER 17: RESPECT

1. "Noah Shuts Up after Skiles' Put-Down," *Chicago Tribune*, November 8, 2007, http://articles.chicagotribune.com/2007-11-08/news/0711080578_1_berto -center-scott-skiles-bulls.

2. "Skiles Says 'Jab' at Noah Was Misconstrued," RealGM Wiretap, November 9, 2007, http://basketball.realgm.com/wiretap/186448/Skiles_Says_Jab_At_Noah _Was_Misconstrued#ixzz20kDh50DG.

3. Randstad, *The World of Work 2009*, 7, http://us.randstad.com/content/about randstad/knowledge-center/employer-resources/World-of-Work-2009.pdf.

4. By the way, Millennials are hardest on themselves. Pew Research found that Millennials think the older generations are more respectful and well-mannered than theirs. "Millennials: A Portrait of Generation Next," Pew Research Center,

February 24, 2010, 6, http://www.pewsocialtrends.org/files/2010/10/millennials-confident-connected-open-to-change.pdf.

5. The generations agree that they want their managers approachable and respectful, but there are subtle differences in some other traits they value in a manager:

If you manage Traditionalists, knock off the authoritative style and go easy on the collaboration, but kick up inspiration and innovation. They are tired of hierarchical organizations.

If you manage Boomers, they want inspiring, collaborative, and innovative management traits. Almost half will like you better if you are kind. Two out of three don't want you to use an authoritative approach.

If you manage Gen Xers, they also want you to be inspiring and collaborative, but not as much as the older two generations do, so don't overdo it.

If you manage Millennials, up the kindness. You don't have to be Mr. Rogers, but they expect kindness more than the other generations. They value it almost as much as collaboration (typically held up as the Holy Grail for managing Millennials). Bursting another myth in the popular press, Millennials don't see respect and kindness at odds with an authoritative style, which 42 percent value. Randstad, *The World of Work 2009*, 7.

6. For more about helping people deal with the emotions of change, see www.mygenerationalcoach.com to learn more about my workshops Leading through the 6 Change Reactions and Working through the 6 Change Reactions.

CHAPTER 18: TRAINING

1. A national sample of 650 CEOs, CFOs, HR executives/managers, and benefit administrators were interviewed by Market Strategies International April 19–23, 2011, on behalf of Bank of America Merrill Lynch Retirement Services. Bank of America Merrill Lynch, *Workplace Benefits Report*, June 14, 2011, 4, http://www.benefitplans.baml.com/Publish/Content/application/pdf/GWMOL/Executive-Summary-BofAML-Workplace-Benefits-Report.pdf.

2. Randstad, "American Workers Feel Overqualified, but Aren't Ready to Stop Learning," news release, May 31, 2011, http://us.randstad.com/content/about randstad/news-and-press-releases/press-releases/2011/20110531001.xml.

3. Ibid.

4. J. Walker Smith and Ann Clurman, *Generation Ageless* (New York: HarperCollins, 2007), 108.

5. Beverly Goldberg with Roberta Fusaro, "Needed: Experienced Workers," *Harvard Business Review* (July 2001), http://hbr.org/2001/07/needed-experienced-workers/ar/1.

6. Michael Gaynor, "Could You Drive a UPS Truck?" *Washingtonian*, December 6, 2010, http://www.washingtonian.com/articles/people/could-you-drive-a-ups-truck/; Jennifer Levitz, "UPS Thinks out of the Box on Driver Training," *Wall Street Journal*, April 6, 2010, http://online.wsj.com/article/SB10001424052702303912104575164573823418844.html.

7. "UPS Moves Driver Training from the Classroom to the Simulator," *Training*, June 15, 2009, http://www.trainingmag.com/article/ups-moves-driver-training-classroom-simulator.

8. Nadira A. Hira, "The Making of a UPS Driver," *Fortune*, November 7, 2007, http://money.cnn.com/magazines/fortune/fortune_archive/2007/11/12/101008310/index2.htm.

9. Gaynor, "Could You Drive a UPS Truck?"

10. Hira, "The Making of a UPS Driver."

11. Gaynor, "Could You Drive a UPS Truck?"

12. Ibid.

13. Ibid.

14. Levitz, "UPS Thinks out of the Box."

15. "Gartner Says Worldwide Hosted Virtual Desktop Market to Surpass $65 Billion in 2013," Gartner Press Release, March 26, 2009.

CHAPTER 19: WORK ETHIC

1. When asked to respond to the statement "I want to achieve a better work-life balance next year," 25 percent strongly agreed; 55 percent agreed; and only 20 percent did not agree or strongly disagreed. Randstad, *Randstad Workmonitor Global Results Wave 4*, December 2010, 29, http://www.randstad.com/press-room/randstad-workmonitor/randstad-workmonitordecember2010.pdf.

2. Paul Taylor and Richard Morin, *Forty Years after Woodstock, a Gentler Generation Gap* (Pew Research Center, August 12, 2009), 8, http://www.pewsocialtrends.org/files/2010/10/after-woodstock-gentler-generation-gap.pdf.

3. For a short article describing lawnmower parents, see "The Pitfalls of Lawnmower Parenting," CBS New York, January 11, 2012, http://newyork.cbslocal.com/2012/01/11/the-pitfalls-of-lawnmower-parenting/.

4. Thom S. Rainer and Jess W. Rainer, *The Millennials: Connecting to America's Largest Generation* (Nashville: B&H, 2011), 130.

5. Ellen Galinsky, Kerstin Aumann, and James T. Bond, *Times Are Changing: Gender and Generation at Work and at Home* (Families and Work Institute, 2011), 1–2, http://familiesandwork.org/site/research/reports/Times_Are_Changing.pdf. Their report of their 2008 study summarizes the results: "When we first started asking this question in 1992, significantly more men under 29 wanted jobs with greater responsibility (80%) than women under 29 (72%). Although the desire to advance to jobs with greater responsibility declined for all young workers between 1992 and 2008, the lowest point we have recorded was in 1997. Since 1997, the desire to move to jobs with more responsibility among young workers has increased. This increase has been greater for young women—from 54% to 65%—than young men—from 61% to 68%."

6. Randstad, "Do Employees Need a Vacation from Their Vacation?" news release, May 20, 2009, http://us.randstad.com/content/aboutrandstad/news-and-press-releases/press-releases/2009/20090520002.xml.

7. Pew Research Center, *Millennials: A Portrait of Generation Next* (February 24, 2010), 5, http://www.pewsocialtrends.org/files/2010/10/millennials-confident-connected-open-to-change.pdf.

8. "Generation Xhausted," *The Economist*, August 18, 2012, 53.

9. Rainer and Rainer, *The Millennials*, 39.

10. Richard Branson, "Give People the Freedom of Where to Work," *Richard's Blog*, February 25, 2013, http://www.virgin.com/richard-branson/blog/give-people-the-freedom-of-where-to-work.

11. See Mary C. Noonan and Jennifer L. Glass, "The Hard Truth about Telecommuting," *Monthly Labor Review* 135, no. 6 (June 2009): 38–45.

12. PricewaterhouseCoopers, *Managing Tomorrow's People* (2007), 18, http://www.pwc.de/de_DE/de/prozessoptimierung/assets/millennials_at_work_report08.pdf.

13. Rainer and Rainer, *The Millennials*, 138. See also Don Tapscott, *Grown Up Digital: How the Net Generation Is Changing Your World* (New York: McGraw-Hill, 2009), 75.

14. Rainer and Rainer, *The Millennials*, 144.

15. Randstad, "Limited Interaction among Generations in the Workplace Indicates New Challenges," news release, May 27, 2008, http://us.randstad.com/content/aboutrandstad/news-and-press-releases/press-releases/2008/20080527001.xml.

16. Claire Cain Miller and Nicole Perlroth, "Yahoo Says New Policy Is Meant to Raise Morale," *New York Times*, March 5, 2013, http://www.nytimes.com/2013/03/06/technology/yahoos-in-office-policy-aims-to-bolster-morale.html?pagewanted=all&_r=0.

17. Even Best Buy, famous in generational literature for their Results Only Work Environment (ROWE) program, which allowed people to work anywhere and anytime as long as they hit their goals, is rethinking flexible schedules—not work flexibility but the lack of communication between managers and employees over when and where they work: Julianne Pepitone, "Best Buy Ends Work-from-Home Program," *CNN Money*, March 5, 2013, http://money.cnn.com/2013/03/05/technology/best-buy-work-from-home/index.html.

APPENDIX: FREQUENTLY ASKED QUESTIONS

1. Paul Taylor and Richard Morin, *Forty Years after Woodstock, a Gentler Generation Gap* (Pew Research Center, August 12, 2009), 3, http://www.pewsocialtrends.org/files/2010/10/after-woodstock-gentler-generation-gap.pdf.

2. Ibid.

3. Pew Research Center, *Millennials: A Portrait of Generation Next* (February 24, 2010), 15, http://www.pewsocialtrends.org/files/2010/10/millennials-confident-connected-open-to-change.pdf.

4. For more on treating people as whole persons, see the Leading Across Generations workshop: http://www.franklincovey.com/tc/solutions/generations-solutions/modular-series-leading-across-generations and Stephen Covey, *The 8th Habit: From Effectiveness to Greatness* (New York: Free Press, 2004), 20–24.

5. D'Vera Cohn and Paul Taylor, "Baby Boomers Approach 65—Glumly," Pew Research Social and Demographic Trends, December 20, 2010, http://www.pewsocialtrends.org/2010/12/20/baby-boomers-approach-65-glumly/.

6. The Futures Company, *Unmasking Millennials: Executive Summary 2011* (2011), 21–25, http://www.tfccontent.com/Freethinking/FP_Unmasking_Millennials_Executive_summary_2011.pdf.

7. Dinah Eng, "Mad Men, Miami-Style," *Fortune*, April 8, 2013.
8. "Census: US Poverty Rate Spikes, Nearly 50 Million Americans Affected," CBS DC, November 15, 2012, http://washington.cbslocal.com/2012/11/15/census-u -s-poverty-rate-spikes-nearly-50-million-americans-affected.

Index

About the Author

HAYDN SHAW has helped clients with his research regarding generational differences for more than twenty years. He is the author of FranklinCovey's bestselling workshops Leading Across Generations and Working Across Generations. Haydn has worked with more than 1,500 businesses (from Fortune 500 companies to start-ups), not-for-profit organizations, and governmental agencies, speaking and consulting on generations, leadership, management, and change with over 100,000 people. The results from his long-term organizational development and change projects have been written up in case studies.

Hailed as a "leadership guru" by the *Washington Post*, Haydn speaks and consults in excess of 160 days each year, serving clients who consistently invite him back. He has worked as a senior consultant with FranklinCovey for more than twenty-one years. He is one of a handful of consultants in FranklinCovey to win the Chairman's Award. He also speaks independently on generations and change.

A popular speaker, Haydn has delivered hundreds of convention keynotes and small, off-site workshops. Known for taking groups from hilarity to deep reflection, he combines rich content with use-tomorrow tools. His work makes an impact because he does his homework, customizing each speech to drive results.

Organizations turn to Haydn for help with (1) designing succession and leadership-development plans for those who will replace the retiring Boomers; (2) adapting communications, policies, and systems to make each generation more productive; and (3) facilitating teams as they work through generational sticking points using the five-step process.

He is also the author of the training workshops Leading through the 6 Change Reactions and Working through the 6 Change Reactions.

Haydn lives in a multigenerational household in a suburb of Chicago. Haydn, his wife, Laurie, and her disabled brother are Boomer/Gen Xer Cuspers. Their four teenagers are Millennials. His mother-in-law is a Traditionalist.

For more information on Haydn, visit www.mygenerationalcoach.com.

Learn how to work and communicate more effectively with other generations.

Bring Haydn Shaw to your organization.

Haydn Shaw has spoken to more than 1,500 organizations and spends 160 days each year speaking and consulting with business leaders and employees. Known for taking groups from hilarity to deep reflection, he combines rich content with practical tools. His presentations on generations, change, and leadership make a powerful impact as he customizes each speech, workshop, or consultation to meet your unique needs. People often refer to his presentation on generations as the best speech they have ever heard.

To bring Haydn Shaw to your organization, visit **mygenerationalcoach.com** *or call 815-469-2617.*

Generational Resources from Haydn Shaw and FranklinCovey.

Leading Across Generations™
FranklinCovey's four-hour, instructor-led module gives leaders the understanding, tools, and practice to deal with generational differences and help their teams stick together.

Working Across Generations
FranklinCovey's four-hour, instructor-led module for all employees provides the understanding and tools they need to speak the languages of other generations and work together effectively.

Also available are additional workshops on the 5 steps of leading through generational differences as well as custom-designed content to fit your needs.

To get more information on workshops, visit www.franklincovey.com/tc/solutions /generations-solutions or call 815-469-2617 or toll-free 1-800-827-1776.

Learn why change initiatives stall, and gain practical tools for helping people deal with the 6 Change Reactions.

Since people respond to change in six different ways, tension and resentment can build between team members as they struggle to process the change.

For a free summary and more information on Haydn Shaw's keynotes on change along with his full- and half-day workshops "Leading through the 6 Change Reactions" and "Working through the 6 Change Reactions," visit **mygenerationalcoach.com** *or call 815-469-2617.*

CP0663